flexicurity
a relevant approach
in Central and
Eastern Europe

flexicurity

a relevant approach
in Central and
Eastern Europe

Sandrine Cazes
Alena Nesporova

International Labour Office • Geneva

Cazes, S.; Nesporova, A. (eds.)
Flexicurity: A relevant approach for Central and Eastern Europe
Geneva, International Labour Office, 2007

Labour flexibility, employment, employment security, wages, labour market, labour policy, trend Eastern Europe

ISBN 978-92-2-119215-2

ILO Cataloguing in Publication Data

Cover design: © Aimery Chaigne 2006
Typeset by Magheross Graphics, France & Ireland www.magheross.com
Printed in Switzerland   PCL

FOREWORD

The research findings presented in this book have been guided by the Global Employment Agenda for the pursuit of Decent Work for all, the main framework of the International Labour Organization's (ILO) Employment Sector, which was approved by the ILO Governing Body in 2003,[1] as well as by the "vision" document on implementing the Agenda.[2] One of the core elements of the Global Employment Agenda (GEA) relates to the contribution of labour market institutions and policies in ensuring successful labour market adjustment as globalization, technological change and competition accelerate. Enterprises have to constantly adjust their operations and their labour force in order to adapt to fluctuations in demand and to productivity growth. But simply responding to enterprises' needs for flexibility, without providing adequate employment and income security for workers, would have not only negative social implications but also micro- and macroeconomic repercussions as job insecurity increases workers' resistance to changes while lower incomes reduce consumer demand and consequently economic growth. Social protection thus becomes a productive factor and as such it is another core element of the GEA. Finding a good balance between flexibility and security is therefore an important issue for social dialogue, as policy-makers and the social partners should agree on institutional and policy reforms that are acceptable to all the parties concerned.

This book is the second to stem from the ILO technical project on the issue of flexibility and security and their impact on employment performance carried out for Central and Eastern Europe (CEE) countries. The first volume[3] explored in detail how

---

[1] ILO: *The Global Employment Agenda* (Geneva, 2003).

[2] ILO: *Implementing the Global Employment Agenda: Employment strategies in support of decent work, "Vision" document* (Geneva, 2006).

[3] Cazes and Nesporova: *Labour markets in transition: Balancing flexibility and security in Central and Eastern Europe* (Geneva, ILO, 2003).

the labour markets of the CEE countries reacted to economic and social reforms accompanying their transition to a market system during the 1990s. Opening up their national economies to global competition forced domestic enterprises to adjust their inputs (including labour) as well as their outputs to market demand. Amended national labour legislation, newly established public employment services and labour market policies facilitated these changes by extending the use of time-bound labour contracts and allowing employment terminations for economic reasons, and by providing laid-off workers with re-employment assistance, unemployment benefits and programmes to improve their employability. This process of flexibilization of the labour market further expanded over the course of the transition period while failing to be properly compensated by increased employment and income security outside the enterprise, leading to negative impacts on labour reallocation, employment level and labour productivity. Within that context, Cazes and Nesporova called for a more balanced policy that would lower adjustment costs for enterprises while at the same time improving security for workers.

In the present book, the authors focus on the new European Union (EU) member and EU accession countries and re-examine their policy recommendations in the light of recent labour market developments. Changes in the regulatory provisions, such as legal regulations on hiring and firing, collective bargaining, labour taxation and labour market policies, are reviewed for the period 1999–2003 to assess whether, in contrast to the 1990s, the labour markets of these countries have converged towards the patterns of those of the EU15 countries taken as a benchmark. The impacts of these reforms on key labour market outcomes are also updated for the period 1999–2003. In line with the EU agenda, which increasingly emphasizes that a better combination of flexibility and security is indispensable to improve competitiveness and at the same time maintain the principles of the European social model, this volume argues that flexicurity strategies are similarly highly relevant for the CEE countries. However, as there is no one-size-fits-all flexicurity model, the publication also comprises a series of national case studies to examine the institutional provisions and policy schemes of the national employment and social protection systems and their interactions, as well as the position of the main actors in designing required labour market reforms. The volume carefully examines whether and how far Bulgaria, Croatia, Hungary, Lithuania and Poland have moved towards a good balance between flexibility and security.

This book will enrich the literature discussing the flexibility–security nexus, the role of labour market institutions and policies on labour market performance, and the flexicurity approach for the countries of Central and Eastern Europe. Providing cross-country perspectives and national experiences, the book suggests innovative policy proposals to policy-makers from government and the social partners on how to better manage labour market changes in a globalized economy from an economic and a social point of view.

José M. Salazar-Xirinachs
Executive Director
Employment Sector, ILO

Friedrich Buttler
Regional Director
EUROPE, ILO

CONTENTS

List of tables

List of figures

ACKNOWLEDGEMENTS

This book is the fruit of collective effort. In particular, our thanks go to the authors of the five country studies: Iskra Beleva, Vasyl Tzanov and Genoveva Tisheva from Bulgaria, Sanja Crnković-Pozaić from Croatia, János Köllő and Beáta Nacsa from Hungary, Boguslavas Gruzevskis and Inga Blaziene from Lithuania, and Gabriela Grołkowska, Mieczyslaw Socha and Urszula Sztanderska from Poland. Thanks are also due to Mirco Tonin for his contribution on wage flexibility and Sylvie Rauffet for providing statistical assistance. The authors also benefited from valuable comments given by colleagues at the Employment Sector and in the Sub-Regional Office in Budapest. Finally, thanks are due to Charlotte Beauchamp for her careful editing of the manuscript, Thomas Cornelissen for compiling the literature, and Aimery Chaigne for the great design of the cover pages.

INTRODUCTION

1

Sandrine Cazes* and Alena Nesporova**

1.1 THE DEBATE ABOUT FLEXIBILITY AND LABOUR MARKET PERFORMANCE

The debate about the effect of flexibility on labour market performance relates to the controversial and ongoing discussion over whether or not labour market institutions matter; or put another way, whether poor labour market outcomes are the consequences of labour market rigidities. Discussions around this issue are inconclusive and unsatisfying, partly because the complexity of the concept of labour market flexibility may feed its ideological dimension: while considered the highly desirable remedy to labour market problems by some, it is seen as the path to instability and insecurity by others. There are indeed different perspectives on labour market flexibility. From the macroeconomic perspective, flexibility refers to the speed of adjustment of the labour market to external shocks or changing economic conditions. Thus, labour market flexibility is the degree to which employment and/or working time (quantitative adjustment) or wages (price adjustment) adjust to economic changes. At the microlevel, and from the employers' perspective, a flexible labour market should not unduly impede the ability of an enterprise to adjust the size, composition and cost of its workforce. From the workers' perspective, a flexible labour market means lower protection at the workplace, and thus a higher probability of job loss (but also the possibility of finding a new job quickly). There is no single criterion of labour market flexibility, as flexibility is multidimensional. Categorizing the three perspectives in this way is a simplistic means of capturing a complex phenomenon, as all dimensions are of course interrelated and flexibility at the micro level is reflected in flexibility at the macro level.

* Senior Employment Specialist, Economic and Labour Market Analysis Department, International Labour Office, Geneva. ** Deputy Regional Director, Regional Office for Europe and Central Asia, International Labour Office, Geneva.

The literature on flexibility usually looks at the different definitions of labour market flexibility: *external* versus *internal* flexibility, the former referring to job changes involving new employment with a different employer and to labour turnover and geographic mobility, and the latter referring to job changes within the same enterprise; and *numerical* versus *functional* flexibility, the former relating to changes in the number of workers, and the latter meaning occupational changes and mobility within the enterprise. A second element for disagreement relates to its assessment, or the perceptions of the level of labour market flexibility. Employers are considered never to find labour markets flexible enough, while workers are believed always to prefer a higher degree of protection. But the most consistently controversial dimension is whether or not flexible labour markets deliver better outcomes. In the influential OECD *Jobs Study* (1994), for example, higher flexibility is clearly seen as the solution to poor economic and employment performance. Other international financial institutions (IFIs) and economists have made labour market deregulation[1] and increased employment and wage flexibility in the labour market the keys to economic success (see, for example, IMF, 2003), in line with what is commonly known as the orthodox view. In insisting on costs and disincentive effects induced by benefits and social security programmes, they recommend a general weakening of labour market institutions in favour of market adjustment. According to this approach, employment protection legislation (EPL),[2] for example, would lead to a reduction in employment, and 'over-generous' unemployment benefit or the minimum wage would create unemployment through work disincentives and obstacles to recruitment. At the same time the adverse role of employment protection on employment and unemployment has been challenged by several labour experts (for example, Pissarides, 2001) and many international organizations have subsequently expressed more nuanced views about the effects of labour market institutions on labour market outcomes: the OECD 1999 *Employment Outlook*, for example, found no influence of employment protection legislation on the level of unemployment.[3]

Economists have thus failed to reach consensus on the potential for deregulation to improve labour market performances: the effects of labour market institutions and policies on labour market outcomes, as they may affect both employers' and employees' decisions, are far from clear-cut from both a theoretical and an empirical perspective. Cazes and Nesporova (2003) provide an overview of theoretical arguments on the impact of employment protection legislation on labour market outcomes. The main findings are ambiguous, as employment protection legislation generates a number of effects on labour costs, employment and productivity: some

---

[1] Labour market regulations include here labour market institutions (such as trade unions, unemployment insurance systems and public employment systems), legislation (such as employment protection legislation and minimum wages) and labour market policies.

[2] EPL refers to regulatory provisions that relate to 'hiring and firing', particularly those governing unfair dismissals, termination of employment for economic reasons, severance payments, minimum notice periods, administrative authorization for dismissals, and prior consultations with trade union and/or labour administration representatives.

[3] Some negative impact was however revealed on the structure of unemployment.

favourable and some unfavourable. Thus the net impact of these effects seems likely to vary by size of firm and type of activity, and according to economic conditions. Empirical analysis has also failed to provide evidence on whether or not tight labour market regulations are to be blamed for poor labour market performance. One of the reasons for this is that measuring the degree of flexibility of a labour market is a difficult task, as there is no single indicator to capture all its dimensions. Moreover, while some aspects of labour market flexibility can be assessed quantitatively, such as the level of severance pay or unemployment benefit, the percentage of persons covered by the unemployment benefit schemes or the weight of the tax burden, other aspects are more difficult to measure, notably in the field of employment protection, such as the willingness of labour courts to accept lawsuits by fired workers or the interpretation of the notion of just cause for termination (see Bertola, Boeri and Cazes, 2000).

1.2   THE CONCEPT OF FLEXICURITY

The flexibility–efficiency argument has strong political implications, since it questions both the access to employment and the quality of this employment. Policy-makers, including the social partners involved in discussions and advocacy on economic and social security systems, are thus facing the crucial challenge of determining the forms of regulation that should accompany rapidly evolving labour markets in the context of a globalized economy. Should they heed the calls for greater flexibility? Or can they place their trust in a more balanced and comprehensive approach that seeks to address the flexibility–security nexus? According to research conducted by the International Labour Organization (ILO), increasing flexibility *alone* has not improved labour market efficiency, as all stakeholders need some degree of stability and security.[4] There is, for example, no convincing evidence that firms themselves would opt for a very high degree of flexibility and high labour turnover. They may prefer stable employment relationships and appreciate experience, as transaction costs such as screening and training would be lower in this case and efficiency wages[5] are counted over the longer term (see Becker, 1964, and Williamson, 1985). In a context of high volatility, there would be no investment in human capital, in new technologies and in capturing new markets. Hence, as both employers and workers need some flexibility and stability, there is a need for new types of institutions and policies in order to mobilize the workforce, improve its employability and adaptability, and more generally improve the efficiency of the labour markets.

Auer and Cazes (2003) provide examples of western industrialized countries which have organized their systems of employment and social protection in such a way as to allow flexibility for enterprises while ensuring income (and broader social)

---

[4] See for example Auer and Cazes (2003); Cazes and Nesporova (2003); Auer, Berg and Coulibaly (2005).

[5] Efficiency wages are set above the level of market-clearing wages.

protection to workers at the societal level. This is done by offering other than permanent, full-time contracts and extending social protection to persons on such contracts, while maintaining employment protection at the enterprise level, or by ensuring only a minimum of employment protection at the enterprise level but a decent level of easily accessible income and social protection in the case of redundancy. This suggests that it is never one institutional setting that on its own determines the question of job flexibility and security, but systemic interaction between the main national labour market institutions, such as the labour legislation, unemployment benefit schemes, active labour market policies (ALMPs) and wage-setting institutions. Thus policy-makers, legislators and the social partners may all have wider policy choices at their disposal. These choices are based on various combinations of the different components of the employment and social protection systems which need to be identified in order to enhance flexibility and security for both workers and employers. The viability of such choices is largely dependent on the willingness and the ability of social partners to become actively involved in defining the right balance of the various components of employment policy through tripartite and bipartite dialogue. It is therefore important to provide the partners with a meaningful role which engages them in the setting up of national employment policies, but also to constantly adjust such policies to the dynamics of the market through dialogue and negotiations at the various levels.

The 'flexicurity' approach combines a more flexible labour market with good social protection, offering high income protection accompanied by active labour market policies. This could provide an answer to the dilemma of how to maintain and improve competitiveness while at the same time preserving an effective policy framework for social inclusion, and also of how to make full use of the potential of social policy as a productive factor. The concept of flexicurity stems originally from a Dutch law (Wet Flexibiliteit en Zekerheid dated 1999), which offers temporary agency workers the prospect of permanent employment after two years of work and thus combines flexible assignment of staff with employment security. However, there is no one-size-fits-all flexicurity model, and different combinations of flexibility and security can be of service to both employers and workers in different national contexts (in terms of tradition and culture but also of variations in the structure of national economy and other factors). Although the balance can be delicate, at the heart of this concept lies the pursuit of win–win strategies for both employers and workers.

Flexicurity policies can be observed in various national and international governance systems: in the European Union (EU) Lisbon Strategy[6] and the ILO Global Employment Agenda, in the systems currently used in Austria and in Belgium, and in the Scandinavian countries. In each country, a different emphasis

---

[6] For European policy-makers, flexicurity has been increasingly seen as a way to preserve the European social model, which has its foundations in a shared commitment to economic prosperity, social cohesion and solidarity, healthcare and education systems that are accessible to all, as well as a broad and reliable social welfare system and social dialogue.

has been put on the types of flexibilization and security, as both are multi-dimensional concepts. In Denmark, for instance, there is a clear trade-off between a high level of external–numerical flexibility and a high level of income security. Danish workers have little protection against dismissal, but with decent income protection they have the security of being able to find a new job quickly, through wide access to training, mediation and reintegration. The Austrian approach has been characterized by a strong emphasis on active labour market policies, involving a shift from job security to employment security: there, employability of the workforce has become a crucial factor, enhancing flexibility through security. Moreover, the Austrian tradition of social partnership, which relies on a well-organized dialogue between the social partners, has smoothed the process of adaptation and helped promote the flexicurity concept.

1.3   LABOUR MARKETS IN TRANSITION: FLEXIBLE BUT JOBLESS

The process of economic and social reform that began in the early 1990s in Central and Eastern Europe has had a profound impact on the functioning and adjustment of the labour markets in these countries. Before transition, enterprises were not exposed to international competition and workers enjoyed extremely high employment protection, job security and stability. With the opening to global markets at the beginning of the 1990s, enterprises were forced to adjust their inputs – including labour and production technology – and their outputs to market demand. Labour market deregulation was thus seen as part of a necessary adjustment process, and it was broadly accepted that full employment and the generous social protection systems could not be maintained any longer. The policy prescription extended in the region, and strongly advocated by IFIs, was thus very much in line with the orthodox view of the labour market: employment protection legislation was amended, leading to a substantial moderation of workers' protection; and unemployment insurance schemes, while very generous at the beginning of transition, were severely reduced in terms of the level of benefits, eligibility conditions and duration of payment.[7] Nevertheless, low activity and employment rates, persistent unemployment and alarming levels of long-term unemployment remained major challenges in most countries of the region (Cazes and Nesporova, 2003). While it was first argued that the poor employment outcomes were due to slow economic recovery, there is now growing evidence that even in those countries where economic growth has since recovered and remained relatively high over a longer period, this has not led to significantly higher employment and lower unemployment.

---

[7] According to the orthodox theory, generous income support influences labour market performances in two ways: it discourages the unemployed from seeking jobs (by increasing their reservation wage) and it reduces the 'fear' of being unemployed, hence increasing the upward pressure on wages from employees (through the trade unions, for example).

Cazes and Nesporova (2003) explored in detail to what extent the labour markets of the Central and Eastern European (CEE) countries adjusted and became more flexible over the course of the 1990s. They analysed changes in the characteristics of employment and found a significant upsurge in flexible forms of employment, mainly in the form of multiple-job holding or second jobs, both formal and more especially informal (held in addition to primary employment, registered unemployment or formal inactivity). Also the frequency of temporary employment rose significantly, but more in the form of non-labour contracts rather than as fixed-term or short-term labour contracts. Using micro-level data, the authors also analysed the job reallocation process and workers' transitions across labour market status. They demonstrated that labour market flexibility measured by labour turnover intensified in connection with enterprise restructuring and that it fluctuated with the economic cycle.

An important result of their analysis was the finding of countercyclical behaviour of labour turnover, in contrast to the pro-cyclical pattern of economically advanced (in this case OECD) countries. The authors explained this result by depressed demand for labour but also by workers' behaviour, which was different in the CEE and OECD countries. In the former region, the weakening of workers' rights, the reduction of employment and income protection, and more generally high perceived insecurity meant that workers were reluctant to quit their jobs voluntarily, even during an economic upswing.[8] The authors also examined regulatory constraints faced by employers: amendments in employment protection legislation were clearly inspired by labour legislation reforms in economically advanced countries, in particular the EU15 countries.[9] Using methodology developed by the OECD (OECD, 1999), Cazes and Nesporova (2003) provided summary EPL strictness indices for the region for the late 1990s. They found that, on average, EPL was similar to the EU15 average and slightly above the OECD average. However, the weaknesses in labour market institutions and collective bargaining, combined with poor law enforcement, contributed to high labour market flexibility and perceived job insecurity.

Finally, the authors identified the possible effects of labour market institutions and policies on the labour market performances of CEE countries. They built on work done by Nickell (1997), Layard and Nickell (1999) and the OECD (1999), and conducted an econometric analysis; they looked at the impact of employment protection legislation, unemployment benefit systems, wage-setting institutions, active labour market policies and payroll taxes on labour market outcomes. The main result of this empirical research for the end of the 1990s was that the strictness of employment protection legislation had no statistically significant impact on unemployment (aggregate, youth and long-term) in CEE countries, but was significantly correlated with the level of the participation rate, suggesting that more

---

[8] This finding was also supported by a strong correlation between economic cycle and labour market flows data, such as moves from employment to unemployment or inactivity for the majority of the CEE countries studied by the authors.

[9] EU15: Austria, Belgium, Denmark, Ireland, Italy, Finland, Germany, Greece, France, Luxembourg, the Netherlands, Portugal, Spain, Sweden and the United Kingdom.

protection could increase labour force participation in the (formal) labour market. The explanation for this should be sought in the widespread non-observance of labour legislation as well as in the large informal employment. Active labour market policies and collective bargaining coverage were the labour market institutions that had an impact in enhancing labour market participation and employment and in lowering unemployment, youth unemployment and long-term unemployment over the period. In addition, all three unemployment indicators tended to increase with higher labour taxation.

It can thus be concluded that the deregulation policy conducted in Central and Eastern Europe did not improve labour market performance and even led in some countries to adverse effects on labour force participation – which had once been among the highest in the world, but is now below the OECD average – and on employment and labour reallocation. As mentioned previously, the enhancement of labour market efficiency involves addressing the complex flexibility–security nexus. Therefore, it is a major task of the policy-makers and social partners in the CEE countries to develop innovative policies to better manage labour market changes from both the economic and the social point of view.

1.4 TOWARDS FLEXICURITY STRATEGIES IN CENTRAL AND SOUTH-EASTERN EUROPE

The search for a better combination of flexibility and security has been increasingly emphasized within the EU as being indispensable to improve competitiveness and at the same time maintain the European social model. The Austrian Government, for example, included flexicurity among the key topics for its EU presidency. With the recent enlargement of the EU to include the CEE countries, the availability of adequate social security and active labour market policies which might enable the labour force to be more flexible and mobile can be questioned. The aim of this book is thus to advocate the relevance of the flexicurity approach for CEE countries and suggest appropriate reforms of both their labour markets and institutional frameworks, and their education and social security systems.

The book consists of nine chapters. After this introductory chapter, Chapter 2 first provides a comparative analysis of labour market developments and adjustment from a cross-country perspective – examining key labour market indicators such as labour market participation, employment, unemployment, underemployment and inactivity and major characteristics of employment relationship – in Central and South-Eastern Europe over the last five years. Then it endeavours to investigate whether new labour market flexibility patterns have emerged in the light of economic and employment developments since the late 1990s. Following the pattern of analysis used in Cazes and Nesporova (2003), it re-examines for the period 1999–2003 the different dimensions of flexibility, analysing flexible forms of employment, labour mobility and its fluctuation over the economic cycle, and the regulatory provisions faced by employers. Multivariate regressions test the impact of labour market institutions on labour market performances for the period, to assess the stage of convergence of the new EU members with the EU15 countries. This comparative analysis is supported by national studies on balancing labour market flexibility and security in Croatia, Bulgaria, Hungary, Lithuania and Poland.[10] For each country, the interactions between the main components of labour market regulation, institutions and policies are carefully examined to reveal whether or not the main elements of labour market institutions and policies have developed in such a way as to provide labour market flexibility without raising the level of insecurity (Chapters 3, 4, 5, 6 and 7).

Chapter 8 deals with the issue of wage flexibility, to reveal to what extent wages are flexible in adjusting to changes in economic conditions. Chapter 9 draws general conclusions and policy recommendations from these analyses to inform future labour market policy orientation for the new EU member and EU accession countries.

Finally, it should be noted that apart from a brief study of the extent and characteristics of employment in the informal economy in CSEE countries provided in Chapter 2, the main analysis in this book concentrates solely on employment in the formal economy for the reasons of availability of statistical data. At the same time it has to be acknowledged that a sharp increase in the informal economy experienced in the 1990s has to be seen as an important part of the process of labour market flexibilization and segmentation.

---

[10] This selection of countries was chosen to present different types of schematic relationships between employment and social protection.

LABOUR MARKETS IN CENTRAL AND SOUTH-EASTERN EUROPE: FROM TRANSITION TO STABILIZATION

2

Sandrine Cazes and Alena Nesporova

2.1 INTRODUCTION

This chapter provides a comparative analysis of changes in labour market characteristics occurring in Central and South-Eastern Europe (CSEE) since the end of the 1990s. The chapter consciously follows the outline of the previous book by Cazes and Nesporova, *Labour markets in transition: Balancing flexibility and security in Central and Eastern Europe* (Geneva, ILO, 2003), thereby updating its major analytical findings for the period 1999–2003/4. It attempts to give an answer to the question whether, in contrast to the developments in the 1990s, the labour markets of the new EU member and accession countries have recently evolved more in line with the trends observed in the EU15 countries or whether to a large extent divergent development still continues, with negative consequences for the European social model.

The chapter first discusses labour market trends and developments in the CSEE countries, identifying positive changes as well as persisting problems and newly emerging challenges. It then studies new evolutions in the incidence of flexible forms of employment. In its third section, it provides an insight into the labour market dynamics of the region – labour turnover, job tenure and outflows from unemployment – and studies the fluctuations in labour turnover, employment and outflows from unemployment over the economic cycle. The subsequent section analyses changes in the strictness of employment protection legislation and its relationship with key labour market indicators. The concluding section summarizes recent changes in the labour market institutions of the region and presents results of an analysis of the impact of institutions on major labour market indicators. Policy implications from this analysis, as well as from the national studies and cross-country wage study presented in the following chapters, are provided in the last chapter of the book.

2.2   RECENT LABOUR MARKET DEVELOPMENTS: POSITIVE TRENDS, PERSISTING PROBLEMS AND NEW CHALLENGES

From an economic point of view, the period of 2000–04 was successful for Central and South-Eastern Europe as all the countries of the region finally embarked on solid economic growth (see table 2.1), after having overcome the negative consequences of the Russian financial crisis (Baltic countries), transient economic recession (Czech Republic and Poland) and the Kosovo crisis (Balkan countries). Nevertheless, by 2004 only the five most advanced economies (Czech Republic, Hungary, Poland, Slovakia and Slovenia) and Albania had managed to exceed their 1989 level of gross domestic product (GDP), albeit in the new sectoral structure of GDP. Other countries had yet to reach their pre-transition levels although, with the exception of Macedonia, they recorded in general higher growth rates in the period under investigation, strengthening their catching-up process. First assessments of the effects of EU accession in May 2004 point to an overall positive impact on the economies of the eight CSEE countries concerned, as accelerating exports contributed additionally to their growth rates for 2004 and 2005.

Table 2.1   Average annual growth rates of GDP and employment, CSEE countries, 2000–04 (percentages)

Country	GDP	Employment
Albania	5.8	−2.65
Bosnia and Herzegovina	4.2	−1.00
Bulgaria	4.9	+1.11
Croatia	4.1	+0.67
Czech Republic	3.1	−0.24
Estonia	7.2	+0.58
Hungary	3.9	+0.46
Latvia	7.5	+1.01
Lithuania	6.7	−0.28
Former Yugoslav Republic of Macedonia	1.3	−3.90
Poland	3.1	−1.14
Romania	5.3	−1.66
Serbia and Montenegro	4.9	−0.92
Slovakia	4.1	+0.35
Slovenia	3.4	+0.63

Source: UNECE database, own calculations.

Figure 2.1 Labour market participation rates (population aged 15–64), EU8+3
countries, 2000 and 2004 (percentages)

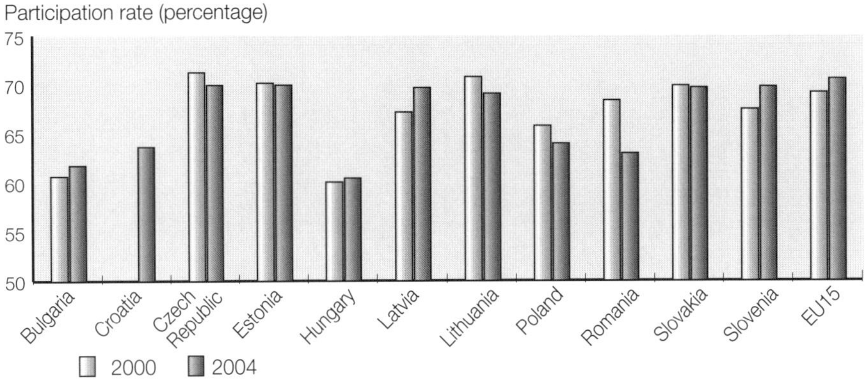

Participation rate (percentage)

Source: Eurostat.

Economic growth, however, has not been adequately translated into employment recovery. Only Bulgaria, Croatia, Estonia, Hungary, Latvia, Slovakia and Slovenia achieved positive, although very modest, net employment growth. All other countries of the CSEE region still face contraction of their employment (see table 2.1). Thus economic growth can still be characterized as nearly jobless growth for the region, despite huge employment losses during the transition crisis in the early 1990s in particular. This is especially worrying for countries such as Albania, Bosnia and Herzegovina, Macedonia, Poland, and Serbia and Montenegro,[1] the labour markets of which are very weak. As a result, the CSEE countries have on average significantly lower labour market participation rates compared with the EU15, and the difference is more pronounced for male than for female workers. Figure 2.1 confirms these findings for the new EU member and EU candidate countries (EU8+3) (comparable gender-specific employment data for Croatia were not available).[2]

Figure 2.1 shows that only four countries – Bulgaria, Hungary, Latvia and Slovenia – recorded increasing participation rates between 2000 and 2004. Moreover, while in 2000 four of the EU8+3 exceeded the average participation rate of the EU15, by 2004 none of them did and even the two countries with the highest activity rates – the Czech Republic and Estonia – remained 0.6 percentage points below the EU15 average. Cross-country differences are substantial at almost 10 percentage points, and cannot be explained away by variances in their economic level and growth rates.

---

[1] Montenegro declared its independence from Serbia on 2 June 2006. However, throughout this book we refer to the common State of Serbia and Montenegro due to data availability.

[2] Due to a lack of data and problems of their comparability for the majority of South-East European countries, we limit our analysis to the group of the new EU member (Czech Republic, Estonia, Hungary, Latvia, Lithuania, Poland, Slovakia and Slovenia) and EU candidate countries (Bulgaria, Croatia and Romania) in order to benefit from comparable Eurostat data.

Figure 2.2 Labour market participation rates by sex (population aged 15–64),
EU8+3 countries, 2000 and 2004 (percentages)

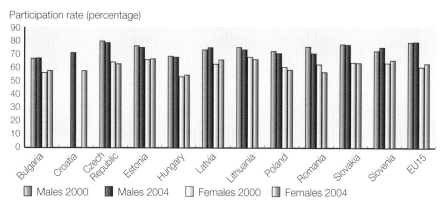

Source: Eurostat.

Three of the four countries with the highest GDP growth rates – Estonia, Lithuania and Romania – actually experienced a reduction in their participation rates, which in the case of Romania was rather steep. Only Bulgaria, Latvia and Slovenia were able to translate high economic growth into a significant increase in economic activity.

In all the EU8+3 countries, male participation rates were higher than female (see figure 2.2). The difference in participation rates ranged from 6.4 to 13.8 percentage points across the region in 2004, with a slight tendency towards a closing gender gap. The reason for this convergence was a tendency for male participation rates to shrink more or increase less than the female ones; in Hungary and Estonia the rates even moved in the opposite direction between 2000 and 2004. While in 2000 the Czech Republic was the only CSEE country which exceeded the average EU15 male participation rate, four years later not a single country reached that level. In contrast, as a legacy of the past high economic activity among women, only three of the EU8+3 countries had female participation rates below the EU15 average in 2000. By 2004, however, this number had increased to six, reflecting rapidly increasing economic activity among women in the old EU which has not been matched in the EU8+3 subregion.

Employment rates evolved more favourably than participation rates over the period 2000–04. This points to an improving employment situation in the subregion, with the exception of the Czech Republic (though its employment rate at least declined slightly less than the participation rate), Poland and Romania (see figure 2.3). The last two countries in particular experienced a sharp reduction in their employment rates, despite good economic growth. Comparisons with the EU15 average reveal that in 2004 only Slovenia found its rate slightly above the EU15 average while all other countries had lower employment rates, including the Czech

Figure 2.3 Employment rates, EU8+3 countries, 2000 and 2004 (percentages)

Employment rate (percentage)

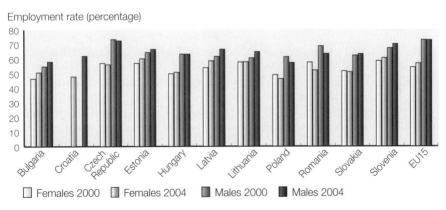

□ 2000 ■ 2004

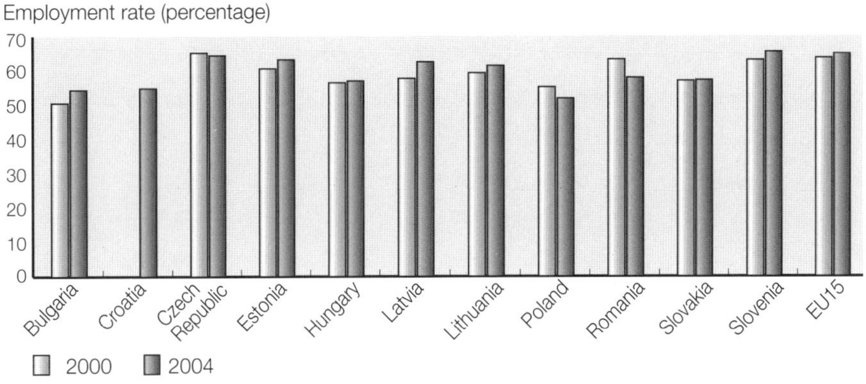

Source: Eurostat.

Republic and Romania, which four years earlier had been above or close to the EU15 average. The breakdown of the employment rates by sex (see figure 2.4) reveals that the main difference between the old and the new EU member and candidate countries is in the relatively low employment of men in the latter group. None of the EU8+3 countries reached the EU15 average for males in 2004 and the gap was significant in Bulgaria, for example, at 15 percentage points. Nevertheless, while the average male employment rate stagnated in the EU15, it slightly increased in the EU8+3 subregion. The EU8+3 female employment rates were more on a par with those of the old EU

Figure 2.4 Employment rates by sex, EU8+3 countries, 2000 and 2004
             (percentages)

Employment rate (percentage)

□ Females 2000 □ Females 2004 ■ Males 2000 ■ Males 2004

Source: Eurostat.

13

Table 2.2   Aggregate (AUR) and youth (YUR) unemployment rates, selected CSEE countries, 2000 and 2004 (percentages)

	2000			2004		
	AUR	YUR	YUR/AUR	AUR	YUR	YUR/AUR
Bulgaria	16.4	33.7	2.05	11.9	24.4	2.05
Czech Republic	8.7	17.8	2.05	8.3	21.1	2.54
Estonia	12.5	23.6	1.89	9.2	21.0	2.28
Hungary	6.3	12.1	1.92	5.9	14.8	2.50
Latvia	13.7	21.4	1.56	9.8	19.0	1.94
Lithuania	16.4	30.6	1.87	10.8	19.9	1.84
Poland	16.4	36.3	2.21	18.8	39.5	2.10
Romania	6.8	17.2	2.53	7.1	21.4	3.01
Slovakia	18.7	37.1	1.98	18.0	32.3	1.79
Slovenia	6.6	16.2	2.45	6.0	14.3	2.38
EU15	7.6	15.3	2.01	8.1	16.6	2.05

Source: Eurostat, own calculations.

countries, although the former countries are losing their position due to rapidly increasing female employment in the latter group. The overall EU8+3 trend was towards a slight increase, but if Croatia is included for 2004 the average female employment rate actually stagnated.

The majority of the EU8+3 countries have recorded declining unemployment, in particular the Baltic States and Bulgaria (see table 2.2). Nevertheless, there have been important differences across the subregion. Lithuania, in particular, seems to be a special case. On the one hand, the steep decline in unemployment in this country has been to some extent the result of a combination of continuous withdrawals from the labour market and rising employment (this issue is elaborated on further in section 2.3 below). Part of this favourable unemployment development should however be attributed to the rather high level of emigration after the country's accession to the EU in May 2004. Most of those leaving have been young people seeking better employment opportunities, mainly in Ireland and the United Kingdom, as is reflected in the sharply declining youth unemployment presented below. This also seems to be the case for Bulgaria and Slovakia, despite the candidate status of the former, as some anecdotal evidence confirms. In Bulgaria, Estonia, Latvia and Slovenia, decreasing unemployment rates are mainly connected with growing employment rates. The Czech Republic has seen both declining employment and unemployment rates due to a continuation of labour market departures. In contrast, the sharp fall in employment in Romania translated into a rapidly declining participation rate while relatively

Figure 2.5 Unemployment rates by sex as percentage of labour force, selected
CSEE countries, 2000 and 2004 (percentages)

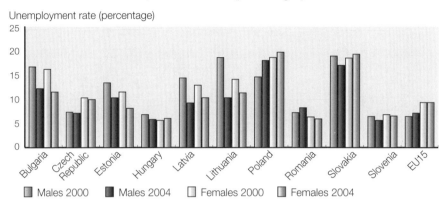

Source: Eurostat.

low unemployment only slightly increased. Changes in Hungary and Slovakia were
positive but small for all three labour market indicators. Labour market developments
in Poland contrasted with other EU8+3 countries, with the exception of Romania.
Despite healthy economic growth, employment in Poland significantly declined and
led on the one hand to a rapid increase in unemployment, reaching the highest level
of all these countries, and on the other to a further decline in economic activity.

Even though total unemployment has on average fallen significantly in the EU8+3
subregion over the period under investigation, while slightly increasing in the EU15,
it has remained well above the average of the 'old' Europe. The differences among
countries are substantial. The Polish unemployment rate is more than three times
higher than that of Hungary and Slovenia, and, what is most worrying, this
particularly high unemployment rate is combined with low economic activity in
Poland. In contrast, Slovenia seems to have the best labour market performance of
the whole region, combining low and declining unemployment rates with relatively
high and increasing participation and employment rates.

Figure 2.5 reveals that in seven out of ten countries of the EU8+3 subregion,
unemployment rates for men were higher than for women in 2000 but this was
reduced to only three countries out of ten in 2004. This indicates that improvements
in the unemployment situation were more beneficial for men than for women.
Nevertheless, despite systematically higher unemployment levels for both sexes in
this subregion, compared with the EU15, the gaps between the new and old Europe
are more profound for men than for women due to significantly lower (albeit
increasing) male unemployment in the EU15.

As table 2.2 showed, youth unemployment rates were on average twice as high
as the aggregate rates across Europe in 2000. However, countries with low aggregate
unemployment rates, such as Romania and Slovenia, had relatively higher youth

Figure 2.6 Youth unemployment rates (population aged 15–24) by sex, selected
CSEE countries, 2000 and 2004 (percentages)

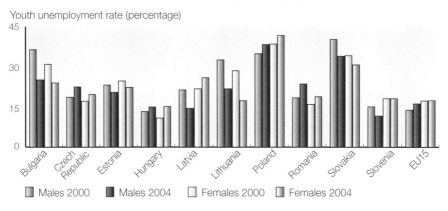

Source: Eurostat.

unemployment rates (see the fourth column of table 2.2), pointing to a disproportionately worse position of young people in their labour markets. Between 2000 and 2004 the ratio of youth to aggregate unemployment deteriorated in the majority of countries in the EU8+3 subregion, providing evidence that improving labour demand benefited mainly the adult population at the cost of young individuals without work experience. Moreover, the youth unemployment rate increased in absolute terms in the Czech Republic, Hungary, Poland and Romania, despite declining overall unemployment in the first two countries. This contrasts with significant declines in youth unemployment rates in Bulgaria, Lithuania and Slovakia, which could at least partially be explained by higher departures of young people from these countries after the May 2004 enlargement of the EU in search for new employment perspectives in richer EU countries. Estonia, Latvia and Slovenia experienced smaller absolute reductions in youth unemployment, which however meant an increase in the ratio of youth to aggregate unemployment. In general, unlike the EU15, which has almost stable youth unemployment, the EU8+3 countries recorded on average absolute reductions in youth unemployment but at the same time saw a relative deterioration of the labour market position of young people compared with their older counterparts.

Comparisons of youth unemployment rates by sex show that in about half of the EU8+3 countries male rates are higher while in the other half female rates are higher, climbing to 41.4 per cent in Poland.

Long-term unemployment (unemployment with duration over one year) remained very high in the EU8+3 subregion, well above the average of the EU15 (see table 2.3). Moreover, unlike in the EU15, it further increased in six out of ten countries between 2000 and 2004, so that only Hungary and Latvia recorded a share of long-term unemployment in total unemployment below 50 per cent. The situation is particularly

Table 2.3   Long-term unemployment as percentage of total unemployment, CSEE
countries, 2000 and 2004

Country	2000	2004
Bulgaria	57.3	59.7
Czech Republic	48.3	50.6
Estonia	45.6	52.2
Hungary	47.6	44.1
Latvia	57.7	43.9
Lithuania	67.0	54.6
Poland	46.3	54.3
Romania	51.4	59.2
Slovakia	54.5	65.0
Slovenia	60.6	51.7
EU15 average	44.7	42.0

Source: Eurostat.

detrimental in Slovakia, where two-thirds of all jobless and 11.7 per cent of the total labour force were without employment for more than one year. Long-term unemployment thus represents a particular problem for the EU8+3 countries due to its very high proportion in total unemployment and its persistence, suggesting that labour market institutions are paying relatively little attention to solving labour market problems of less competitive jobseekers. There is also a higher incidence of long-term unemployment among men: only the Czech Republic and Poland had higher female long-term unemployment rates in 2000, while Slovakia and Slovenia had the same rates for both sexes. However, this changed in 2004 when the proportion was reversed for Latvia, Lithuania, Slovakia and Slovenia, and the rates equalized in Bulgaria.

In sum, although the EU8+3 countries have finally embarked on sound economic growth, the majority of them have not been able to reverse the low and still declining labour market participation. The Baltic States, Bulgaria and Slovenia were the only countries to finally benefit from new job creation and improve their employment performance as unemployment began to decrease (though part of this decline should probably also be attributed in some countries to emigration in the wake of EU enlargement), but their employment rates remained low compared with the EU15 average and unemployment levels remained high for many of them. In other countries shrinking unemployment occurred as a consequence of the withdrawal of less competitive jobseekers from the labour market. In contrast, Poland and Romania faced significant deterioration of their labour market situation in terms of economic activity, employment and unemployment. Poland and Slovakia are the two countries with the highest unemployment rates in the subregion. Youth unemployment and long-term unemployment remain very high for the subregion, showing that less competitive individuals are seriously disadvantaged in the labour market and need intensive assistance from labour market institutions.

2.3   Increasing flexibilization of employment relations in Central and South-Eastern Europe

The main finding of our analysis of the CSEE labour market characteristics in the 1990s was a relatively low incidence of 'classical' flexible forms of employment such as part-time employment, fixed-term contracts or self-employment (this with the exception of Poland and Romania) in this region, compared with the old EU countries. Therefore it is interesting to check whether this characteristic has changed in the period of economic boom after 1999.

As far as self-employment is concerned, in most countries the acceleration of economic growth has led towards a decline in the proportion of own-account workers in total employment (see table 2.4). The only exceptions are the Czech Republic and Slovakia, where there is rapidly growing self-employment, and Estonia and Romania,

Table 2.4   Self-employment as percentage of total employment by sex, CSEE countries, 2000 and 2004

	2000			2004		
	Total	Men	Women	Total	Men	Women
Bulgaria[1]	11.4	..	..	10.4	..	..
Czech Republic	15.0	18.8	10.1	18.8	24.0	12.2
Estonia	9.0	11.5	6.4	9.6	12.9	6.3
Hungary	15.1	18.8	10.5	14.2	17.6	10.1
Latvia	14.9	16.3	13.5	13.3	14.4	12.1
Lithuania[2]	20.0	23.1	16.9	18.4	20.7	16.0
Poland[3]	37.7	40.6	34.1	29.0	31.4	26.1
Romania	46.2	44.4	48.2	46.8	47.3	46.3
Slovakia	8.3	11.3	4.8	12.3	16.5	7.2
Slovenia[4]	18.0	20.3	14.4	16.7	19.0	14.0
EU15	14.9	17.8	11.0	14.9	18.1	10.8

Notes: .. = not available. [1] 2003 instead of 2004. [2] 2002 instead of 2000. [3] Break in the series in 2003. [4] 2001 instead of 2000.

Source: Eurostat.

which have slightly increasing shares of self-employment. In the case of Romania, however, this was combined with sharply falling employment, i.e. the absolute number of self-employed actually fell in Romania. There are wide differences across the subregion in percentages of self-employed workers in total employment, ranging from 9.6 per cent in Estonia to 46.8 per cent in Romania. A large part of these variations can be explained by the high proportion of farming in total employment and the fact that agriculture is mostly based on family farms in countries such as Lithuania, Poland and Romania. With new job opportunities outside agriculture, younger people leave small-scale farming and accept wage employment, which contributes to declining self-employment. This is not the case for Romania, however, where the deteriorating labour market situation generally is not conducive to leaving agriculture.

Quite frequently, self-employment hides regular employment relationships between employers and workers, as employers force workers to accept civil contracts that permit employers to disguise an employment relationship and thus avoid paying costs such as social contributions and insurance against occupational accidents. Some anecdotal evidence points to an increasing incidence of this phenomenon in the Czech Republic and perhaps also in Slovakia, and this could partially explain the increasing share of self-employment in both countries. There have been serious efforts by the EU8+3 governments to reduce this misuse of civil contracts,[3] which could also contribute to an overall decline in self-employment figures. However, there have been other factors such as tough competition from the major international retail, catering and hotel chains, which drive out local shops, restaurants and hotels and limit self-employment.

The breakdown of self-employment by sex reveals that with the exception of Romania men are significantly more involved in self-employment than women. This is particularly true for countries with low proportions of employment in agriculture. Moreover, in countries such as the Czech Republic, Estonia, Romania and Slovakia, male self-employment increased relatively fast in the period under study, while female self-employment saw a slower rise or even a decline. This contrasts with the rest of the 'new' European countries facing declining shares of self-employed persons in total employment, but there the reduction for men was more pronounced than for women. Comparison with the EU15 shows that the EU8+3 countries tend to have on average a higher proportion of own-account workers, as this proportion stagnated after 2000 in the old EU member countries. Both country groups have also experienced an increasing gap between male and female self-employment levels.

An interesting development has occurred with regard to fixed-term contracts (see table 2.5). Eight out of eleven countries have seen a growing incidence of fixed-term contracts, although the development has not been dramatic so far, with the exception of Poland. Although we have only very limited information on newly concluded

---

[3] The Hungarian Government introduced new labour legislation on the use of independent contractors and on so-called 'labour loan' arrangements (where workers are lent by one enterprise to perform work for another) as of 1 January 2006. This includes specific definitions of the differences between regular contracts and independent or civil contracts, which can be concluded only for the provision of one precise product or service. Labour law violations can be fined up to HUF 20 million.

Table 2.5   Fixed-term contracts as percentage of total employment, CSEE countries, 2000 and 2004

	2000			2004		
	Total	Men	Women	Total	Men	Women
Bulgaria[1]	6.3	6.6	5.9	7.4	7.7	7.0
Croatia	..	..	..	12.2	12.1	12.4
Czech Republic	8.1	7.1	9.4	9.1	7.8	10.7
Estonia	3.0	4.4	1.7	2.6	3.5	1.8
Hungary	7.1	7.7	6.5	6.8	7.5	6.1
Latvia	6.7	8.8	4.6	9.5	11.6	7.3
Lithuania	4.4	5.9	3.1	6.3	8.7	3.9
Poland	5.8	6.5	4.9	22.7	23.7	21.5
Romania	2.8	2.8	2.8	2.5	2.9	2.0
Slovakia	4.8	5.1	4.5	5.5	6.0	5.1
Slovenia	13.7	12.7	14.8	17.8	16.7	19.1
EU15	13.7	12.8	14.7	13.6	12.9	14.4

Note: .. = not available. [1] 2001 instead of 2000.

Source: Eurostat.

contracts (see Chapter 4), it points to a sharp increase in the offer of fixed-term contracts in Croatia (while their share in all contracts grows more slowly) and also to their shortening duration; in Croatia over half of new contracts were concluded for a period of less than six months in 2002 compared with less than one-quarter five years earlier. Anecdotal evidence points to the existence of such a phenomenon in at least some other EU8+3 countries as well. These trends seem to reveal increasing labour market segmentation, with certain workers (usually young people and lower-skilled workers) confined to this type of precarious jobs, subject to high job turnover, while the majority of workers enjoy permanent contracts and thus more stable and secure jobs. There has been a rapid increase in the use of fixed-term contracts in Poland, where their share in total employment increased four times between 2000 and 2004. This is another sign of the sharp deterioration of the Polish labour market: in a context of high economic insecurity employers are resorting to temporary contracts, facilitated by changes in labour legislation (see Chapter 7). This rapid flexibilization of employment has not contributed to significant labour market improvements, however, as might be expected by neo-liberal economists. Besides Poland, Slovenia is the only CSEE country to have achieved a proportion of temporary contracts in total employment above the EU15 average, while Croatia is approaching that level.

Table 2.6   Part-time employment as percentage of total employment, CSEE
            countries, 2000 and 2004

	2000			2004		
	Total	Men	Women	Total	Men	Women
Bulgaria[1]	3.2	2.9	3.6	2.4	2.1	2.7
Croatia	..	..	..	8.5	6.3	11.2
Czech Republic	5.3	2.2	9.3	4.9	2.3	8.3
Estonia	8.1	5.3	10.9	8.0	5.4	10.6
Hungary	3.5	2.0	5.2	4.7	3.2	6.3
Latvia	11.3	9.7	12.8	10.4	7.7	13.2
Lithuania	10.2	9.2	11.1	8.4	6.5	10.4
Poland	10.5	8.2	13.4	10.8	8.2	14.0
Romania	16.5	14.6	18.6	10.6	10.2	11.2
Slovakia	2.1	1.1	3.1	2.7	1.4	4.2
Slovenia	6.5	5.3	7.8	9.3	7.9	11.0
EU15	17.7	6.1	33.2	19.4	7.2	35.1

Note: .. = not available. [1] 2001 instead of 2000.

Source: Eurostat.

Interestingly, the use of fixed-term contracts has stagnated in the old EU after 2000 while the overall tendency in Central and South-Eastern Europe is towards higher temporary employment.

Unlike in the EU15, where fixed-term contracts are on average more often held by women, in the 'new' European region fixed-term employment is more frequent among men, with the exception of the Czech Republic and Slovenia. Both countries have also experienced faster growth of temporary employment of women compared with men. All other countries have experienced the opposite trend, with an increasing gap in their incidence between both sexes to the detriment of men.

The last flexible form of employment for which data are available, part-time employment, has so far been underrepresented in the EU8+3 countries in comparison with the EU15 (table 2.6). The share of part-time employment in total employment in the EU15 subregion is almost double that of three EU8+3 countries with the highest level of part-time employment, namely Latvia, Poland and Romania. Moreover, while it has further increased in the EU15, in most countries of the former subregion part-time employment has declined (notably in Romania) or stagnated. The only country which registered a more significant increase in part-time employment was Slovenia, followed at some distance by Hungary. The main reasons for the low incidence of part-time employment remain the same as described in Cazes and Nesporova (2003). Employers claim that, due to high labour taxation and other fixed labour costs, part-time employment (including job-sharing) is not profitable for them and is not perceived favourably by customers. Workers state that due to increasing living costs they cannot afford shorter working hours and corresponding wage losses. Low birth rates on the one hand and availability of long maternity and parental benefits in a situation of relatively expensive childcare facilities also contribute to low part-time employment, as women (only very rarely men) prefer to stay at home with their children for longer rather than combining an early return to work and shorter working hours. In terms of gender differences, although the incidence of part-time employment is clearly higher for women than for men, the gap between the sexes is less profound than in the EU15, where the female share was five times higher in 2004. Thus, while the share of men with part-time employment was on average the same for both subregions, that for women was approximately three times higher in the EU15. No information was available on the proportion of involuntary part-time employment.

While in the late 1990s multiple-job holding was a significant flexible form of employment, the national studies (Chapters 3–7) report a significant decrease in its use for the period under study.

Although data on informal employment are scanty, they suggest its decline due to recent improvements in national legislation and its enforcement, as well as tighter control of informal activity by the public employment services and better tax collection.

One can conclude from the above analysis that in the majority of the new EU member and candidate countries there is indeed a trend towards increasing flexibilization of employment. This is mainly manifested in the growing incidence of contracts with limited duration, which are more widespread among men and involve young people and low-skilled workers in particular, who often remain stuck in these insecure types of employment. In contrast, part-time employment is still not popular in the subregion and its low availability can in fact contribute to unfavourable demographic developments: as long parental leaves can result in employers discriminating against workers with small children, families may decide to have one child or none at all. There has not been any clear trend in self-employment across the subregion, with the exception of family (subsistence) farming, which is evidently in decline as a result of improving employment opportunities. Two opposing trends have affected the development of self-employment. On the one hand are factors such as international retail, catering and hotel chains squeezing out small local firms; multinational enterprises often relying on their own suppliers from abroad; or emerging better wage employment opportunities for those who would have been forced to turn to self-employment for want of a job. On the other hand there are factors contributing towards an increase in self-employment such as new information and communication technologies, which allow highly skilled specialists to start their own profitable businesses; or imperfect legislation that allows the substitution of labour contracts by service (civil) contracts. Informal employment seems to be still high in South-Eastern Europe in particular, but the available information suggests a declining trend.

2.4 LABOUR MARKET DYNAMICS IN THE REGION: RECENT TRENDS

This section examines the dynamics of labour markets in CSEE countries and their relation to economic and employment developments over the last five years. More specifically it checks how labour mobility and labour reallocation have evolved recently after the period of massive restructuring of the enterprise sector in the 1990s. It goes on to examine job stability on the basis of job tenure data and destinations of outflows from employment to determine the extent to which employment has recently become more stable and secure. Finally, it assesses whether labour dynamics in these countries have been converging towards OECD patterns in recent years.

2.4.1 Declining labour turnover in the 2000s

Two sources of employment flow data are available to assess labour mobility and the intensity of reallocation: those based on establishment surveys (ES) and those originating in labour force surveys (LFS). Labour turnover based on the former source is calculated as a sum of recruitments and separations by individual establishments over a given year divided by their initial or average employment levels for that year. As establishment surveys only cover enterprises with over a certain number of employees, they may exclude an important segment of the enterprise sector as well as certain categories of workers with irregular contracts. Hence we have based our analysis on LFS, whenever it was possible.[4]

Labour force surveys were introduced gradually into the region during the 1990s; and more recently, national statistical offices have begun to estimate selected aggregate flow data regularly and provide them to Eurostat. Additional flow data have been provided by researchers based on their own calculations.[5] Labour turnover is a sum of the aggregate accession and separation rates. The accession rate is calculated as a sum of aggregate flows from unemployment to employment, from inactivity to employment and from one employment to another, divided by initial or average employment in a given year.[6] The separation rate is a sum of aggregate flows from

---

[4] For a comprehensive presentation of data and sources, as well as their characteristics, see Cazes and Nesporova (2003).

[5] For example, Haltiwanger and Vodopivec (1998); Arro et al. (2001); Kwiatkowski, Socha and Sztanderska (2001); and Večerník (2001), who provided data calculated by them for Estonia, Poland and the Czech Republic. More recent data for these countries as well as for Hungary and Slovenia have been calculated and kindly provided to us by departments responsible for labour force surveys in the national statistical offices.

[6] Similarly to establishment surveys, a vague definition of job-to-job changes may be an important source of data distortions, especially in comparative studies. For this reason we could not use all the available data, in particular when there was a strikingly wide difference between the results of establishment surveys and labour force surveys, as in the case of Slovenia.

employment to unemployment, from employment to inactivity and from one employment to another, divided by initial or average employment in a given year.

Available data from both sources of information (ES for Bulgaria and Poland; and LFS data for Croatia, the Czech Republic, Estonia, Hungary, Lithuania and Poland – see table 2.7) indicate a general stabilization – and in some countries even a decrease – of labour turnover in the region over the 1999–2003 period. Previous findings already indicated such a trend: they showed that after an initial phase of intensive labour reallocation following the introduction of economic reforms in the early 1990s, labour turnover subsequently declined and stabilized in all countries, with some periodic surges due to specific structural changes or economic shocks, such as the Russian financial crisis in 1998 (Cazes and Nesporova, 2003). Hence the period under review (1999–2003) seems to correspond to a phase of enterprise stabilization, rather than a restructuring period. Bulgaria stands out as an exception, however, with outstanding labour mobility rates,[7] as explained in more detail below. Another remarkable pattern is the convergence of separation and accession rates over recent years; moreover, while in the 1990s separation rates exceeded hiring rates (mostly due to downsizing of large enterprises), the reverse can be observed since the early 2000s in Bulgaria, the Czech Republic and Hungary.

In Poland the dynamics of the labour market weakened quite significantly after 1998. Separation rates and turnover data, from both sources, show that job destruction, but also labour churning,[8] have been dominating labour market dynamics. However, data and patterns diverged between ES and LFS for accession rates, in particular over the last five years: they suggest that, in contrast to the 1990s, the job creation capacity of small enterprises (which are better captured by LFS) has slowed down significantly since 1998. As detailed in Chapter 7, the Polish labour market has been characterized by a fall in participation and employment rates between 1998 and 2003; changes in the level of employment were also combined with changes in employment structure, with two groups particularly hit on the labour market: workers in the public sector and employers whose numbers dropped by about 12.2 per cent; in addition, employment in firms employing between one and five workers decreased between 1998 and 2004.

Bulgaria experienced very high labour mobility rates over the 1990s, indicating massive job destruction in large and medium-sized enterprises (see table 2.7). The establishment of the Currency Board in 1997 forced the Government to accelerate the privatization of large state enterprises; this led to restructuring and large-scale downsizing, particularly in 1999. Simultaneously, the hiring rate increased substantially, pointing to strengthening structural changes, with a positive effect on economic growth. In 2001, for the first time, the hiring rate exceeded the separation rate, but due to a sharper decrease of separation rates, since then both rates have been increasing, with hiring rates accelerating in 2003. Macroeconomic stability and

---

[7] Data for Bulgaria, from ES, do not seem fully comparable with other figures however.

[8] Labour churning refers to labour mobility connected with non-structural reasons.

Table 2.7   Accession rates, separation rates and labour turnover, selected CSEE countries, 1990–2003 (percentages)

Country	Source	1990	1993	1996	1998	1999	2000	2001	2002	2003
				Accession rates						
Bulgaria	ES	..	..	..	18.6	19.5	23.5	22.0	24.2	27.7
Croatia	LFS	..	..	..	..	15.7	16.3	16.3	14.1	..
Czech Republic	LFS	..	22.6	12.2	10.5	11.6	11.8	9.9	9.8	10.9
Estonia	LFS	14.9	25.6	20.8	16.0	15.2	16.5	16.2	16.2	18.2
Hungary	LFS	..	..	..	..	16.4	15.4	14.4	14.5	15.4
Lithuania	LFS	..	..	..	..	..	..	13.4	16.0	14.0
Poland	ES	12.2	20.6	25.0	24.6	23.9	20.5	19.5	17.5	.
Poland	LFS	..	22.8	28.5	19.6	17.2	18.0	16.4	14.8	..
				Separation rates						
Bulgaria	ES	..	..	..	21.3	24.4	26.7	21.8	22.3	24.4
Croatia	LFS	..	..	..	..	18.0	18.9	17.6	13.8	..
Czech Republic	LFS	..	22.0	12.6	11.8	12.3	11.4	9.9	9.3	11.1
Estonia	LFS	15.9	30.0	22.1	19.0	19.6	19.9	18.0	17.0	18.0
Hungary	LFS	..	..	..	..	14.5	13.7	12.9	12.7	13.9
Lithuania	LFS	..	..	..	..	..	..	14.4	14.3	12.0
Poland	ES	23.0	21.0	22.3	22.8	24.6	23.0	23.6	19.0	21.6
Poland	LFS	..	21.2	24.9	16.8	13.6	15.2	13.2	13.2	..
				Labour turnover						
Bulgaria	ES	..	..	..	39.9	43.9	50.2	43.7	46.5	52.1
Croatia	LFS	..	..	..	..	33.7	35.2	33.9	27.9	..
Czech Republic	LFS	..	44.6	24.8	22.3	23.9	23.2	19.8	19.1	22.0
Estonia	LFS	30.8	55.6	42.9	35.0	34.8	36.4	34.2	33.2	36.2
Hungary	LFS	..	..	..	..	31.0	29.1	27.3	27.2	29.3
Lithuania	LFS	..	..	..	..	..	..	27.8	30.3	26.0
Poland	ES	35.2	41.6	47.3	47.4	48.5	43.5	43.1	36.5	..
Poland	LFS	..	44.0	53.4	36.4	30.8	33.2	29.6	28.0	..

Notes: ES = establishment survey. LFS = labour force survey. .. = not available.

Sources: National statistics, calculations by national statistical offices.

positive economic growth over the last years (over 4 per cent for 2000–03) have created a favourable environment for increased job creation and higher demand for labour. This led to a positive impact on employment[9] and a general improvement of

[9] However with a total employment figure of 3,020,000 in 2003, employment in Bulgaria did not even reach its 1993 level.

Figure 2.7 Accession and separation rates within selected CSEE countries, 1990–2003 (percentages)

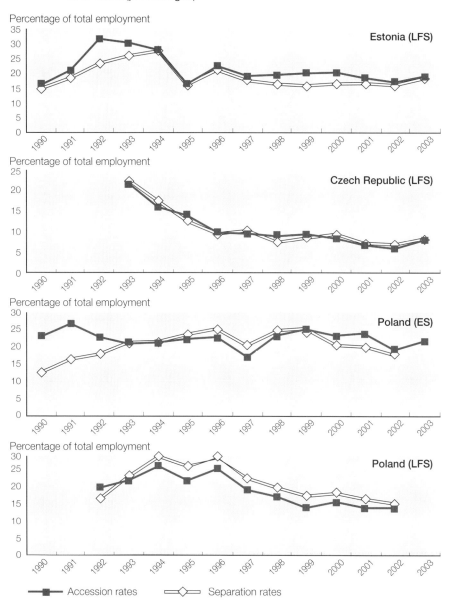

Notes : ES = establishment survey; LFS = labour force survey.

Source: See table 2.7.

labour market performance in this period: unemployment has been decreasing from its peak level of 1999 (19.2 per cent) to a lower 11.9 per cent in 2004.

Estonia and the Czech Republic recorded the lowest labour turnover in the early 2000s (figure 2.7).[10] In Estonia, the accession rate slightly exceeded the separation rate for the first time in 2003, after massive restructuring of the enterprise sector and intensive reallocation of labour over the whole transition period. The overall effect of structural changes translated into a slight improvement of labour market performance. In the Czech Republic, accession and separation rates have followed a quasi-similar (synchronized) pattern, in level and tendency. The Czech employment growth rate was negative for the 2000–04 period, despite economic recovery, but its level was still among the highest in the region. Turnover data for Croatia, Hungary and Lithuania have been available only recently. They point to an overall stabilization of the labour dynamics of these countries, with some differences in their relationship between accession and separation rates. In Hungary,[11] hiring and firing rates have been synchronized but at rather low levels, with the former always exceeding the latter. This has been the case in Lithuania only since 2002 and in Croatia since 2003. Declining separation rates – in particular outflows from employment to unemployment – reflected the recovery of the Lithuanian economy (which began in 2000); they were followed by a slight decrease in unemployment levels.

2.4.2 Labour turnover, job tenure and employment outflows

How is labour turnover affected by economic fluctuations? In industrialized countries, it typically accelerates in periods of economic growth: enterprise start-ups and expansions create new jobs, attracting newcomers to the labour market and increasing hires of unemployed jobseekers. At the same time, though dismissals for economic reasons abate, the growing number of job opportunities encourages more people to change their jobs *voluntarily*. In contrast, in economic downturns, labour turnover declines: enterprises seek to cut costs by reducing hires and by resorting to redundancies, yet the consequent sharp reduction of voluntary quits more than counterbalances the increase in dismissals. Hence, largely for supply-side reasons, labour turnover tends to behave pro-cyclically (Boeri, 1995; ILO, 1996). An important finding of Cazes and Nesporova (2003) was the countercyclical behaviour of labour turnover in CEE countries over the transition decade. Table 2.8 presents the correlation coefficients of labour turnover to both GDP and employment growth rates

---

[10] It is important to note that labour turnover data for the Czech Republic are not fully comparable with those for other countries, as they underestimate job-to-job moves. For methodological reasons it was not possible to separate job-to-job moves from continuous employment for some 20 per cent of persons covered by the LFS (see Večerník, 2001). Moreover, unlike Poland, where calculations sum up quarterly flows, the data for the Czech Republic as well as for Estonia are annual and do not take into account multiple changes during the year. The data therefore underestimate aggregate labour market flows.

[11] Small enterprises not taken into account.

Table 2.8   Correlations between GDP and employment dynamics (E) versus labour turnover (LT), selected CSEE countries, 1999–2003

Country	LT vs GDP	LT vs GDP (–1)	LT vs E	LT vs E (–1)
Bulgaria	0.63	–0.32	0.16	0.37
Croatia[1]	–0.49	–0.79	–0.73	–0.91
Czech Republic	0.20	–0.87	–0.65	–0.82
Estonia	0.12	–0.53	–0.19	–0.42
Hungary	0.25	0.07	0.98	0.27
Lithuania[2]	–0.75	–0.03	0.32	–0.77
Poland[1]	0.80	0.70	–0.28	–0.22

Notes: [1] 1999–2002, LFS. [2] 2001–2003. (–1) = data lagged by one period.

Sources: For labour turnover data see table 2.7. GDP and employment data from UNECE. Own calculations.

for a new set of CSEE countries, which slightly differs from our previous research; hence results are not fully comparable. Cross-country comparisons are impaired by the fact that the labour turnover data series are rather short for some countries and the results should therefore be interpreted with caution. Bearing these caveats in mind, the same correlations have been calculated with a time lag of one year, as labour adjustment to new economic performances may take a while.

The correlation between labour turnover and GDP shown in table 2.8 do not indicate clear-cut patterns: coefficients indicate a negative correlation for Croatia and Lithuania and a significant positive correlation for Bulgaria, Hungary and Poland. For the other countries there seems to be no significant correlation between the two indicators. However, the time-lagged coefficients (column three) show the correlation to *be negative for almost all the countries* – with the exception of Poland (the correlation being non-significant for Hungary). Correlations with employment growth (see last two columns) confirm this pattern, in particular with the time-lagged variable which is more strongly correlated to labour turnover. These findings suggest that in general labour reallocation has been more responsive to employment changes than to fluctuations in GDP growth and point to a weaker link between employment and economic fluctuations; while strong economic performances did not translate into more significant employment creation, they contributed to decreases in unemployment. Poland is again the exception, with, on the one hand, a strong pro-cyclical labour turnover and, on the other, a mild countercyclical fluctuation of turnover to employment growth. This result could be explained by labour churning, in a context of depressed demand for labour.

In Croatia, negative correlations exist between employment growth and labour turnover, on the one hand, and between economic growth and labour turnover, on the other. The same goes for Hungary, though the correlations are in this case positive.

This pattern suggests a rather strong relationship between economic and employment developments in these two countries. For the rest of the region, the overall picture is less clear-cut: labour turnover may be positively correlated to GDP and negatively to employment growth or vice versa, suggesting a rather peculiar link between economic and labour market developments. However, when a time lag is introduced, a strong negative correlation emerges between labour turnover and the employment dynamics in all countries, except in Bulgaria and Hungary (last column of table 2.8). The pro-cyclical behaviour of turnover in these two countries can be explained by the recent improvement of their labour market outcomes, in particular the growing labour force and employment rates.

Overall, the calculations presented in table 2.8 invite the tentative conclusion *that labour turnover still tends to have a countercyclical development in the region*, with the exception of Bulgaria and Hungary, which continues to contrast with the situation in industrialized countries. This pattern coincides with the simultaneous decrease of accession and separation rates, with a stronger deceleration for the latter. As indicated previously, the explanation can be found in a certain stabilization of the labour markets since 2000, as defensive restructuring[12] and massive withdrawals from the labour markets have come to an end. Enterprises are not dismissing workers more, but they have not opened new positions, as indicated by the continuing rather poor employment performance.

The distribution of employment by job tenure,[13] as well as average tenures, provides a general summary of job stability across countries. Table 2.9 presents these indicators for some countries (unfortunately data on job tenures are quite scarce in the region) in 2003. Average job tenure in these countries was 9.0 years in 2003, below the 2002 average of 10.5 years for the EU14[14] and 12.2 years for Japan, but above the United Kingdom level of 8.4 years (2005) and the United States average of 6.9 years (2004) (see Auer, Berg and Coulibaly, 2005). Table 2.9 shows the differences between countries in average tenure. The lowest job tenures are held in Estonia, Bulgaria and Lithuania respectively (slightly above the United States level, but still below that of the United Kingdom), followed by Hungary and the Czech Republic with tenures below ten years (levels similar to those in Denmark and the Netherlands).[15] The longest average tenure is still to be found in Poland.

Cross-country differences are even more pronounced when the distribution of employment across some job tenure classes is considered, notably the share of workers with long tenures. There are significant differences in the proportion of workers with ten or more years of tenure, between Poland (43.8 per cent) and the

---

[12] 'Defensive restructuring' is within-enterprise reform and rationalization, resulting largely in labour shedding, while 'strategic restructuring' should lead to the revival of the firm through innovations, with possible new recruitments.

[13] Defined as the length of time currently employed individuals have spent with their present employer.

[14] EU14: Belgium, Denmark, Finland, France, Germany, Greece, Ireland, Italy, Luxemburg, Netherlands, Portugal, Spain, Sweden and the United Kingdom.

[15] According to Eurostat, average job tenure was 8.4 years in Denmark and 9.9 years in the Netherlands in 2002.

Table 2.9   Distribution of employment by job tenure, selected CSEE countries, 2003 (percentages)

Country	Job tenure									
	<6 months (%)	6–12 months (%)	1–2 years (%)[1]	2–5 years (%)[1]	5–10 years (%)	10–20 years (%)	>20 years (%)	Average tenure (years)	Total <1 year (%)	Total >10 years (%)
Bulgaria	..	16.9[2]	8.6	23.2	21.6	29.7[3]	..	7.6	16.9	29.7
Croatia	..	..	..	..	..	..	..	11.0	..	..
Czech Republic	5.7	5.3	16.1	14.3	25.4	21.1	12.2	9.0	11.0	33.3
Estonia	..	18.0[2]	12.0	23.0	24.0	23.0[3]	..	7.3	18.0	23.0
Hungary		13.3[2]	8.7	26.6	20.8	30.6[3]	..	8.7	13.3	30.6
Lithuania	6.7	6.3	11.3	18.2	29.3	19.6	8.7	7.7	13.0	28.3
Poland	7.0	5.0	7.8	17.1	19.3	22.0	21.8	11.7	12.0	43.8
Unweighted average	..	..	..	..	..	..	..	9.0	13.5	31.8
EU14[4]	..	..	..	..	..	..	..	10.5	14.8	41.5

Notes: [1] The breakdown provided by the Czech Statistical Office differs slightly for two sub-periods, as it refers to 1–3 years and 3–5 years. [2] <1 year. [3] >10 years. [4] 2002. For average tenure: European Union, the United States and Japan; for the distribution of employment by tenure: European Union and the United States. .. = not available.

Sources: Eurostat; Czech data from the Statistical Yearbook of the Czech Republic, 2004.; data in Auer, Berg and Coulibaly (2005).

Baltic States (23.0 per cent in Estonia and 28.3 per cent in Lithuania in 2003). As detailed in Cazes and Nesporova (2003), these striking differences can be partly explained by the sectoral distribution of job tenure. A comparison of average tenure data between 1999 and 2003 points to a slight lengthening of job tenure over the period, except for Poland, where it slightly decreased from 11.9 to 11.7 years (table 2.10). This finding would be consistent with the previous result that labour turnover declined in the region over the last years of the period and labour markets stabilized. However, analysing job tenure patterns is a complex task, because of two factors: the composition effect (average tenure is a weighted sum with respect to groups of workers with different characteristics, so changes in the weights can mask the actual variation in tenure within each group and average tenure may also reflect changes in the demographic composition of the labour force) and the effect of the economic cycle.[16] While data and evidence are unfortunately insufficient here to detect any clear-cut picture of employment stability through average tenure, the comparison of

---

[16] For a detailed presentation of this issue, see Auer, Cazes and Spiezia (2001).

Table 2.10 Distribution of employment by job tenure, selected CSEE countries, 1999 and 2003 (percentages)

Country	1999	2003
Czech Republic[1]		
Average tenure	8.2	9.0
Under 1 year	14.6	11.0
Over 10 years	25.5	33.3
Estonia		
Average tenure	6.9	7.3
Under 1 year	18.4	18.0
Over 10 years	19.9	23.0
Hungary		
Average tenure	8.8	8.7
Under 1 year	12.6	13.3
Over 10 years	30.9	30.6
Lithuania		
Average tenure	7.6	7.7
Under 1 year	12.8	13.0
Over 10 years	24.1	28.3
Poland		
Average tenure	11.9	11.7
Under 1 year	10.5	12.0
Over 10 years	44.2	43.8

Notes: [1] For 1994: December to February of the following year; for 1999: October to December.

Sources: Eurostat; for Slovenia, national data; for Czech Republic, national data.

the employment distribution by job tenure between 1999 and 2003 suggests that some significant changes occurred, such as a shift of the distribution towards shorter tenure in most countries. In Estonia, for example, the proportion of workers with tenure of less than two years increased, while that of two to five years decreased; in Hungary, the proportion of two-to-five-year tenure increased, while that of five to ten years decreased. These findings should of course be examined in the light of the national economic context and labour market developments in order to come up with straightforward conclusions in terms of employment stability. However, they are generally consistent with the hypothesis of a general stabilization of the labour markets – seen in the general decline of labour turnover and lengthening of job tenure – and of an increase in flexibilization of the employment relations as indicated in

Table 2.11 Separation rates by destination of outflows from employment, selected CSEE countries, 1990–2003 (percentages)

Country	1990	1991	1993	1996	1997	1998	1999	2000	2001	2002	2003
Employment to unemployment (EU)											
Croatia[1]	..	..	..	..	..	..	3.3	3.6	3.3	3.0	..
Czech Rep.[1]	..	..	1.7	1.5	1.8	3.0	4.1	3.4	2.6	2.5	2.7
Estonia[2]	0.7	1.7	5.4	4.8	4.6	6.0	5.1	5.7	4.7	3.7	4.0
Lithuania	..	..	..	..	..	..	..	6.3	4.7	3.9	3.1
Poland	..	..	8.4	6.2	5.0	5.2	4.8	6.0	6.0	6.0	..
Employment to inactivity (EI)											
Croatia[1]	..	..	..	..	..	..	5.3	5.3	4.1	3.4	..
Czech Rep.[1]	..	..	5.3	4.0	3.8	3.7	3.2	3.1	2.6	2.9	3.2
Estonia[2]	5.6	6.4	7.5	5.0	4.0	4.6	4.7	4.6	4.9	4.9	4.7
Lithuania	..	..	..	..	..	..	..	3.5	2.2	1.7	1.2
Poland	..	..	12.8	8.3	7.7	6.4	5.6	5.6	4.0	4.4	..
Employment to employment (EE)											
Croatia[1]	..	..	..	..	..	..	9.4	10.0	10.3	7.4	..
Czech Rep.[1]	..	..	14.9	7.1	6.5	5.0	5.0	4.9	4.7	3.9	5.1
Estonia	9.7	12.2	17.0	12.2	9.8	8.4	9.8	9.6	8.4	8.4	9.3
Lithuania	..	..	..	..	..	..	..	..	7.5	8.7	7.7
Poland	..	..	..	10.4	6.0	5.2	3.2	3.6	3.2	2.8	..

Notes: [1] Own calculations. .. = not available.

Source: Labour force surveys.

section 2.2, with Poland again the exception. The findings would also confirm that despite economic recovery in the region there have been generally fewer hires, and that there has been a reduction in the number of dismissals (which tends to lengthen average tenure).

LFS data on outflows from employment by destination (exit to another job, to unemployment and to inactivity) are presented in table 2.11. As indicated previously, outflows from employment have continued to decrease in all countries under review except Poland, until 2003; this deceleration has been particularly significant for outflows to unemployment and inactivity (and sharper for the former). Both flows have been converging over 1998–2003, but outflows to inactivity still exceed those to unemployment in most countries (except in Lithuania and in Poland since 2000). This confirms previous findings of a general stabilization of the labour markets in the region, reflecting economic recovery and the end of the restructuring phase. Outflows from employment to employment (job-to-job moves), on the other hand, stagnated over the same period, suggesting rather cautious labour supply behaviour. There are of course differences amongst countries in job-to-job moves, which were still high in the Baltic States and increased in the late 1990s in Croatia, after the acceleration of

Table 2.12 Correlation coefficients of GDP and outflows from employment by destination, selected CSEE countries, 1999–2003

Country	EE vs GDP	EI vs GDP	EI vs GDP (–1)	EU vs GDP	EU vs GDP (–1)
Croatia	−0.31	−0.82	−0.77	−0.25	−0.99
Czech Republic	0.47	0.12	−0.85	−0.21	−0.92
Estonia	−0.48	−0.04	0.80	−0.22	−0.79
Lithuania	−0.25	−0.92	−0.92	−0.92	−0.92
Poland	0.64	0.99	0.51	−0.59	−0.52

Notes: EE is a flow from one job to another, EI a flow from employment to inactivity and EU from employment to unemployment. (–1) = data lagged by one period.

Sources: For flow data see table 2.11. GDP data from UNECE. Own calculations.

structural changes. This contrasts with the situation in Poland, where the number of direct job-to-job moves has been much lower than the number of redundancies and withdrawals from employment to inactivity since 1998, which goes to explain the very poor employment performance of this country in the period under study.

Job-to-job moves as well as exits from employment to unemployment and inactivity are obviously affected by the economic performance of a country. As already mentioned, in Western industrialized countries in periods of economic upswing, demand for labour increases and employers tend to offer higher wages in order to attract new and more qualified workers. The latter, in turn, are more inclined to avail themselves of better job opportunities so that, besides new labour market entries and re-employment of previously unemployed persons, job-to-job moves also accelerate. In contrast, in periods of economic decline workers become more hesitant to change their jobs voluntarily in fear of eventually remaining jobless. Enterprises endeavour to cut production costs in order to maintain or restore their competitiveness, and resort if necessary to redundancies, early-retirement schemes and similar measures to cut their workforce.

Table 2.12 presents the correlation between GDP growth rates and flows from employment to each of the three destinations. As job-to-job moves are usually voluntary, while outflows from employment to unemployment and to inactivity are mostly involuntary (such as forced withdrawals from employment, de-registration from unemployment, early retirement), one would expect positive correlation of the former flows and negative correlation of the two latter flows with the economic cycle. Again, as employment protection rules may delay outflows from employment to unemployment and to inactivity, the same correlations have been calculated with a time lag of one year.[17]

---

[17] Again, these results should be interpreted with caution, due to rather short and incomplete data series, with differences among countries.

Figure 2.8 Labour market flows and GDP growth, selected CSEE countries, 1990–2005 (percentages)

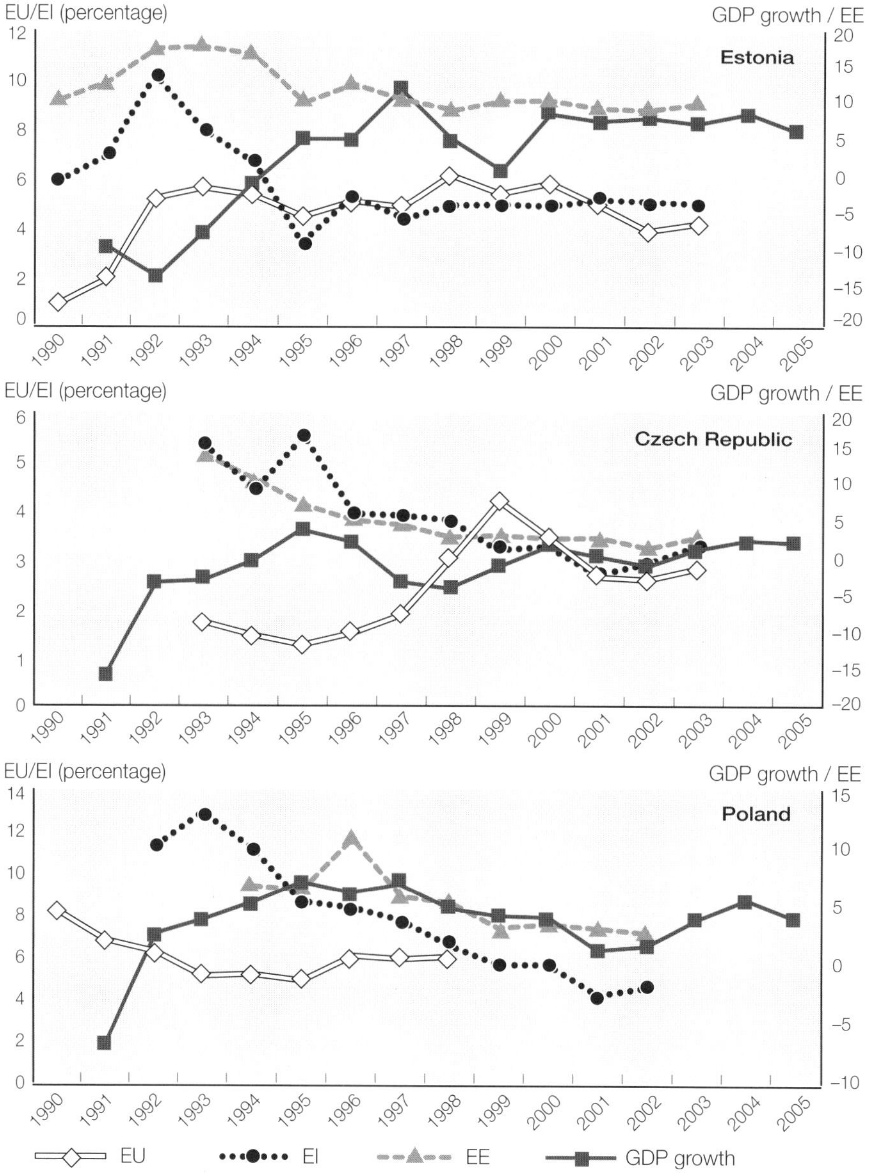

Note: EE is a flow from one job to another, EI a flow from employment to inactivity and EU from employment to unemployment.

Source: GDP data from UNECE; for labour market flow data see table 2.11.

In line with expectations, table 2.12 shows strong negative correlation between GDP growth and exits to unemployment for all countries under review. The correlation is even more pronounced if exits to unemployment are correlated with lagged GDP. The general picture for moves from employment to inactivity is less clear cut: correlations tend to show a countercyclical pattern in Croatia and Lithuania, and in the Czech Republic for the time-lagged variable; in contrast, a pro-cyclical pattern seems to characterize outflows to inactivity in Estonia and Poland. Job-to-job moves also present contrasting trends. Correlations fit with our previous finding on countercyclical behaviour of job-to-job flows for Estonia (Cazes and Nesporova, 2003), and here also for Croatia and Lithuania, which would indicate involuntary quits while new jobs are often not secure. In the Czech Republic and Poland, however, job-to-job flows increase with economic upswings; these developments of job-to-job flows have to be interpreted differently in the two countries, reflecting a large amount of labour churning in the Polish case, but rather voluntary moves in the case of the Czech Republic. Figure 2.8 depicts the evolution of GDP and employment outflows, including job-to-job moves, for the Czech Republic, Estonia and Poland.

These results do not differ widely from our earlier findings for the 1990s. They point to generally countercyclical movements of labour market flows: higher outflows from employment in periods of depressed demand for labour and lower outflows during employment upswings. Clearly, the economic recovery that characterized the region over recent years contributed to a significant decrease of flows into unemployment; however, due to the weak link between economic and employment growth, outflows to inactivity and/or employment have been different in the various countries. Poland displays a particularly worrying picture, as high economic growth coincides with high outflows to inactivity and shrinking employment.

2.5 EMPLOYMENT PROTECTION LEGISLATION AND ITS IMPACT ON LABOUR MARKET DEVELOPMENTS

2.5.1 Trends towards further liberalization of EPL

Cazes and Nesporova (2003) examined the nature and extent of changes in national labour legislations in the CEE countries over the course of the transition process until the end of the 1990s. The objective of these profound modifications was to enable enterprises to terminate employment for economic reasons, including financial problems, bankruptcy, and complete or partial liquidation of the enterprise, but at the same time to protect workers against unjustified or unfair termination, give them time to look for a new job during the notice period and compensate them in the form of severance pay. The regulation of temporary employment was also extended to make it possible for employers to recruit workers for a time-bound period only and at the same time to prevent any misuse of temporary contracts. Finally, in view of the adverse social consequences of large-scale enterprise restructuring, many countries launched special rules for collective dismissals, to restrict massive redundancies and give particular protection to workers hit by such an event. Modifications to labour legislation were clearly inspired by labour legislation reforms in economically advanced countries, primarily the old EU countries.

When unemployment deepened in the region, neoliberal economists started blaming over-restrictive employment protection legislation as one of the main reasons for its depth and persistence. According to them, strict legislation is limiting new hires, especially for permanent jobs, as termination of permanent contracts becomes too costly for employers. The situation further aggravates if the regulation of temporary contracts is also so strict that they can only be issued exceptionally or their repeated conclusion is not allowed.

To confirm or reject this statement with empirical evidence, a methodology for measuring the strictness of EPL has been developed by the OECD. It permits comparisons of strictness of national EPL across countries and identification of the possible impact of strict EPL on the level of unemployment as well as on other labour market indicators. The OECD methodology (OECD, 1999) covers both permanent and temporary contracts, as well as collective dismissals. In the case of permanent contracts it includes procedural inconveniences, notice and severance pay for no-fault individual dismissals, and difficulty of dismissal. It quantifies their strictness directly (for example, the length of notice period or severance pay measured in the number of months) or indirectly (for example, by the definition of unfair dismissal), converting them into a scale of cardinal numbers ranging from 0 (no restriction) to a maximum figure (full restriction). The quantified indicators are then allocated weights and aggregated in two steps. A similar procedure is used for measuring the strictness of temporary contracts – both fixed-term contracts and employment through temporary work agencies – and for their aggregation in two steps. The same procedure is applied for collective dismissals. The summary EPL strictness index aggregates the indices for permanent contracts, temporary contracts and collective dismissals, attributing to them the weights of, respectively, 5/12, 5/12 and 2/12. The value of all three partial indices as well as of the summary EPL index moves from 0, indicating very liberal EPL, to 6, meaning very restrictive EPL.

Cazes and Nesporova (2003) calculated the EPL strictness index for eight selected CEE countries at the end of the 1990s and compared them with 19 OECD countries and 15 EU countries. The calculations revealed important differences across countries both within the CEE group (ranging from 1.8 for Hungary to 3.3 in Slovenia) and the OECD group (from 0.7 in the United States to 3.7 in Portugal). In general, they showed that in the late 1990s the CEE countries tended to have more restrictive labour legislation than the OECD countries (the CEE average was 2.5 versus the OECD average of 2.0)[18] but they were almost on a par with the EU15 average (2.4).

Since the end of the 1990s practically all the CEE countries have further modified their labour codes in response to complaints from employers that labour regulation was

---

[18] The value 2.5 refers to the selection of countries in Cazes and Nesporova (2003), which includes the Russian Federation. The relevant value for the EU8+3 is 2.4.

Table 2.13 EPL strictness indices in selected new EU member and candidate countries, 2003 compared with the late 1990s

Country	Index for permanent contracts	Index for temporary contracts	Index for temporary and regular contracts	Index for collective dismissals	EPL summary index 2003	EPL summary index late 1990s
			2003			
Bulgaria	2.1	0.9	1.50	4.1	2.0	2.8
Croatia	2.7	2.8	2.75	2.5	2.7	..
Czech Republic	3.0	0.3	2.20	2.6	1.8	2.2
Estonia	2.7	1.3	2.10	4.0	2.3	2.4
Hungary	2.1	0.4	1.25	3.4	1.6	1.8
Lithuania	2.9	2.4	2.65	3.6	2.8	..
Poland	2.0	1.8	1.90	3.3	2.1	2.0
Slovakia	2.9	0.3	1.60	3.0	1.8	2.3
Slovenia	2.7	1.8	2.25	3.3	2.4	3.3
CSEE average	2.6	1.3	2.00	3.3	2.2	2.4
			Late 1990s			
CSEE average	2.7	1.5	2.1	3.9	...	2.4
EU average	2.4	2.0	2.2	3.4	...	2.4
OECD average	2.0	1.8	1.9	2.5	...	2.0

Notes: The EPL indices reported in the table are measured on a scale from 0, indicating very liberal EPL, to 6, meaning very restrictive EPL. Country averages are weighted averages. .. = not available. ... = not applicable.

Sources: For 2003, calculations by Mirco Tonin on the basis of an OECD methodology. For late 1990s, see Cazes and Nesporova (2003).

still too strict, disadvantaging them in competition with other goods or service providers. The five country-study chapters in this book analyse in more detail these changes in national labour legislation. A detailed analysis of EPL in 2003[19] has indeed revealed a clear tendency towards further liberalization of EPL in the new EU member and candidate countries compared with the late 1990s, as evidenced in table 2.13.

Table 2.13 shows that the cross-country differences in the strictness of EPL are lower for permanent, regular contracts but more significant for temporary contracts

---

[19] The authors would like to thank Mirco Tonin for undertaking this analysis of national labour legislation and for calculating EPL strictness indices for 12 CEE countries.

and collective dismissals. With regard to legislation on the termination of permanent contracts, Bulgaria and Hungary are the two countries with the least restrictive regulation, while the Czech Republic, closely followed by Lithuania and Slovakia, has the strictest. However, the picture changes when it comes to regulation of temporary contracts: the Czech Republic, Hungary and Slovakia have almost fully liberal legislation while Croatia has the most rigid. In terms of collective dismissals, their regulation is on average more than that of individual termination of contracts. Croatia and the Czech Republic are the most liberal and Bulgaria and Estonia the most strict in this regard. The index combining regulation of individual termination of both permanent and temporary contracts emphasizes Hungary as the most liberal country, as presented in the fourth column of table 2.13. Finally, the summary index reveals that Hungary, the Czech Republic and Slovakia respectively have the most flexible labour legislation among the new EU member and candidate countries, while Lithuania and Croatia seem to have the most restrictive.

A comparison of the EPL strictness in 2003 with the situation in the late 1990s reveals that all these countries further liberalized their EPL in this period, with the exception of Poland. Regulation has been mainly relaxed for collective dismissals, indicating that many countries, after having completed the restructuring and privatization process in the majority of large enterprises, no longer accentuated special protection of workers against collective dismissals. Regulation of temporary contracts was also further liberalized, primarily through reforms of existing provisions in Bulgaria, Hungary, Slovakia and Slovenia, though in Poland the rules were made stricter. With regard to regulation of termination of regular or permanent contracts, the change seems negligible but it actually hides an important relaxation of legislation in Slovenia and a reinforcement of regulations in Poland.

Comparing the CSEE average for 2003 with the EU and OECD averages for the late 1990s, the CSEE group remained stricter than the EU in its regulation of termination of permanent contracts and stayed well above the OECD average. The regulation of temporary contracts, on the other hand, was already more liberal on average in the CSEE countries than in the EU and OECD in the late 1990s and this trend has continued. In contrast, collective dismissals, which at the end of the 1990s had been more strictly regulated in the CSEE than the two other country groups, were in 2003 less strictly regulated than the EU average, though remaining well above the average level of the OECD. Finally, the summary EPL index for the CSEE countries fell below the late 1990s EU average but still remained above the OECD average. Whether and to what extent this overall move in EPL strictness has had any significant impact on labour market trends is analysed below on the basis of bivariate regressions.

2.5.2 Effects of EPL on labour market indicators

First we calculated the bivariate regression, attempting to depict any association between the aggregate unemployment rate (averaged over the period 1999–2003 to smooth cyclical fluctuations) and strictness of EPL. According to neoliberal

Figure 2.9 Relationship between EPL strictness and aggregate unemployment, selected CSEE countries, 2003

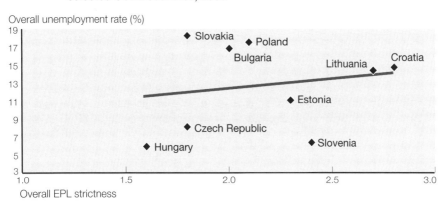

Notes: Unemployment rate = 2.1 * EPL + 8.1; R^2 = 0.032. The overall unemployment rates are computed from LFS data as averages over the period 1999–2003.

Source: EPL indices from table 2.13; unemployment (data based on LFS) from Eurostat.

economic theory, strict labour market regulation should have a negative impact on the level of unemployment, and in particular that of vulnerable groups, such as youth unemployment. It should also lead to higher long-term unemployment as employers would not be willing to recruit less competitive persons from the unemployment pool. Figure 2.9 shows that indeed the unemployment level tends to increase with stricter EPL; however, the regression is not statistically significant. No correlation has been found between long-term unemployment and the EPL strictness index. In contrast, youth unemployment seems to increase quite sharply with stricter EPL but again the regression is not statistically significant. Therefore it can be concluded that strictness of EPL does not have any statistically significant effect on unemployment indicators and there is no justification for claims that high aggregate, youth and long-term unemployment can be attributed to strict labour regulation in the EU8+3 countries. This result is similar to that found for selected CEE countries in the late 1990s.

We also plotted the summary EPL strictness index against the employment-to-population ratio, again averaged over the period 1999–2003. The outcome suggests no correlation between the two indicators, which is to say that strict labour regulation does not contribute to any change in the employment rate. This is different from the relationship estimated at the end of the 1990s, which was positive, but the regression was statistically insignificant.

Figures 2.10 and 2.11 present the relationship between strictness of EPL and, respectively, temporary employment and self-employment. Standard economic theory suggests that stricter EPL should lead towards lower permanent employment, pushing employers to offer and workers to accept temporary employment and/or pushing

Figure 2.10   Relationship between EPL strictness and temporary employment,
selected CSEE countries, 2003

Temporary employment (percentage of total employment)

Overall EPL strictness

Note: Temporary employment = 1.6 * EPL + 5.6; R^2 = 0.018.

Source: EPL indices from table 2.13; temporary employment (LFS) from Eurostat.

Figure 2.11   Relationship between EPL strictness and self-employment, selected
CSEE countries, 2003

Self-employment (percentage of total employment)

Overall EPL strictness

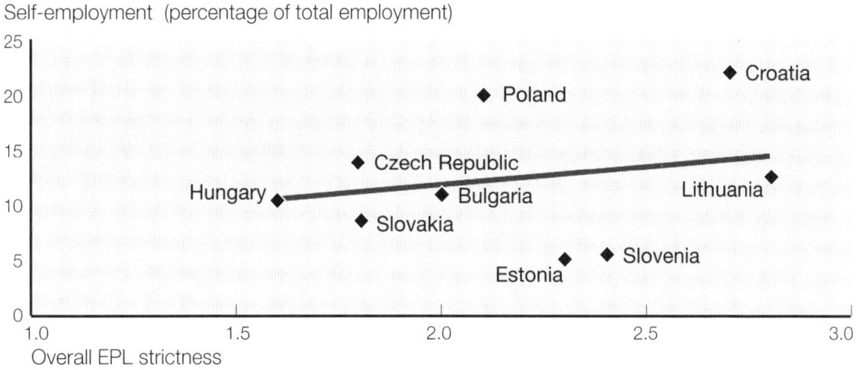

Note: Self-employment = 2.5 * EPL + 9.4; R^2 = 0.050.

Source: EPL indices from table 2.13; self-employment (LFS) from Eurostat.

workers to start self-employment, with higher shares of workers in temporary
employment and self-employment as a result. Our estimates could indeed indicate these
conclusions, but with the reservation that neither regression is statistically significant.
Nevertheless, the result for 2003 differs from that for the late 1990s, when stricter
EPL was related to a decline in the share of self-employment, though the positive
link for temporary employment seems to have persisted across time.

Figure 2.12   Relationship between EPL strictness and labour turnover, selected
CSEE countries, 2003

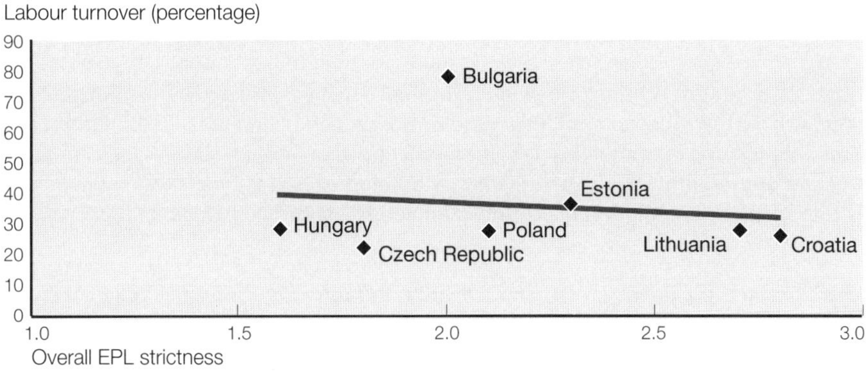

Labour turnover (percentage)

Overall EPL strictness

Note: Labour turnover = 6.9 * EPL + 50.5; R^2 = 0.025.

Source: EPL indices from table 2.13; labour turnover data from table 2.7.

Finally, we tested the links between EPL and labour market dynamics represented by labour turnover and average job tenure. Economic theory suggests that stricter EPL should slow down labour mobility measured in terms of labour turnover. This was also confirmed by our estimate from the late 1990s, which was statistically significant at the level of 10 per cent. The estimate based on 2003 data has led to the same negative association between EPL and labour turnover, with practically the same value of the EPL regression coefficient (see figure 2.12). However, this time the regression is not statistically significant.

In contrast, the correlation of average job tenure and EPL strictness should be positive, indicating that stricter employment protection regulation contributes towards increasing length of employment relationships. Indeed, the estimate from the late 1990s was consistent with this expectation, although it was not statistically significant. The new estimate based on 2003 data, however, shows no correlation between the two indicators.

2.5.3   Conclusions

This section analysed changes in employment protection legislation and their possible effect on labour market developments. A detailed study of modifications in employment protection legislation has confirmed an overall trend towards its liberalization. In general, it concerned mainly deregulation of collective dismissals, which reached the EU15 level but remained high in comparison with the OECD average. The already quite liberal regulation of the application of temporary contracts has been further relaxed to be now well below average practice in both the OECD and

EU15 groupings. On the contrary, termination of permanent contracts still remains more restrictive compared with the EU and the OECD average.

Bivariate regressions between EPL strictness and labour market indicators – both static and dynamic – have indicated tendencies consistent with economic theory, such as higher unemployment and lower employment rates as well as higher labour turnover, temporary employment and self-employment associated with stricter labour regulation. However, none of these relationships has been statistically significant. This implies that in reality stricter employment protection legislation does not seem to have any significant influence on labour market trends, and advice on further labour market deregulation is not substantiated by empirical evidence.

2.6   DO LABOUR MARKET INSTITUTIONS STILL MATTER IN CSEE COUNTRIES?

2.6.1   Recent changes in labour market institutions

Cazes and Nesporova (2003) found that in the second half of the 1990s there was no substantial difference between the OECD and the CEE countries in terms of the nature of the adopted labour market institutions. Nevertheless, there were important variations between the two country groups as to the extent or intensity of their use. In general, the CEE countries tended to have on average slightly stricter employment protection legislation and higher labour taxes than the OECD countries, while their unemployment benefit systems tended to be less generous in terms of the length of payment of benefits and replacement rates. The former countries also allocated fewer resources to active labour market policies, despite considerably higher unemployment rates. Moreover, although the level of unionization in the CEE countries was still high, the coverage by collective agreements and coordination of collective negotiations in these countries was more or less in line with the average of the OECD19, pointing to proportionally less powerful trade unions.

With the progressive adaptation of national labour legislation, institutions and policies to EU practice as the date of entry into the EU approached, the picture described above was also changing considerably. As already mentioned, the majority of countries, which are now the new EU members and membership candidates, liberalized their employment protection legislation further. If we compare the EPL strictness index for the seven countries, which were analysed in Cazes and Nesporova (2003) on the basis of data for the late 1990s and then for 2003, the index declined from 2.4 to 2.0. The only country where it slightly increased (from 2.0 to 2.1) was Poland, while in Bulgaria, Slovakia and Slovenia the extent of liberalization was substantial.

As to changes in the characteristics of the national unemployment benefit systems, two parameters were considered – the unemployment benefit replacement rate (measured as a ratio of average unemployment benefits to the gross average wage) and the duration of payment of benefits (we took the maximum duration). While there were no significant changes in the replacement rates between the end of the 1990s and 2003 (for the seven CSEE countries represented in both samples), there was a slight tendency towards increasing the maximum duration of benefits for certain categories of workers (older workers as in the Czech Republic or workers in depressed regions as in Poland). Nevertheless, both parameters of the benefit systems of the new EU member and candidate countries remained on average below the OECD average.

Comparison of expenditure on active labour market policies per unemployed person (ALMP expenditure as a percentage of GDP divided by the LFS unemployment rate) at the end of the 1990s and 2003 showed a significant increase in some countries such as Bulgaria and the Czech Republic, but simultaneously a rather sharp decline in others such as Poland or Slovenia, while in the rest of the countries the spending more or less stagnated. In 2003 this indicator ranged from 0.004 in Croatia and 0.005 in Estonia to 0.88 in Hungary. Reasons for these recent changes varied: in Bulgaria it was the result of a determined effort on the part of the Government to reduce persistent high unemployment by a large-scale labour market programme and thus strengthen the positive employment impact of high economic growth. As the programme combined community works and subsidized employment with improving employability of participants through training and promotion of self-employment, the outcomes were relatively good and indeed contributed toward reducing unemployment. In Slovenia the decline in spending was justified by decreasing unemployment and growing employment boosted by solid economic growth. In contrast, in Poland, despite a dramatic deterioration in unemployment during the period analysed, allocations to labour market policies increased only marginally and the bulk of them went to mandatory spending on passive policies. Spending on ALMP per 1 per cent of unemployment was thus sharply reduced and certainly contributed towards the unfavourable labour market situation.

Information available on collective bargaining and the impact of trade unions on wages and employment in the new EU member and candidate countries points to their considerable weakening. Membership in trade unions has declined dramatically. If in the mid-1990s the unionization of workers exceeded 50 per cent in Bulgaria, Hungary, Slovakia and Slovenia and approached that level in the Czech Republic, in 2003 only Croatia and Slovenia reported a unionization rate exceeding 40 per cent, while in other countries this share ranged from 35 per cent in Slovakia to less than 20 per cent in the Baltic States and Poland. The coverage of workers by collective agreements was systematically higher than the union density, with the exception of Latvia and Lithuania, where it coincided with the low level of unionization. However, only Slovenia reported very high, 98 per cent collective bargaining coverage of workers, while in all other countries the coverage was below 50 per cent. No information exists on the degree of coordination between trade unions' and employers' organizations.

Systematic pressure from employers to bring down labour taxes, stressing their negative effects on total labour costs and thus decisions on hiring and firing, has brought about considerable cuts in labour taxes in the majority of the new EU member and candidate countries. Nevertheless, the level of taxes still remained on average significantly higher compared with the OECD average (37.4 per cent as opposed to 23.4 per cent in 2003). The level of payroll taxes (measured as the sum of employers' and employees' social contributions as a percentage of wages) ranged from 46 per cent in Lithuania to 28.6 per cent in Latvia in 2003.

In sum, substantial changes in labour market institutions of the new EU member and candidate countries did occur in the period under investigation, with potentially important implications for labour market trends. They concerned first of all the collective bargaining system, as both the power of trade unions in terms of workers' membership and coverage of workers by collective agreements weakened considerably. The level of labour taxation declined, nevertheless remaining significantly higher than in the OECD countries on average. While the degree of protection of jobseekers through unemployment insurance schemes has slightly increased in terms of longer payment of benefits to vulnerable groups, expenditure on active labour market policies in relation to the unemployment rate increased in some countries but declined in others. All these parameters of labour market policies remain on average well below the average level for the OECD countries.

2.6.2   Impacts of labour market institutions on labour market performance: Evidence from multivariate regressions

The main result of multivariate regressions explaining labour market developments in relation to changes in labour market institutions and policies for the end of the 1990s was that indeed labour market institutions and policies did have an impact on labour market performance of the transition countries (Cazes and Nesporova, 2003). It turned out that active labour market policies contributed significantly towards an increase in labour market participation and employment, and a decline in aggregate, long-term and youth unemployment. Though significant in most regressions, the role of collective bargaining was not clear-cut. In addition, unemployment rates tended to increase with higher labour taxation. However, although testing of the hypothesis of no behavioural differences between the group of transition countries and the OECD countries confirmed no differences for all three unemployment indicators, in the case of the participation rate this hypothesis was not valid (for employment it was close to the limit of invalidity) and the two groups of countries developed in opposite ways. In respect of the OECD countries, employment and participation rates decreased as a result of stricter employment protection legislation, while they seemed to increase for the CEE countries. The explanation should be sought in frequent non-observance of labour legislation as well as in the large informal economy in the latter countries, which push workers outside formal employment. If employment protection legislation is stricter or better enforced, employers have to offer workers regular labour contracts rather than irregular or no contracts, with the result that employment and participation rates increase and informal employment declines.

Since the end of the 1990s, however, the labour market institutions of the CSEE countries have matured as a result, inter alia, of the completion of legislative changes required for the accession of the first eight countries to the EU and the advanced stage of adjustment in the EU candidate countries. They have also been increasingly

Table 2.14 Main characteristics of labour market institutions and policies in the CSEE countries, 2002–03

Country	Unemployment benefit as % of average wage (replacement ratio)	Share of registered unemployed receiving benefits	Total expenditure on labour market policies		Payroll tax as % of wages contributed by employers and workers	Trade union density as % of TU members among all workers
			% of GDP	% on active measures		
Bulgaria	33	20	0.97	0.67	42.7	25.0
Croatia	25	22	0.55	0.06	37.2	42.5
Czech Rep.	22	34	0.44	0.17	35.2	30.0
Estonia	7	50	0.30	0.08	35.0	15.0
Hungary	26	34	0.88	0.51	36.8	25.0
Latvia	21	44	0.64	0.14	28.6	19.0
Lithuania	16	11	0.28	0.16	46.0	14.0
Poland	22	19	1.25	0.11	38.1	18.0
Romania	23	23	0.88	0.03	n.a.	n.a.
Slovakia	26	17	0.96	0.47	36.2	35.0
Slovenia	39	24	1.00	0.44	38.0	42.0

Sources: National data sources.

influenced by the European Employment Strategy and its role in coordinating national employment action plans. Table 2.14 summarizes the main parameters of labour market institutions and policies in the EU8+3 countries in 2002–03 (EPL was presented in table 2.13).

Table 2.14 shows significant differences among the CSEE countries with regard to parameters of the unemployment benefit schemes (unemployment benefit replacement rates and shares of benefit recipients among jobseekers), expenditure on labour market policies and its distribution between active and passive policies, labour taxation and trade union coverage. A comparison of these variations with unemployment rates (see figure 2.5) shows that they are only weakly correlated, which points to an uneven attention given by the decision-makers to employment challenges and their frequent lack of trust in their effective solution by labour market institutions and policies. It also suggests that the trade unions are rather weak in many of these countries, so that social dialogue may be of limited help in addressing high unemployment.

However, there are some important characteristics shared by EU8+3 countries which may distinguish them from the EU15 and OECD. First of all, the unemployment insurance schemes in these countries are not generous either in terms of the benefit replacement rates, which do not even reach the level of 40 per cent of the average national wage in any of these countries, or in coverage: the share of unemployment benefit recipients among all jobseekers, including those not covered by unemployment registers, is very low.[20] Second, the funds devoted to labour market policies as a percentage of GDP are very limited. Moreover, in the majority of the CSEE countries but in particular in those with high unemployment, the share of these funds spent on active labour market programmes is also low as passive labour market policies, which are considered as entitlements required by law, absorb most of the available resources. The tax burden on labour is very high, and employers and economists never miss an opportunity to blame it for depressed labour demand and poor job creation. Despite recent reductions in payroll taxes in a number of these countries, their levels compare unfavourably with most other EU and OECD countries.

Therefore it can be concluded that increased flexibilization of the labour markets of the EU8+3 countries has not been sufficiently compensated by stronger protection of workers affected by redundancy, through better assistance in re-employment provided by public employment services, broader access to active labour market programmes or decent income support in unemployment. This is despite high taxes on labour, which may work against new recruitments and raise the level and duration of unemployment.

To find out whether these differences in labour market institutions between the EU8+3 countries and the OECD countries still have the same impact on labour market performance as revealed at the end of the 1990s or whether important changes can be traced, we again ran multivariate regressions. The dependent variables were the log unemployment, log long-term unemployment and log youth unemployment rates, as well as employment rates and labour market participation rates. Explanatory variables describing the institutional package of the labour market were employment protection legislation, unemployment benefits, active labour market policies, collective bargaining and labour taxation plus the output gap. The year analysed was 2003. The specification of the variables remained the same as in the computations for the end of the 1990s (see annex 2.1). The only explanatory variable missing was the indicator on the degree of union and employer coordination, as this information was not available.

Again, the regression was first run for all the variables and then only for those that had been found to be statistically significant. While the number of the OECD countries (19) has remained the same in our sample and only one country has changed, the sample of the CEE countries has been modified: the Russian Federation and Ukraine were replaced by the rest of the new EU member and candidate countries, making ten in total.[21] As before, in the second step we estimated the regression only for 19 OECD countries and tested the hypothesis of stability of coefficients between the two sets of countries (29 versus 19) with the use of the Chow test. The results are presented and

---

[20] The difference between the numbers of registered unemployed persons and those identified as unemployed by the LFS is small in the Czech Republic, Hungary, Poland and Slovakia but very high in Croatia and Slovenia (where registered unemployment exceeds LFS unemployment), as well as Estonia, Latvia and Lithuania (where LFS unemployment is much higher than registered unemployment).

[21] The 19 OECD countries included Australia, Austria, Belgium, Canada, Denmark, Finland, France, Germany, Ireland, Italy, Japan, Netherlands, New Zealand, Norway, Portugal, Spain, Sweden, the United Kingdom and the United States (Ireland replacing Switzerland in the original sample), while the CSEE countries covered Bulgaria, Croatia, the Czech Republic, Estonia, Hungary, Latvia, Lithuania, Poland, Slovakia and Slovenia.

commented on below. As the sample of the CEE countries has changed, the estimates are not fully comparable. Despite this, they can reveal any important modifications in development trends that may have occurred in the CEE country group.

Unemployment

As the first column in table 2.15 shows, the two statistically significant variables explaining changes in aggregate unemployment are active labour market policies, which contributed to a decline in unemployment, and labour tax, which led to an increase in unemployment. Collective bargaining coverage has the highest coefficient and thus would seem to have a major impact on reducing the unemployment rate, but it is not statistically significant. Trade union density does not have any measurable impact. Neither employment protection legislation nor the parameters of the unemployment benefit scheme are statistically significant.

If all non-significant variables are omitted, the new estimate presented in the second column shows a small reduction in the regression coefficient for active LMP and no change for labour tax. However, statistical significance of both these factors

Table 2.15 Regressions explaining the log unemployment rate (dependent variable) for selected CSEE and OECD countries, 2003 compared to the late 1990s

Independent variables	Log unemployment rate (dependent variable)			
	All independent variables	Only statistically significant independent variables		
	OECD + CSEE 2003	OECD + CSEE 2003	OECD + CEE end 1990s	OECD 2003
Employment protection	0.06 (0.45)	..	..	..
Replacement rate		..	..	..
Benefit duration	0.04 (0.80)	..	..	..
Active LMP	–0.05 (–3.36)	**–0.04 (–4.50)**	–0.02 (–1.98)	–0.03 (–3.18)
Union density	0.00 (1.09)	..	..	..
Collective bargaining coverage	–0.11 (–0.70)	..	0.18 (1.59)	..
Labour tax	0.02 (2.15)	**0.02 (3.58)**	0.01 (1.59)	0.01 (2.44)
Output gap	0.01 (0.11)	..	–0.10 (–2.33)	..
Adj. R^2	0.53	**0.57**	0.50	0.38
Number of countries	29	**29**	27	19
Chow test	..	**0.46****	0.90**	..

Notes: Estimation is by Ordinary Least Squares (OLS). t-statistics are presented in parentheses. For the Chow test, ** means that the hypothesis of coefficients stability is accepted at the 5 per cent level. .. = not applicable.

Table 2.16 Regressions explaining the log long-term unemployment rate
(dependent variable) for selected CSEE and OECD countries, 2003
compared to the late 1990s

Independent variables	Log long-term unemployment rate (dependent variable)			
	All independent variables	Only statistically significant independent variables		
	OECD + CSEE 2003	OECD + CSEE 2003	OECD end 1990s	OECD 2003
Employment protection	0.06 (0.29)	..	..	..
Replacement rate	0.02 (0.99)	..	..	..
Benefit duration	0.10 (1.14)	**0.14 (2.05)**	0.12 (1.32)	0.14 (2.14)
Active LMP	−0.07 (−2.97)	**−0.06 (−4.28)**	−0.04 (−1.54)	−0.05 (−2.88)
Union density	0.00 (0.48)	..	..	..
Collective bargaining coverage	−0.14 (−0.52)	..	0.75 (3.02)	..
Labour tax	0.06 (3.88)	**0.06 (6.88)**	0.02 (1.95)	0.06 (5.04)
Output gap	0.03 (0.26)	..	..	..
Adj. R^2	0.67	**0.72**	0.53	0.57
Number of countries	29	**29**	27	19
Chow test	..	**0.48****	0.75**	..

Notes: Estimation is by Ordinary Least Squares (OLS). t-statistics are presented in parentheses. For the Chow test, **
means that the hypothesis of coefficients stability is accepted at the 5 per cent level. .. = not applicable.

further increases. The same regression run only for the OECD countries brings no
change of coefficients of the two independent variables, suggesting no particular
discrepancy in the explanation of variations in aggregate unemployment between the
OECD and the CSEE countries. This conclusion is also confirmed by the Chow test.

A comparison with the estimate made for the end of 1990s shows several
important differences. First of all, the impact of active LMP on unemployment
reduction has further increased but so has the impact of labour taxation on unemployment expansion. Collective bargaining coverage, which used to have a rather strong
and negative effect on unemployment (contributing to its increase), has lost its
significance. The influence of the output gap has disappeared, too.

With regard to long-term unemployment (see table 2.16), regression coefficients
for active LMP and labour tax are again statistically significant, of almost the same
absolute value, which is higher than for total unemployment, and again with opposite
signs. This shows an even higher importance of both factors for long-term unemployment but also suggests that the positive influence of active LMP on pulling people
out of long-term unemployment could be completely offset by higher labour tax.
However, when running the regression while deleting one statistically insignificant

Table 2.17 Regressions explaining log youth unemployment rate (dependent variable) for selected CSEE and OECD countries, 2003 compared to the late 1990s

Independent variables	Log youth unemployment rate (dependent variable)			
	All independent variables	Only statistically significant independent variables		
	OECD + CSEE 2003	OECD + CSEE 2003	OECD + CSEE end 1990s	OECD 2003
Employment protection	0.05 (0.47)	..	..	..
Replacement rate	0.01 (0.85)	..	..	..
Benefit duration	0.06 (1.39)	**0.07 (2.11)**	0.11 (2.28)	0.08 (2.44)
Active LMP	−0.06 (−4.85)	**−0.05 (−6.59)**	−0.02 (−2.02)	−0.05 (−5.80)
Union density	0.01 (2.13)	**0.01 (2.28)**	..	0.01 (2.48)
Collective bargaining coverage	−0.09 (−0.68)	..	..	..
Labour tax	0.02 (2.83)	**0.02 (4.88)**	0.02 (3.60)	0.02 (4.19)
Output gap	−0.02 (−0.37)	..	0.10 (2.17)	..
Adj. R^2	0.67	**0.71**	0.56	0.66
Number of countries	29	**29**	26	19
Chow test	..	**0,09****	2,01**	,,

Notes: Estimation is by Ordinary Least Squares (OLS). t-statistics are presented in parentheses. For the Chow test, ** means that the hypothesis of coefficients stability is accepted at the 5 per cent level. .. = not applicable.

factor after another, the significance of unemployment benefit duration starts to increase and confirms that this factor contributes to an increase in long-term unemployment in the sample of 29 OECD and CSEE countries. This outcome seems to be driven more by the OECD countries, as on average unemployment benefits are paid for longer periods in that country group, and the option of depending on unemployment benefits instead of taking up available, usually low-paid, jobs may indeed contribute towards an increase in long-term unemployment. However, it also reflects the fact that less competitive people face particular difficulties finding a new job in a context of low demand for labour in general. The unemployment benefit system then has to provide some income support to those who are eligible. If the same regression is estimated only for OECD19, the coefficients remain almost without change and the Chow test confirms that at a 5 per cent significance level. Comparison with the estimate on the basis of the late 1990s data again shows the loss of influence of collective bargaining on long-term unemployment as this factor has become statistically non-significant. EPL and benefit replacement rates remain non-significant too. Again, limiting the regression estimate to the OECD countries gives no change in the level of coefficients, which is confirmed by the Chow test.

In the case of youth unemployment, the picture is again slightly different from the previous two unemployment indicators (see table 2.17). Active LMP and labour tax remain statistically significant and keep their opposite signs, showing that higher expenditure on active LMP contributes to a decline in youth unemployment while higher labour taxation tends to increase youth unemployment. In addition, the trade union density coefficient is this time statistically significant and positive, although low. This could indicate that stronger trade unions protect their members, usually older workers, to a greater extent, at the cost of young people who are then more exposed to job losses or face more difficult access to employment and finally end up in unemployment (or inactivity). Neither employment protection legislation nor unemployment benefit schemes have any statistically significant impact on youth unemployment.

Running regressions and gradually omitting statistically non-significant variables, the benefit duration variable becomes statistically significant while the regression coefficient for active LMP slightly declines and others remain unchanged. This confirms a negative impact of the length of benefit payment on the level of youth unemployment. There could be two explanations for this result. Young people eligible for unemployment benefits may use them to the maximum, utilizing the time to improve their skills or taking temporary or informal employment while they wait for better jobs. Or, it may again show that in the situation of low demand for labour and high unemployment, young people suffer more than adult workers and the unemployment insurance system then has to provide income support to the jobless for longer periods. Active LMP remains a significant factor contributing towards reduction of youth unemployment. In turn, union density and labour taxation exhibit a negative impact on youth unemployment. Testing the hypothesis of stability of regression coefficients when constraining the database only to the OECD countries confirms its validity.

Comparison with the estimates based on data from the late 1990s shows that the impact of the benefit payment duration actually declined after 1999, most probably due to the cuts in benefit payment for young people without work experience in some countries. In contrast, the influence of trade union density has increased, pointing to the fact that trade unions have strengthened their activity in defending their core staff, with adverse consequences for young jobseekers. The impact of the output gap variable has disappeared.

Labour input

We estimated the regression with the employment rate as the dependent variable while keeping all other factors that had been used for explaining log unemployment rates in the previous regressions. The results presented in table 2.18 show that active LMP and labour tax retain their statistical significance and logically now have opposite signs (employment rate rises as a consequence of higher expenditure on active LMP but contracts with higher labour tax). The coefficients of employment protection legislation and both collective bargaining variables stay insignificant, showing a negligible effect of labour regulation and social dialogue on employment performance in the countries

Table 2.18 Regressions explaining the employment rate (dependent variable) for selected CSEE and OECD countries, 2003 compared to the late 1990s

Independent variables	Employment rate (dependent variable)			
	All independent variables	Only statistically significant independent variables		
	OECD + CSEE 2003	OECD + CSEE 2003	OECD + CEE end 1990s	OECD 2003
Employment protection	1.54 (0.96)	..	−2.93 (−1.74)	..
Replacement rate	−0.17 (−1.45)	..	..	..
Benefit duration	−1.30 (−1.97)	**−1.41 (−2.77)**	..	−1.49 (−3.27)
Active LMP	0.83 (4.75)	**0.64 (5.96)**	0.52 (3.18)	0.63 (5.25)
Union density	−0.03 (−0.57)	..	..	..
Union coordination	..	..	2.27 (1.29)	..
Collective bargaining coverage	0.93 (0.47)	..	−5.91 (−3.17)	..
Labour tax	−0.52 (−4.68)	**−0.49 (−6.82)**	..	−0.48 (−5.95)
Output gap	0.25 (0.31)	..	−0.87 (−1.40)	..
Adj. R^2	0.73	**0.75**	0.63	0.71
Number of countries	29	**29**	27	19
Chow test	..	**0.25****	2.77**	..

Notes: Estimation is by Ordinary Least Squares (OLS). t-statistics are presented in parentheses. For the Chow test, ** means that the hypothesis of coefficients stability is accepted at the 5 per cent level. .. = not applicable.

concerned. However, according to the results of the estimations, the main length of payment of unemployment benefits again appears to be significant: an increase in the average payment of unemployment benefits leads to a contraction of the employment rate. This seems indeed to indicate that the long duration of payment of unemployment benefits prevalent in a number of the OECD countries but less so in the new EU member countries does not force unemployed individuals to take up new jobs if these are of low quality and poorly paid.

Nevertheless, it is a little surprising to see that this factor is significant for the employment rate while remaining insignificant for the aggregate unemployment rate, although highly significant for long-term and youth unemployment. One explanation could be that many benefit recipients are actually passive jobseekers and therefore not classified as unemployed according to the ILO definition (or they may work informally and then be classified as neither unemployed nor employed if they do not disclose this information in LFS questionnaires). In contrast, long-term unemployed persons or unemployed young people are probably more careful to appear to be active jobseekers in order not to lose income support. This is why in their case the significance of unemployment benefit payment duration for the level of long-term and youth unemployment is important. The hypothesis of stability of the coefficients when reducing the sample of countries only to the OECD group has been confirmed, pointing to a convergent trend in development between the OECD and the CSEE countries in the last five years of the period under study.

Comparison with the late 1990s estimates reveals important differences. Both employment protection legislation and collective bargaining coverage have lost their significance in the last five years. Active labour market policy has become an even more important factor. However, two new factors have gained importance: labour tax and (maximum) unemployment benefit duration, both with negative impact on the employment rate. While between the late 1990s and 2003 social dialogue factors lost their impact on labour market developments, high labour tax and parameters of the unemployment benefit schemes seem to have played an increasing role when it comes to employment performance. This is influenced on the one hand by hiring and firing decisions by employers and on the other hand by decisions by workers whether or not to actively seek new jobs and accept them, taking into consideration the local labour demand, availability and quality of jobs, and access to social transfers. However, the estimates also confirm

Table 2.19 Regressions explaining the labour force participation rate (dependent variable) for selected CSEE and OECD countries, 2003 compared to the late 1990s

Independent variables	Labour force participation rate (dependent variable)			
	All independent variables	Only statistically significant independent variables		
	OECD + CSEE 2003	OECD + CSEE 2003	OECD + CEE end 1990s	OECD 2003
Employment protection	1.37 (0.78)	..	−2.87 (−1.97)	..
Replacement rate	−0.12 (−0.95)	..	..	..
Benefit duration	−1.21 (−1.77)	**−1.38 (−2.46)**	..	−1.58 (−2.46)
Active LMP	0.48 (2.50)	**0.39 (3.33)**	0.26 (1.70)	0.50 (3.00)
Union density	0.06 (1.13)	..	..	..
Union coordination	n.a.	**n.a.**	2.69 (1.69)	n.a.
Collective bargaining coverage	−0.66 (−0.35)	..	−3.92 (−2.28)	..
Labour tax	−0.42 (−3.65)	**−0.42 (−5.42)**	..	−0.51 (−4.46)
Output gap	−0.11 (−0.22)	..	−0.39 (−0.86)	..
Adj. R^2	0.55	**0.58**	0.57	0.52
Number of countries	29	**29**	27	19
Chow test	..	**0.45****	3.20	..

Notes: Estimation is by Ordinary Least Squares (OLS). t-statistics are presented in parentheses. For the Chow test, ** means that the hypothesis of coefficients stability is accepted at the 5 per cent level. .. = not applicable. n.a = not available.

that active LMP can make a difference and activate passive jobseekers by improving their employability and/or giving them access to subsidized jobs.

Regressions with the participation rate as the dependent variable show very similar results as those for the employment rate (see table 2.19). Again, the maximum length of payment of unemployment benefits has a significant impact on the participation rate, indicating that payment of benefits over a long period seems to lead towards factual inactivity of registered jobseekers as defined by the ILO, who may be discouraged or uninterested in seeking new jobs if these are unavailable or of very low quality. High labour taxation further strengthens this negative impact. Active labour market policies can partially offset these two factors as they contribute towards an increase in the participation rate. Employment protection legislation and collective bargaining indicators again proved to be statistically insignificant.

The Chow test confirmed the hypothesis of stability of coefficients at the 5 per cent significance level if run only on the sample of the 19 OECD countries, indicating that the labour markets of the new EU member and EU candidate countries increasingly follow the same patterns as the old OECD countries. This result is notably different from the late 1990s estimate when the stability of the regression coefficients was rejected, suggesting that the OECD countries behaved differently from the CEE countries at that time. Another difference between the two estimates reflecting changes in factors affecting the labour force participation rate is the rising significance of unemployment benefit duration and labour taxation – the two factors influencing individual decisions of employers and workers. In contrast, social dialogue indicators – factors stemming from collective negotiations and decisions – have become insignificant.

2.6.3 Conclusions

As confirmed throughout this chapter, labour market institutions of the new EU member and candidate countries have undergone significant changes since 1999. Employment protection legislation has been further liberalized to reach OECD levels, and protection of workers through collective bargaining has weakened as a result of declining unionization and the decreasing coverage by collective agreements. However, this lower level of job security has only partially been counterbalanced by increasing employment and income security through longer paid unemployment benefits (for less competitive workers in particular) and higher expenditure on active labour market policies in some countries (others have reduced their spending). Moreover, payroll taxes have been reduced in the majority of these countries but have still remained high in comparison with the OECD average.

In order to test whether these modifications in institutions and policies have exhibited any significant influence on labour market trends in the last five years, we turned to econometric calculations. The multivariate regressions using parameters of the crucial labour market institutions (employment protection legislation, unemployment insurance, active labour market policies and collective bargaining) to explain participation, employment and unemployment trends have indeed confirmed their importance. The main result is that no difference has been found between the OECD countries and the new EU countries as to the overall effects of labour market institutions on labour market performance.

Employment protection legislation continues to have no significant impact on unemployment levels on average. Diversity between the two groups of countries with regard to the impact of employment protection legislation on economic activity and employment trends identified in the late 1990s has disappeared.

Active labour market policies have contained and even strengthened their positive effect on reducing unemployment and promoting employment and labour market participation over the two periods. In contrast, not only unemployment as in the late 1990s but also employment and economic activity now seem to be negatively affected by high payroll taxes.

Social dialogue has lost its impact on employment and labour force participation, unemployment, and long-term unemployment since the late 1990s. Moreover, in the case of youth unemployment the results even point to a negative role of union density, suggesting that strong protection of core workers against a loss of their jobs could actually lead to more frequent dismissals and less hiring of peripheral workers, primarily young and inexperienced ones, and thus contribute to higher youth unemployment.

The duration of unemployment benefits has negatively affected all labour market indicators except aggregate unemployment. This rather surprising outcome may be mainly driven by the OECD countries, where the benefit system is much more generous than in the new EU countries. However, it may also indicate that in a context of low overall demand for labour, particular difficulties in finding a job and very poor-quality available employment, less competitive persons are compelled to stay on unemployment benefits as long as possible. Many of these people may also accept informal employment in order to supplement their low income. Long-term dependence on the benefit system contributes to lower labour market participation, as beneficiaries are actually discouraged jobseekers or even informally employed without disclosing this to LFS interviewers and thus figuring as inactive according to the ILO definition. It also results in higher youth unemployment and long-term unemployment, and in lower employment.

ANNEX 2.1 EMPLOYMENT PROTECTION INDEX: SELECTION OF INDICATORS AND WEIGHTING SCHEME

Level 4	Level 3	Level 2	Level 1		
EPL overall summary indicator	Regular contracts (5/12)	Procedural inconveniences (1/3)	Procedures		(1/2)
			Delay to start notice		(1/2)
		Notice and severance pay for no-fault individual dismissals (1/3)	Notice period after	9 months	(1/7)
				4 years	(1/7)
				20 years	(1/7)
			Severance pay after	9 months	(4/21)
				4 years	(4/21)
				20 years	(4/21)
		Difficulty of dismissal (1/3)	Definition of unfair dismissal		(1/4)
			Trial period		(1/4)
			Compensation		(1/4)
			Reinstatement		(1/4)
	Temporary contracts (5/12)	Fixed-term contracts (1/2)	Valid cases other than objective		(1/2)
			Max. number of successive contracts		(1/4)
			Max. cumulated duration		(1/4)
		Temporary work agency (1/2)	Types of work for which is legal		(1/2)
			Restrictions on number of renewal		(1/4)
			Max. cumulated duration		(1/4)
	Collective dismissals (2/12)		Definition of collective dismissal		(1/4)
			Additional notification requirements		(1/4)
			Additional delays involved		(1/4)
			Other special costs to employers		(1/4)

Note: Weightings given in parentheses.
Source: OECD (1999, table 2.B.2).

BULGARIA

3

Iskra Beleva,* Vasil Tzanov* and Genoveva Tisheva**

3.1 INTRODUCTION

The importance of labour market flexibility and security is increasing in Bulgaria as economic and social reform reaches a new stage of development. The established legal and institutional framework of the market economy and the market mechanisms in place in all spheres of socio-economic development indicate that the transition period is over. The new stage of development creates new priorities, namely the combination of economic and employment growth with stability and sustainability. From the labour market point of view this means not only more job opportunities and more flexible access to jobs, but also better jobs, improvements in the skills of the labour force and in the protection of human capital development. The quality of the combination of flexibility and security is therefore clearly a problem that needs more attention and the implementation of appropriate policies.

Over the period 1993–98, the labour market in Bulgaria underwent a significant evolution in an unstable and harsh economic environment and at a time of negative demographic tendencies. These adversely affected economic activity and created the conditions for an expansion of employment in the informal or 'shadow' economy. Stable economic growth after 1998 has contributed to a stable increase in employment since 2000 and better conditions for labour market development.

3.1.1 Data sources

The analysis in this chapter is based on different sources of information, namely: labour

---

* Institute of Economics, Bulgarian Academy of Sciences. ** Bulgarian Gender Research Foundation.

force surveys (LFS),[1] monthly data on unemployment registrations with the National Employment Agency, and national statistical annual data. In addition, the National Statistical Institute specially prepared the labour market flow data used here (data cover only 2003 and cannot be expanded because of the rotation of the sample). Other sources of information are the annual reports of the Agency for Small and Medium-Sized Enterprises, the National Action Plan for Employment, the National Bank reports and Household Budgets. Because of the different methodologies used for data collection, the different sources of information present different data for one and the same indicator; these variations must be borne in mind when comparing the data presented here. Despite these imperfections, all the cited sources of information are important for our analysis because of the different sub-indicators they provide.

The legislation in force has also been reviewed, including the amendments and supplements in force in the relevant period. The pace of legislative change is rather rapid, and this made it necessary to cite briefly successive amendments and the philosophy behind them.

3.2 MAIN CHARACTERISTICS OF THE NATIONAL LABOUR MARKET

3.2.1 Recent demographic and labour market trends

Bulgaria's demographic development is characterized by unfavourable trends related to the declining birth rate and the rising death rate. According to census data the country's population decreased from nearly 9 million in 1985 to fewer than 8 million in 2001. As a result, a lasting process of population ageing is under way. Active emigration, particularly over the last 12 years, has also contributed to this. As young people occupy a significant share in the structure of emigration, this is an additional contributor to the declining birth rate.

A number of other negative tendencies, such as the deteriorating levels of education, qualifications and health, have also been observed. The most alarming feature is the deterioration in the educational level of the population and the high rate of annual school dropouts. The share of dropouts for 2004–05 varied around 3 per cent for the different levels of education (Ministry of Labour and Social Policy, 2005, p. 8).

At the beginning of transition, Bulgaria undertook very radical economic reforms in the sphere of price and trade liberalization and mass privatization. As a result, economic performance deteriorated significantly. Over the period of transition (1989–2003), Bulgaria suffered a sharp decline in employment (figure 3.1). There

---

[1] At the beginning of 2003 the methodology and the organization of the LFS were brought into line with Eurostat requirements, requiring changes in the periodicity of the survey, the survey methodology and the questionnaire. The sample used in the survey was reduced from 24,000 to 18,000 households; persons performing their compulsory military service were no longer distributed by labour status; and the coverage of unemployed people was widened by including people whose job search consisted of studying job advertisements in newspapers and magazines.

Figure 3.1 Annual GDP and employment growth, Bulgaria, 1990–2005
(percentages)

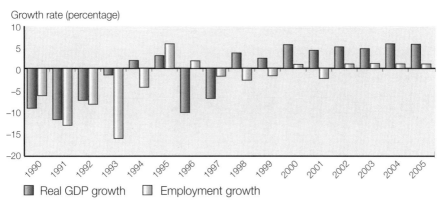

Sources: Statistical Yearbook and National Employment Agency.

was a net loss of more than 1.3 million jobs during this time, the vast majority of which occurred in the first three years of transition (over 1.1 million). Most of these people moved from employment to unemployment. Unemployment peaked in 1993, affecting 814,000 people. By that time, after the liberalization of the conditions concerning travelling abroad, many people emigrated.

Since 1998, the negative trend in economic development has reversed, leading to recovery. The positive economic growth over recent years (3.5 per cent in 1998; 2.3 per cent in 1999; over 4 per cent for 2000–05), and the macroeconomic stability (low level of inflation, balanced budget, increasing foreign investment and so forth) have created a favourable environment for increased job creation and high demand for labour. Thanks to the gross domestic product (GDP) growth accumulated in earlier years, 2002–05 saw a net employment increase, as shown in figure 3.1. Despite the positive tendency outlined above, employment has recently still been only 69.1 per cent of its pre-transition (1989) level.

3.2.2 Structure and development trends of main aggregates

Labour force participation

The economic and demographic impacts on labour demand and supply described here have had a considerable influence on labour force participation and have resulted in a decline in the coefficient of economic activity (ratio between the labour force and the population aged 15 and over), illustrated in figure 3.2.

The total labour force participation rate over the period 1993–2005 decreased by 4.3 percentage points, that of males by 3.5 percentage points and that of females by 4.8 percentage points. Decreasing labour force participation is mainly a result of the

Figure 3.2 Labour force participation, total and by sex, Bulgaria, 1993–2005
(percentages)

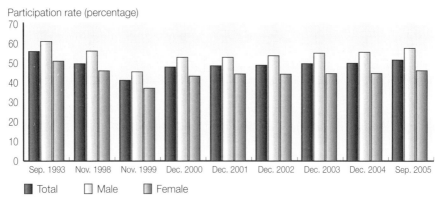

Source: LFS.

depressed labour demand and increasing discouragement of potential workers. It also reflects increasing employment in the informal economy. However, over the last few years participation has increased from 48 per cent in 2003 to 51 per cent in 2005, indicating an increased labour demand.

Employment

Between 1989 and 1993, employment decreased in absolute numbers by 1.14 million. Over this period the problem of employment security was completely neglected, while increasing employment flexibility was considered to be a reasonable way of reducing high unemployment.

According to LFS data published by the National Statistical Institute, employment increased over the period 1995–96 (figure 3.3). This upswing was caused by the delayed privatization of the large public enterprises and the recovery of their employment, as well as by the boom in the development of small and medium-sized enterprises (SMEs). Over this period, employment security increased for those employed in the public sector, while the newly established SMEs suffered high employment insecurity and high employment flexibility.

After the financial crisis in 1996 and the introduction of the currency board regime in 1997, employment decreased steadily until 2001. According to LFS data, employment stagnated in 2001–02 and then began to pick up again, such that by 2005 the number of employed persons had returned to its pre-crisis level.

LFS employment data can be broken up by sex, age, sector, enterprise size, form of ownership and education of employees. Annual changes in total employment disaggregated by sex show that female employment varied between 47.1 and 43.3 per cent of total employment the period 1989–2004, and that in some periods (1995–97)

Figure 3.3 Employment, Bulgaria, 1993–2005 (thousands and percentages)

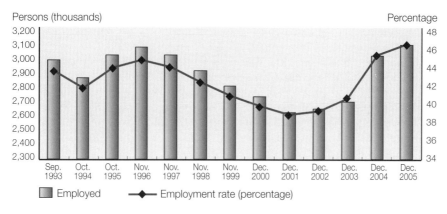

Source: LFS.

it decreased faster than male employment. The changes in employment during the transition varied for men and women, depending mainly on which sector was undergoing restructuring. The privatization process of traditionally 'female' sectors (textiles, for example) meant that in some periods there was a more significant decline in female employment, while the restructuring of the steel industry had a greater impact on male employment. The ongoing reform in the education and health systems, where female employment predominates, explains the more modest female employment growth in 2002 and 2003. In 2004, female employment represented 47.1 per cent of total employment.

The analysis of employment by age group shows that over the last three years of the period (2001–04) employment in absolute numbers stagnated among the 15–24 age group and increased among the remaining age groups.

The very intensive intersectoral and interbranch flows of labour over 1989–2004 caused high job insecurity. Sectoral and interbranch labour redistribution was due mainly to industrial restructuring. As a result, the main labour inflow was from the industrial sector to services or agriculture, or to unemployment and inactivity. Employment in industry decreased from 44.7 per cent in 1990 to 23.6 per cent in 2003, while employment in services increased from 36.7 per cent to 51.3 per cent over the same period and employment in agriculture also increased in relative terms, from 18.4 per cent to 25.1 per cent.

The contribution of the SME sector to employment growth in Bulgaria increased over the transition period, so that in 2002 the SME sector accounted for 99 per cent of all enterprises and 54 per cent of total employment. Micro-enterprises in Bulgaria represented 91 per cent of the total SME sector, but contributed only 48 per cent of SME employment. This means that the majority of SMEs are micro-enterprises with just one or two employees. Small businesses represented 6.7 per cent of SMEs by number and

34 per cent of total SME employment, while medium-sized enterprises represented 1.1 per cent of total SMEs by number and 17 per cent of total SME employment.

The dynamics of employment structure by form of ownership over the transition period indicate that the employment status of employees has remained relatively stable, with their share in total employment over a ten year period at 88.7 per cent in 1993 and 83.6 per cent in 2003. The most important change in the structure by ownership has been the increasing share of employees in the private sector, from 11.2 per cent in 1993 to 50.4 per cent in 2003. There has also been an increase in the share of self-employed people, from 8.5 per cent in 1996 to 10.4 per cent in 2003, while the share of employers increased relatively modestly, from 2 per cent to 3.4 per cent. The share of unpaid family workers has also increased over the period, from 1.4 per cent to 2.1 per cent.

Within private sector employment, more men are self-employed than women (63.9 per cent for men, 36.1 per cent for women, in September 2004), while there are relatively equal shares of men and women among employees in private firms (52.9 per cent for men and 47.1 per cent for women, for the same period). Among unpaid family workers, women have the predominant share of employment: in September 2004, women were twice as numerous as men and represented 68.4 per cent of total unpaid family workers.

An interesting point of note is the educational structure of employees in the public and private sectors. Data clearly highlight the different interest taken by public and private employers in the educational structure of the people they employ. Public sector employers prefer people with higher education, while private sector employers are more interested in employing people with secondary technical, vocational or general education. The private sector also hires more people with lower secondary education. The educational structure of employers and self-employed people as of September 2004 shows that 55.5 per cent of employers have a secondary education and 38.6 per cent have higher education. Among self-employed people, 39.1 per cent have secondary education but only 17.1 per cent have higher education and 43.7 per cent have lower secondary and primary education.

Unemployment and inactivity

Bulgaria suffered very high and persistent unemployment after 1989 up until 2002. According to LFS data, average annual unemployment over the period 1993–2004 stood at 567,000 and the average unemployment rate was 16.1 per cent, with more men unemployed than women in absolute numbers. Average annual unemployment figures gathered from the official registers of the employment service were lower for the same period, at 542,000, while the average registered unemployment rate was 14.2 per cent (table 3.1). The positive feature is the downward tendency that began in 2003, mainly due to active labour market programmes.

Figure 3.4 shows the increasing number of people who have withdrawn discouraged from the labour market. In 1994 the share of these people in the total inactive population was 6 per cent, while by 2004 it had increased to 11.3 per cent.

Table 3.1 Registered and total unemployment in Bulgaria, 1993–2005 (thousands and percentages)

	1993	1994	1995	1996	1997	1998	1999	2000	2001	2002	2003	2004	2005
Total unemployment (thousands)	814.7	740.2	520.8	490.8	534.1	556.1	576.9	549.1	632.4	584.5	426.3	373.0	312.9
Unemployment rate (%)	21.4	20.5	14.7	13.7	15.0	16.0	17.0	16.2	18.6	17.3	12.7	11.0	9.2
Average annual registered unemployment (thousands)	600.8	537.0	434.6	422.5	536.7	466.4	490.4	693.4	669.6	655.9	530.5	469.2	424.4
Registered unemployment rate (%)	16.1	12.8	10.7	12.0	14.0	11.1	13.7	18.1	17.5	17.3	14.3	12.6	11.4

Notes: For 1993 and 2000–05, September; for 1994–95, October; for 1996–99, November.

Source: LFS.

In absolute terms, the number of discouraged doubled over the period in question, with discouraged males more numerous than females. In 2005 this trend began to reverse and the share of discouraged people dropped significantly to 6.6 per cent

The 2004 *National Action Plan for Employment* (Ministry of Labour and Social Policy, 2004, p. 14) identified as vulnerable groups the long-term unemployed (representing 50.5 per cent of total average unemployment in 2004); unemployed youths (26.4

Figure 3.4 Discouraged workers as a percentage of inactive population and by sex, Bulgaria, 1994–2005

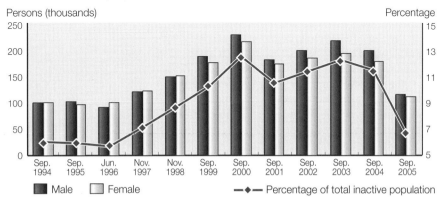

Source: LFS.

63

per cent); unemployed people over 50 years of age (26.4 per cent); unemployed women (54.9 per cent); disabled unemployed (5 per cent);[2] low-educated unemployed (68.8 per cent); and discouraged jobseekers (counted as inactive population).

Atypical (flexible) forms of employment: Incidence and trends

Employment flexibility results from the legal norms facilitating or limiting workers' exit from, or entry into, employment, as well as from the legal conditions under which employers are able to hire and fire workers. The indicators used to measure flexible forms of employment include the types of employment contract, the length of working time, and the flows from and into employment.

The LFS in Bulgaria identifies four forms of contract, based on Labour Code norms, namely: the employment contract, the civil contract, 'other' contracts, and employment without a written contract. The last three forms are considered to be more flexible because they are temporary, clearly indicate the points of agreement between the contracting parties and are easier to terminate. For the period 2001–05 the share of employees with an employment contract has increased insignificantly, from 91 per cent to 93.8 per cent. The share of employees with a civil contract decreased by 2.5 percentage points, while the share of the other two forms did not change. These figures seem to point to slowly declining flexibility related to the type of employment contract.

Differences exist between the sexes regarding the type of employment contract. A higher share of women was working on an employment contract, namely 95.5 per cent of women compared with 92.2 per cent of men, in September 2005. The difference is more significant between men and women hired without an employment contract, namely 5.4 per cent of men and 2.9 per cent of women.

There are also gender differences in the type of contract when comparing public and private enterprises in the period 2001–03. In private enterprises the share of men hired on an employment contract was 88.5 per cent and that of women 91.3 per cent, while in the public sector the gap was smaller, with 97.5 per cent of men and 98 per cent of women. Men without employment contracts accounted for 7.5 per cent of total employees in private enterprises, while the share of women without employment contracts was 4.9 per cent.

Age and education levels are other factors which influence the type of contract used. Young people between 15 and 25 years of age and older persons over 65 years were found to work more frequently without a contract or under civil contract than other age groups. Data indicate that the lower the level of education, the higher the proportion of employed without contract or under civil contract.

The last feature related to the type of employment contract is its use by sector of employment. Workers without an employment contract in September 2003 accounted for 19.1 per cent of the total number of workers in the agricultural sector, with another

---

[2] National Employment Agency: *Labour Market 2005* (Sofia).

6 per cent employed under 'other contracts'. The share of workers without employment contracts in industry was 3.4 per cent and in services it was 3 per cent.

Over the period 1994–2003, the employment structure on the basis of normal working hours indicates increasing numbers of full-time employees in Bulgaria, with the majority working 40–49 hours per week. Part-time employment is concentrated mainly in the private sector (79.5 per cent of total part-time employees in September 2003) and represented an insignificant and declining share of total employment in this period, decreasing from 2.9 per cent to 1.9 per cent.

In absolute figures, part-time employment has decreased dramatically from 98,600 in March 2001 to 35,800 in September 2005. It is interesting to see the reasons for part-time employment, which the LFS identifies as lack of work or of an available full-time job; attending school or training; personal reasons or family responsibilities. In September 2003, 60.7 per cent of all part-time employees cited the lack of work or of an available full-time job as the reason for their reduced hours: this share grew to 74.9 per cent in 2005. This means that most part-time employment is not a personal choice, but a response to the absence of other job opportunities.

Some differences exist between men and women in terms of their normal working hours. In September 2003 the share of male employees working full time was 89.5 per cent of total male employees, while 1.5 per cent were employed part time; another 8.9 per cent failed to classify their type of working time. Among female employees, 91.9 per cent were employed full time and 2.3 per cent part time, while 5.6 per cent failed to classify the type of working time.

It should be noted that the number of workers not classifying their working time in 2003 was four times higher than that of part-time employees. This means that there are other types of working time that are not covered by the classification used by the LFS and it is most likely that these types are more flexible forms of employment.

Flow data[3]

According to data from the National Statistical Institute and the Statistical Yearbook, labour outflows and inflows varied significantly over the transition period, depending on the speed of economic restructuring. Changes in the private sector had a significant impact, since more than half of the outflows and the inflows are in this sector.

The balance between the number of people leaving and entering the labour market was negative and stayed negative over a ten-year period (1990–2000). Only in 2001 was there a positive balance, with more people entering than leaving the labour

---

[3] Three sources of information will be used for the analysis of labour flows. The first source is the annual national statistical data on labour outflows and labour inflows. This source of information regarding labour outflows includes all separations from firms (including separations due to economic restructuring), while labour inflows represent all recruitment. The second source is the monthly unemployment flow data, registered by the employment agency and published in the monthly information bulletin. In this case the data include the newly registered unemployed representing the inflow into unemployment, while the outflow consists of those who were recruited during the month on the primary labour market or under active labour market measures. The third source is LFS data. For more details, see Beleva et al. (2005).

market. In the first three years of transition (1990–92), the number of people withdrawing from the labour market was very high: more than 1 million per year for the first two years and about 800,000 people in 1992. About one-third of withdrawals from the labour market in 1991 and 1992 were the result of economic restructuring. The number of people who entered the labour market was relatively high in 1990 and started to decline in 1991 and 1992.

After 1993, outflows started to decline, mainly owing to the abovementioned delay in the privatization process. As a result the outflow numbers stabilized at about 450,000 people and the inflows at 400,000. However, a new wave of increased outflows followed the economic crisis in 1996 and the subsequent financial stabilization through the implementation of a currency board regime. The acceleration of the economic restructuring resulted in about 700,000 people per year moving out of employment for the period 1997–2001. The inflows then started to increase, with the result that the balance between the outflows and the inflows became positive in 2001.

According to LFS labour market flow data for 2003–05, the labour market has become more flexible in terms of transitions between employment, unemployment and inactivity. Employment has become more stable, while unemployed workers' chances of entry into employment have decreased to between 16 per cent and 11 per cent, and the probability of exiting from inactivity has slightly decreased. The stability of the improvement process seems to be questionable, since third–fourth-quarter data show a deterioration related to exits from unemployment and inactivity and entry to employment.

The analysis of monthly inflows and outflows from unemployment, presented in table 3.2, shows that over the period 1992–2000 the labour market situation was very difficult, with an average annual inflow into unemployment of about 50,000 (varying between 35,000 and 61,000 according to the year), and an average annual outflow of 45,000 (varying between 29,000 and 51,000). After 2000, however, employment prospects progressively improved, as can be seen by the decline in inflows to unemployment after this date, and the increasing outflows from unemployment into employment. In percentage terms, the share of the outflow from unemployment that moved to employment was 19 per cent in 1992 and increased to 47 per cent in 2003. The number of individuals who move to and/or stay in inactivity is still disturbing.

Job tenure data

During transition the pressure of a high supply of labour in relation to the very limited labour demand increased job insecurity.[4] According to the tenure data available for 2001–03, employment of less than one year with one employer increased from 14.1 per cent in 2001 to 17.5 per cent in 2003.

---

[4] Increasing job insecurity is defined not only by decreasing job tenure, but also by much other evidence reported in the mass media, such as longer working time without additional payment, work without labour contracts, and delays in payment of wages.

Table 3.2 Unemployment flows, Bulgaria, 1992–2003 (numbers)

Indicators	1992	1993	1994	1995	1996	1997	1998	1999	2000	2001	2002	2003
Total unemployment	499 765	600 800	537 025	434 627	422 532	536 703	466 493	490 495	693 481	669 609	655 998	530 529
Inflows	53 279	44 932	41 410	45 224	51 975	60 907	35 695	58 050	61 217	44 973	44 595	45 730
Outflows	28 990	35 568	51 028	50 612	47 392	48 099	50 545	46 720	50 528	51 856	50 810	54 219
Outflows to employment	5 539	6 202	6 980	10 412	12 446	17 368	15 726	18 078	17 421	17 706	21 624	25 750
Ratio of inflows/ outflows	1.83	1.26	0.81	0.89	1.09	1.26	0.70	1.24	1.21	0.86	0.86	0.84

Source: Authors' calculations on the basis of monthly registration data from *Monthly Bulletin*, Ministry of Labour and Social Policy.

As an indicator of job stability, employment of less than one year with the same employer is only to be considered as a positive element of labour market development in cases where it reflects increasing job creation rather than higher labour churning. The second assumption is perhaps more valid in the case of Bulgaria since job tenure of between one and two years with the same employer decreased from 9.5 per cent to 7.9 per cent between 2001 and 2003. The largest group consisted of employees with tenure of two to five years (25 per cent in 2001 and 23.3 per cent in 2003), but this share also showed a downward tendency.

Average job tenure decreased from 7.7 to 7.6 years between 2001 and 2003. There are no significant differences in job tenure for men and women: on average female employees have only 0.5 years longer tenure than male employees. More significant differences are revealed if job tenure is analysed by economic sector: average job tenure was lowest in agriculture, at 5.4 years, while in industry it was 7.9 years and in services it was 7.6 years. Compared with other sectors of the economy, job insecurity in the service sector increased substantially between 2001 and 2003, as there was a decrease in job tenure in all groups except five to ten years of tenure and less than one year.

Informal employment

Hidden or informal employment is defined as employment without an employment contract or for which the real amount of remuneration goes unreported. Social insurance contributions and taxes on labour are high, and employers use informal employment to avoid paying these costs.

According to some estimates, the informal economy in Bulgaria accounted for 20 per cent of GDP in 2000 (Ministry of Labour and Social Policy/European Commission, 2002). More recent estimates put it at 25 per cent in 2005 (Ministry of Labour and Social Policy, 2006). The informal economy employs a significant share of the labour force, mainly in precarious and low-productivity jobs, without labour protection. The main sectors with high levels of hidden employment are agriculture, services, construction and trade (Hristoskov et al., 1997). In 1999, according to one study (Kyle et al., 2001), 3 per cent of employment, or about 80,000 people, were not registered as employed. The same study concluded that firms did not declare about 35 per cent of labour expenditures and that between 10 per cent and 50 per cent of incomes were not declared either.[5]

The relatively high hidden employment induced the Government to take steps to reduce it, through such measures as stricter controls on the payment of social security contributions and on labour conditions, and by lowering income taxation. In January 2003 the Obligatory Social Insurance Code (OSIC), aimed at ensuring better coverage of employees through the re-registration of employment contracts, was adopted and came into force. As a result, many new employment contracts emerged

---

[5] The study covered 530 enterprises from selected branches, accounting for 56 per cent of total GDP.

and more employed people were covered by the social insurance system. Recently, as part of the ongoing reform in the health system, the health insurance system has also been revised, thus increasing the number of health-insured people.

3.3 FLEXIBILITY AND SECURITY: INSTITUTIONAL BACKGROUND

Over the transition period Bulgaria saw major evolutions in its labour market flexibility and income security. The economic and social reforms undertaken completely destroyed the previous labour market model – in some cases step by step, in others by radical action – and as a result the present labour market is characterized by a relatively high degree of flexibility and relatively low levels of job protection and income security.

The liberalization of the labour market through the changes in the legal basis created more freedom for employers to react to internal and external economic shocks by increasing labour flexibility at the expense of job and income security. In fact, employers managed to survive in business competition mainly by keeping labour costs low and limiting any additional expenditure on providing decent working conditions or any social benefits. Meanwhile, depressed labour demand in conditions of an over-represented labour supply weakened the trade unions (as seen in their declining membership) and thus restricted the opportunities of achieving a better balance between flexibility and employment security through social dialogue.

3.3.1 Employment protection legislation

Employment protection legislation has been the subject of dynamic transformation during the whole transition period, but the most radical reforms were carried out in 1992 and 2001. The approach adopted by the legislators has been one based on a neoliberal view of the State's role in the social sphere. Some of the reforms have dealt exclusively with the individual employment relationship, the burdens of which are shared by employers and workers; many also touch on issues of general social policy.

Generally the changes in the legislation regarding employment protection are aimed, on the one hand, at liberalizing the termination of the employment relationship on the initiative of the employer, and, on the other, at protection against dismissal.

Liberalizing the termination of the employment relationship by the employer

Amendments were introduced in order to balance the needs of flexibility and security and were tested out in practice for a short period of time. With the amendments made in 1992 several new texts were introduced (concerning dismissal of managers for economic or related reasons with a notice period of two months (art. 328a) and dismissal of managers or members of artistic staff in cultural institutions (art. 328b) which were then repealed in 1995 as not being adequate to the requirements of protection against termination of employment.

Following the amendments, the Labour Code introduced a new rule in March 2001 (art. 331). Its objective is to introduce flexibility and adaptability into the grounds for dismissal under conditions of dynamic social and economic change. The idea is to make the employer free to terminate employment, where there is mutual consent, against a generous agreed compensation. The important features of the provision, which differentiate it from the general rule for mutual consent of the parties, are as follows:

- The employer initiates and submits a written proposal to terminate the relationship.

- The employer is not obliged to give justification for the proposal. The Labour Code does not envisage prior limitations or preconditions.

- The proposal shall contain information on the compensation offered, in exchange for which the employer expects to gain the consent of the employee to terminate the relationship.

- The compensation cannot be less than the sum of the last four gross monthly remunerations. (As there are no further indications in the text, we may assume this is the sum on which the compensation is calculated.)

At the time of adoption of this text, the Unemployment Protection and Employment Promotion Act envisaged certain insurance rights for the unemployed when the termination of the employment was based on mutual consent.[6] The new regulation stipulates that unemployed persons whose employment relationships have been terminated at their own request, with their consent, or due to their own fault, receive the minimum extent of the unemployment cash benefits for four months.[7]

Protection against dismissal

Protection against dismissal as an instrument for employment protection concerns special groups of employed people. An employer may not dismiss the following categories of employee without the prior consent of the labour inspectorate for each specific case:[8]

---

[6] Art. 69(3) of this act stipulates that those unemployed whose employment has been terminated at their own request, with the exception of the cases of art. 327, paras. 1, 2 and 3 of the Labour Code, as well as in cases of disciplinary dismissals, received unemployment benefits equal to 80 per cent of the minimum wage, for a period of four months.

[7] Art. 54b of the Social Insurance Code.

[8] Under art. 328, para. 1, items 2, 3, 5 and 11, and art. 330, para. 2, item 6.

- pregnant women, mothers of children younger than three years of age, or spouses of persons who have entered their compulsory military service;

- employees who have been reassigned due to reasons of health;

- employees suffering from certain diseases listed in a Regulation of the Minister of Health (in these cases the opinion of an expert medical commission must also be considered prior to dismissal);

- employees who have commenced a period of permitted leave.

In these cases, the employer may not dismiss an employee who is a member of the enterprise trade union leadership belonging to a territorial, industrial or national elected trade union body, throughout the period of occupation of the trade union position and not earlier than six months after that, without the prior consent of the trade union body, acting on the decision of the central leadership of the respective trade union organization. The prior consent of the respective trade union body of an enterprise is also needed before dismissing an employee due to staff cuts or reduction of the volume of work, where provided for in a collective agreement. The dismissal of a female employee who uses leave for pregnancy and childbirth may be permitted only in the case of enterprise closure.

Employment protection legislation is implemented voluntarily in most cases. In some cases, however, enforcement is realized by litigation in the country's general system of civil courts. The predominant claims in courts deal with unlawful dismissals; this happened in more than 50 per cent of all rulings issued by the courts in 2002 and 2003. Next come claims for unpaid or delayed wages and salaries, employment injuries, and occupational illness. Although the Civil Procedures Code has been amended in order to speed up labour claims procedures, the claims pending in the general judicial system are numerous. In 2003 more than 16,000 such claims were brought to court and the average time taken to reach a settlement was between one and three years. This long period is inconvenient both for the workers and for the employers. The only way out of this situation is the establishment of specialized labour courts, and this option is being discussed by the social partners.

Overall control over compliance with labour legislation in all sectors and activities is exercised by the General Labour Inspectorate, an executive agency under the Minister of Labour and Social Policy. Other state authorities, in addition to the labour inspectorate, exercise overall or specific control over compliance with labour legislation by force of law or an act of the Council of Ministers. Ministers, heads of other agencies and local government authorities exercise control over compliance with labour legislation through their own special bodies.

Within their own competence, controlling bodies have the right to visit ministries, other agencies, enterprises and other places of work, at any time, and to demand explanations and documentary information from employers, as well as information from workers. Other elements of employment protection legislation in use in Bulgaria include compulsory administrative measures and the appeal against them, labour inspection record books and administrative penal liability. Violations of labour legislation are established by statements issued by state controlling bodies, while penal decrees are issued by the head of the respective controlling body or authorized substitutes.

3.3.2   Additional protection through collective bargaining

Collective agreements regulate issues concerning the labour and social security relations in the case of employees who are not covered by compulsory statutory rules, and should not contain clauses that are more unfavourable to employees than the provisions of the law or of other collective agreements binding upon the employer.

Collective agreements may be concluded at enterprise, branch, industry and municipal levels, with only one agreement permitted at each level. Within an enterprise, the collective agreement should be concluded between the employer and a trade union organization, the draft of which should be prepared and submitted by the trade union.[9] At higher levels, a draft agreement is prepared by the representative organizations of the employees and submitted to the representative organizations of the employers. Where the collective agreement at industry or branch level has been concluded between all representative organizations of the employees and of the employers in the industry or the sector, the Minister of Labour and Social Policy may, upon their joint request, extend the application of the agreement or its individual clauses to all enterprises in that industry or sector.

The draft agreement is then negotiated between the individual employer, the group of employers, or their organizations, and the employees' representatives to conclude a collective agreement. Certain information must be made available to both parties: namely, collective agreements concluded which already bind the parties on the basis of affiliation, and relevant information on their economic and financial position (any information which could cause harm to the employer if disclosed may be refused or granted subject to a requirement of confidentiality). Employers in default of disclosure are liable to pay compensation. For their part, trade unions can be requested to provide membership figures.

The collective agreement comes into force on the date of its conclusion for one year, in so far as it does not provide otherwise, but for no longer than two years, and new collective agreements shall be negotiated no later than three months prior to the expiry of the term of the current agreement. Coverage extends to the trade union's membership, though other employees may accede to the agreement upon request.

Several amendments have been made to the regime of collective agreements in order to improve their regulation and their effectiveness. Judicial experience indicates that there are cases in which the collective agreements have been more explicit and

---

[9] Where more than one trade union exists within an enterprise they shall submit a common draft. In the event that they fail to do so, the employer concludes the collective agreement with the trade union organization the draft of which has been approved by the general meeting of the employees (meeting of proxies) by a majority of more than half of the members thereof (Beleva et al., 2005).

rigid in the area of dismissals than the labour legislation, or have introduced additional preliminary protection against dismissals for enlarged groups of workers. Examples of this might include the reintroduction of certain clauses that existed in the older regulations, now formulated in the collective agreement, such as clauses that prohibit the dismissals in cases of staff reductions of workers who have one, two or even three years to go before retirement; or preliminary consent of the trade union committee even in cases of disciplinary dismissals. In such cases the Supreme Court has consistently ruled invalid those clauses that go beyond the Labour Code.

Regulations regarding working time, which tend to be restrictive, set precise rules regarding daily hours and weekly holidays, and forbid overtime work except under certain circumstances. These have been liberalized with the amendments in 2004–06. Daily working hours have been increased to allow a maximum of ten hours, for example, and the working week has been expanded to a maximum of 48 hours.[10] Further liberalization has been pursued by the employers, but at present the debate is concentrated on annual seniority bonuses which automatically increase the remuneration with each year of employment both in the public and the private sector. Because of the practical difficulties in checking employment conditions through labour inspection and the slow progress of labour law cases through the civil courts, there appears to be a significant degree of non-compliance with employment protection legislation.

3.3.3 Labour market policy

Labour market policy is an important instrument for balancing flexibility with employment and income security in the labour market. Its protective role refers not only to the income protection of the unemployed (passive labour market policy, PLMP) but also to the stimulation of job creation and improvement of skill levels and qualifications among the unemployed (active labour market policy, ALMP).

Passive labour market policy

The priority of labour market policy during the period under consideration has changed with the successive stages of economic and social transformation. At the beginning of transition, passive labour market policy played a very important role at a time when unemployment was emerging as a new social phenomenon. The identification, registration and payment of unemployment benefits as compensation for wage income was a key aim of the labour market institutions. The prevailing passive and reactive character of the labour market policy of that time can be seen in the types of expenditure of the specially established Retraining and Unemployment Benefits Fund (see table 3.3). The amounts accumulated from employers' and

---

[10] Hours in excess of the 40-hour general limit up to a maximum total of 48 hours are permitted for reasons related to the production process during some working days, to be compensated for by reduced hours on other days.

Table 3.3   Expenditure on ALMP and PLMP as a percentage of total labour
market policy spending, Bulgaria, 1993–2003

	1993	1994	1995	1996	1997	1998	1999	2000	2001	2002	2003
Total expenditure	100.0	100.0	100.0	100.0	100.0	100.0	100.0	100.0	100.0	100.0	100.0
Expenditure on ALMP	17.3	19.9	27.3	30.8	27.8	31.2	25.9	25.8	24.0	42.4	66.3
Expenditure on PLMP	82.7	80.0	72.6	69.1	60.1	57.4	58.0	73.6	75.0	57.6	33.6
Other expenditure	..	..	..	..	12.1	11.4	..	0.6	1.0	..	..

Note: .. = not applicable.

Source: National Employment Service.

employees' contributions which were used for funding labour market policy until 2000 show that the share of PLMP within total expenditure in 1993 was 82.7 per cent, declining further to 58 per cent in 1999.

It subsequently became important for the criteria for unemployment compensations to be more precise and for unemployed persons to be stimulated to engage in active job search. Meanwhile, the legal and institutional systems of unemployment administration were established and developed. Later efforts advanced the development of active labour market policy, including packages of regional and branch programmes for alternative employment, temporary employment and programmes promoting self-employment.

At the end of 1997 the Council of Ministers approved the Unemployment Protection and Promotion of Employment Act (UPPEA), which came into force in January 1998. The evolution of priorities continued and this act was replaced by the Employment Promotion Act (EPA, in force since January 2002). With this act, unemployment was clearly identified as a social risk. The National Social Security Institute (NSSI) was put in charge of payment of unemployment benefits. The above-mentioned fund was renamed the Unemployment Fund and is currently managed by the NSSI, while ALMP is implemented by the Ministry of Labour and Social Policy together with the Employment Agency and is funded by the state budget, donors or international programmes. In 2004 the expenditure on unemployment benefits amounted to BGN 102 million (0.3 per cent of GDP) and in 2005 it dropped to BGN 91.8 million (0.2 per cent of GDP).

The number of recipients of unemployment benefits and unemployment assistance fluctuates cyclically (figure 3.5). Up to the mid 1990s there was a substantial downward trend, following which it rose again before declining after 2000. The costs of passive labour market policy as a proportion of GDP remain low (less than 1 per cent) and have closely tracked changes in the number of unemployed receiving unemployment benefits. This trend is a result of the more restrictive policy regarding the access criteria and the payment period for unemployment benefits. The increase in the number of beneficiaries during 1997–2001 was the result of the

Figure 3.5   Number of unemployment benefit recipients (thousands) and the share of PLMP spending in GDP (percentages), Bulgaria, 1994–2005

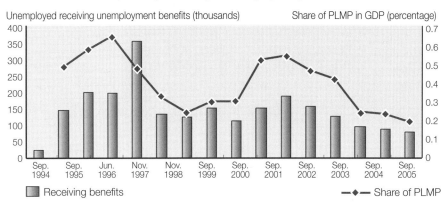

Source: National Employment Agency.

rise in the number of newly unemployed, but by 2005 the number of unemployed receiving unemployment benefits was a quarter of that in 2001.

No evaluations have been made of the impact of unemployment benefits on the intensity of job search. An econometric investigation of the matching function for Bulgaria (Tzanov and Lukanova, 2000, p. 88) shows that the efficiency of job search is low. This result may be explained by the weak impact of unemployment benefits on the matching process. It also means that there is no substantial connection between the restrictive unemployment benefits policy and the intensity of job search.

Active labour market policy

The development of active labour market policy in Bulgaria during the transition has evolved significantly in terms of priorities and overall design. The mechanisms and instruments for its implementation have also been enriched and continue to improve.

The Governmental Programme of 2000 identified active labour market policy as one of its priorities, with the aim of reducing unemployment and increasing human welfare. The New Social Policy Strategy (Ministry of Labour and Social Policy, 2003) underlined the importance of active policies in improving the functioning of the labour market.

In accordance with the provisions of the European Union Accession Partnership of 2002, the Government of Bulgaria and the European Commission prepared a Joint Assessment of Employment Priorities paper (Ministry of Labour and Social Policy/ European Commission, 2002). This paper includes a detailed analysis of the active labour market policy in force, identifies the advantages of the various measures and programmes, and draws recommendations for their improvement.

The Employment Strategy (2004–10) and its *National Action Plan for Employment* (Ministry of Labour and Social Policy, 2004) define the path towards achieving the goals of the European Employment Strategy in Bulgaria, namely full employment, quality and productivity of labour, and social cohesion. Taking into account these recommendations and the assessment of the efficiency of active policies, the two documents set out in detail active labour market programmes and measures for the short and medium term, as well as guidelines for their further development. The Employment Strategy also includes a package of new programmes and measures to be implemented for strengthening equal opportunities and incentives for lifelong learning. The types of active labour market policy proposed in the *National Action Plan for Employment* have four main aims: increasing employability; development of entrepreneurship; incentives for business development and job creation; and strengthening equal opportunities. These follow the general thrusts of the European Employment Strategy: improving employability; providing incentives for employment; development of conditions for lifelong learning; business development and employment; and strengthening equal opportunities.

Active labour market policy development

The growth of active labour market policies is evidenced by the increase in relevant expenditure from 0.1 per cent of GDP in 1994 to 0.21 per cent in 1999, 0.27 per cent in 2001 and 0.67 per cent in 2003 (figure 3.7). This is an indicator showing the priority given to active policies in recent years as a tool for increasing the efficiency of labour and the social reintegration of unemployed people. In 2004 the share of active labour market policies in GDP was 0.55 per cent and in 2005 it was 0.49 per cent.

Since 2001, precedence has been given to active programmes, improving their flexibility with regard to the design and financing of the activities, such that by 2003 labour market programmes covered 82.5 per cent of active labour market policies. Most of these programmes were designed on the module principle, combining work with training or qualification. As illustrated in table 3.4, the programmes implemented during this period targeted separate vulnerable groups or a range of these. For example, priority in accessing programmes was given first to young long-term unemployed, then to long-term unemployed receiving social benefits, then to single mothers, and so on. The programmes and measures targeting specific vulnerable groups offered different forms of support, such as subsidized employment, training or qualification, and incentives to employers for hiring unemployed people and creating jobs. There are also national programmes and programmes targeting one specific region or group of regions, such as those with high unemployment rates.

The figures shown in table 3.4 illustrate the priorities of the programmes in total active labour market policy in 2001–03 and the intensive process of programme review over the period. Some programmes were closed during this time and others, where the number of participants decreased, were being wound up, while many new programmes have since been designed or are in the process of pilot implementation.

Table 3.4   Participation in centrally funded ALMP programmes and measures,
Bulgaria, 2001–03 (numbers and percentages)

Type of programmes and measures	2001	2002	2003
Total number of participants in programmes and measures	86 244	108 200	178 262
Share (percentages)	(100.0)	(100.0)	(100.0)
Participants in selected ALM measures	7 728	19 385	31 057
Share of total participants	(8.9)	(17.9)	(17.4)
Youths, participating in measures	3 612	7 047	8 830
	(4.1)	(6.5)	(4.8)
Long-term unemployed, participating in measures	2 257	2 108	1 289
	(2.6)	(1.9)	(0.7)
Qualification and motivation for unemployed	4 557	14 239	22 117
	(5.2)	(13.2)	(12.4)
Territorial mobility	694	128	362
	(0.8)	(0.1)	(0.2)
Self-employment measures	820	583	704
	(0.9)	(0.5)	(0.3)
Subsidized employment under different measures	4 854	6 244	5 087
	(5.6)	(5.7)	(2.8)
Participants in selected ALM programmes	70 557	88 815	147 205
Share of total participants	(81.8)	(82.1)	(82.6)
From Social Benefits to Employment programme	..	55 293	117 761
	..	(51.1)	(66.0)
Regional employment programmes	24 922	11 009	..
	(28.9)	(10.2)	..
Temporary employment programme	31 797	654	..
	(36.8)	(0.6)	..
National Assistance for Retirement programme	..	96	780
	..	(0.0)	(0.4)
Increasing Employability and Entrepreneurship of Youths project	..	148	880
	..	(0.1)	(0.4)
Job clubs and structural development	7 767	5 229	10 647
	(9.0)	(4.8)	(5.9)
From Social Assistance to Employment programme	5 505	9 497	..
	(6.3)	(8.7)	..
ALMP in cooperation with international institutions	35 672	25 730	12 584
	(41.4)	(23.8)	(7.0)

Notes: As not all programmes and measures are included here, totals do not add up to 100 per cent. .. = not applicable.

Source: Employment Agency, *Information Bulletins* 2001, 2002 and 2003.

The improved coverage of the new programmes is shown by the increasing number of participants, which more than doubled over the three years. The regional approach, which was widely implemented over 2001–03, has been supported by the programme approach whereby significant regional disparities are taken into account and the financial resources distributed among regions are linked to unemployment rates.

The majority of programme participation over the period is concentrated in the From Social Benefits to Employment programme (replacing the From Social Assistance to Employment programme in 2002), targeted at increasing the employability of the socially excluded – that is poor people receiving benefits and the long-term unemployed. Education and training are a key element of these reintegration programmes.

Subsidized employment and training predominate within the active labour market policy package as a whole. The most important source of subsidized employment over the period is the From Social Benefits to Employment programme. This programme targets long-term unemployed people who are not eligible for unemployment benefit and receive social support; individuals under 20 years old not eligible for unemployment benefit; single mothers not receiving social benefits; and long-term unemployed who have been registered for 24 or more months and have received social benefits over the last 18 months. These people are offered subsidized community work and are paid by employers for the work done. They are also entitled to additional payments in accordance with the Labour Code at a minimum level, and social and health insurance. The share of participants in subsidized employment of various kinds is the highest in both programmes and measures. This fact marks one of the main challenges facing active labour market policy today – how to transform subsidized jobs into stable employment.

In spite of the very intensive improvement of active policies, the labour flows presented above indicate that the opportunities for unemployed people to move from unemployment to stable employment are still relatively limited, while the flows from unemployment to inactivity have increased from year to year. The flow from unemployment to inactivity as a result of personal choice has a reasonable explanation when informal employment is taken into account. It is also the case that those unemployed who have been registered with the labour office for six months can apply for general social assistance, while those who participate in active labour market programmes cannot.

The National Action Plan for Employment 2006 highlights the equal treatment of the rights and obligations of workers, whether hired on permanent or atypical contracts, as one of the priorities in the area of labour market flexibility. Thus a widespread information campaign has been launched to inform employers about the new opportunities offered by the law for flexible working hours, including organizing work in shifts, prolonging working time or determining part-time work in certain circumstances. It is considered that in this way employers will be able to adapt the workforce according to the needs of the business. The calculation of working time in hours (in force since January 2005) also makes employers better able to adapt to the insurance system. The same campaign also identifies action being taken to reduce informal employment and increase compliance with labour regulations:

- Working extra hours as part of the insurance service will encourage workers to participate in legal flexible labour forms.

- Eliminating red tape from the process of hiring and firing employees and introducing tax and insurance incentives will encourage compliance on the part of employers.

- Improving the quality of labour inspection and increasing the level of its sanctions tenfold will have an impact on formalization of employment.

Participants in qualification, training and retraining programmes and measures

The high share of unemployed people with low levels of education and the priority given to high-quality employment necessitate an intensive labour market policy in the field of qualification, training and retraining. The incentive for economic restructuring has completely changed job profiles. Hence gaining, improving and changing skills have become the key means through which the unemployed can find a job, but also represent an important preventive step against unemployment for employed people.

There are four types of qualification, training and retraining measures and programmes: professional qualification, additional professional qualification, requalification, and motivation. The development of these programmes and measures is presented in table 3.5. The data show that over the period 1996–2002 the most significant increase in numbers was in those seeking additional skills and qualifications.

Table 3.5 Participation in training and retraining measures and programmes for the unemployed as percentage of total participants, Bulgaria, 1996–2004

Years	Professional qualification	Additional professional qualification	Requalification	Motivation
1996	6.5	48.4	22.7	22.4
1997	11.4	41.8	27.9	18.9
1998	16.4	25.4	24.6	33.4
1999	8.9	65.0	26.1	..
2000	11.2	45.9	42.9	..
2001	11.7	61.8	26.5	..
2002	11.1	61.8	27.1	..
2003	9.7	67.4	22.9	..
2004	18.2	51.8	30.0	..

Notes: .. = not available. With the UPPEA, motivation was included in the activities of the employment offices and was not funded as a specific measure. The number of people completing motivation courses was 2,251 in 2000; 1,639 in 2001; 1,829 in 2002.

Source: Annual report of the National Employment Agency for the respective years.

This fact once again shows the intensive economic restructuring process that has induced people, even those already employed, to change their career orientation. The increasing importance of skills and qualifications is also worth noting.

In 2004 the Ministry of Labour and Social Policy studied the staffing needs of employers to better understand the requirements of the labour market. Its conclusions published in the *National Action Plan* support the targeting of active programmes and measures towards those types of training and professional qualifications demanded on the labour market. A new classification of professions was developed to support this process.

Increased workforce mobility and adaptability is dependent to a large extent on the professional skills and qualifications of workers. The programmes and measures in this respect include careers advice and orientation for the unemployed, employed and students. The latest amendments to the Employment Promotion Law regulate the right of the unemployed to join training courses for a profession in demand on the labour market although the candidate may have other professional skills and qualifications currently not needed. This change creates more opportunities for the unemployed to react to the real needs of the labour market. The training and qualification programmes pay special attention to those people without skills or who are not competitive on the labour market, as well as to young people emerging from the secondary education system. The latter are provided with full-time work as interns or apprentices for up to three months, covering one-third of school-leavers.

Several conclusions can be drawn from the analysis of active labour market policy in Bulgaria. First, over the transition period, active labour market programmes went through substantive changes related to their design, targeting and incentives for participation, aimed at increasing the opportunities for unemployed people to be reintegrated into employment. Second, by 2003 active labour market policy had been expanded to include a wide range of measures and programmes designed to cover the most vulnerable groups and to improve their position in the labour market by social inclusion and labour market integration. Third, the amount of money allocated for these activities increased significantly over the period, reaching 0.67 per cent of GDP by 2003. However, the skill mismatch still remains a problem for the transition of unemployed people from subsidies to stable employment.

3.4 INTERACTION BETWEEN EMPLOYMENT PROTECTION AND LABOUR MARKET POLICIES

3.4.1 Analysis of linkages in the labour market

The relationship between employment protection legislation (EPL) and labour market policy (LMP) has important significance for determining the behaviour of the suppliers and demanders of labour. The links between employment protection legislation and labour market policy are usually defined as trade-offs and complementarities. In the first case one element compensates the other. For example, strong employment protection is combined with low social protection, or weak EPL is compensated by strong social protection. A complementarity, on the other hand, is related to the existence of both forms of protection, with explicit emphasis that the link should be close. The existence of a 'weak' or 'strong' complementarity is defined as the existence of a positive correlation (weak complementarity) or the fact that one cannot exist without the other (strong complementarity) (Auer and Cazes, 2003).

We shall examine here the type of linkage that exists between EPL and LMP in Bulgaria, analysing the following concrete relationships between EPL strictness and PLMP; EPL strictness and ALPM; EPL, LMP and the protection of the inactive of working age; EPL and wage flexibility; and collective bargaining and income protection.

The link between EPL strictness and LMP

EPL in Bulgaria is characterized by relatively short notice periods: the minimum notice period is one month, with possibilities for extension up to three months. There is relatively high severance pay for workers employed for more than ten years (up to six months' salary); in other cases the amount of compensation is two months' salary (individual dismissals) and one month's salary (collective dismissals). Dismissal procedures are also relatively straightforward. In the case of individual dismissals there is no obligation to obtain the consent of trade unions except when trade union representatives are concerned, while with collective dismissals the local organization for tripartite cooperation and local government must be informed three months in advance. In all cases, certain categories of workers (pregnant women, disabled people, mothers of children under three years old, persons on sickness leave, etc.) enjoy strong protection. In terms of contracts, fixed-term contracts can be transformed relatively easily into permanent contracts. If the worker continues working for at least five days after the termination date and the employer does not protest in writing, the contract becomes permanent.

These characteristics of the EPL can be considered as moderate and similar to the other European countries. Confirmation of this is the measurement of the EPL strictness given by Cazes and Nesporova for the end of the 1990s (2003, p. 100). The overall indicator for EPL strictness was 2.8 points, with the following partial indicators: difficulty of dismissal – 2.9 points; index for regular contracts – 2.3 points; index for regular and temporary contracts – 2.5 points.[11] In comparison with other countries, Bulgaria ranked above the average level for the EU15 (2.4 points) and slightly above the average for the CEE countries (2.5). In this sense the strictness of Bulgarian EPL cannot be considered as either high or low.

Linkage between EPL and PLMP

The identification of the linkage between EPL and PLMP requires a similar evaluation of the latter. Unfortunately there is no overall quantitative indicator for the

---

[11] The integer values range from 1 to 6, with low values indicating very flexible EPL and high values very strict legislation.

PLMP. In qualitative terms we shall refer here to some partial indicators, such as coverage, spending and duration, summarized as follows:

- low coverage by unemployment benefits. The proportion of people who receive unemployment benefits is relatively low. Their share in total registered unemployment was 17.9 per cent in 2003, 18.6 per cent in 2004 and 18.4 per cent in 2005. There is a downward tendency which is expressed in a reduction of this share by two-thirds during the entire period 1991–2005 (figure 3.6);

- low replacement rate of unemployment benefits in relation to the average wage. Unemployment benefit in 2003 was a little above one-third of the average wage. Over the last three years there has been a tendency for the replacement rate to decrease, implying a faster increase in the average wage (figure 3.6);

- relatively short duration of unemployment benefits. The period varies between 4 and 12 months, depending on the last period of employment;

- relatively low spending on PLMP. The ratio of spending on PLMP to GDP is less than 1 per cent (0.29 per cent in 2003). From 1993 to 2003 the proportion has moved in parallel with the changes in outflow from employment to unemployment. During the period 1993–96 spending on PLMP as a share of GDP declined from 0.73 per cent to 0.27 per cent because of the decreasing number of unemployed. In 2000, the share rose to 0.62 per cent before declining again in 2003.

A comparison of the characteristics of EPL strictness and PLMP shows that the relationship combines moderate EPL with a low level of PLMP. The relative ease

Figure 3.6 Coverage rate of unemployment benefits and ratio of benefits to the average wage, Bulgaria, 1991–2005 (percentages)

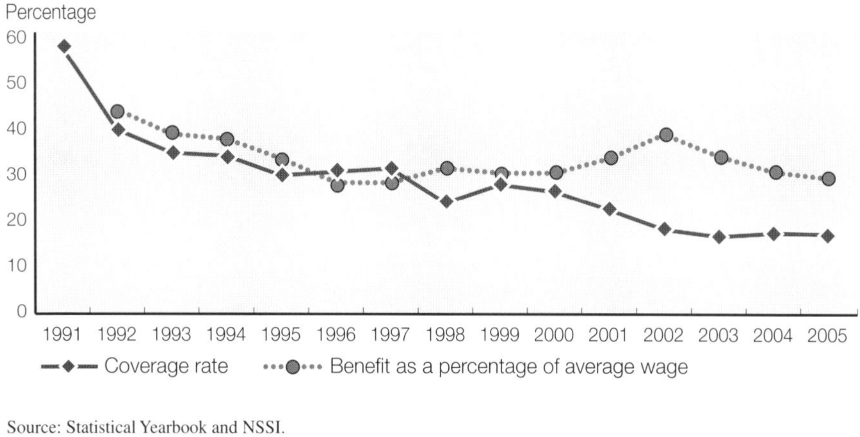

Source: Statistical Yearbook and NSSI.

with which employers can dismiss workers is not compensated by more generous social protection of the unemployed. Dismissed workers receive unemployment benefits for no longer than one year and the amount of the benefits does not exceed 60 per cent of the last earnings before dismissal.

The linkage between EPL and PLMP in Bulgaria cannot be regarded as a trade-off, as the moderate level of EPL strictness is not compensated by a high level of social protection. Nor can this relationship be considered to reflect a strong complementarity, because there is no correspondence between strong EPL and a high level of PLMP. The most probable conclusion is that there is a weak positive connection between EPL and PLMP.

Linkages between EPL and ALMP

The relationship between EPL and active LMP can be analysed using two basic parameters of this policy: spending on ALMP and coverage.

The spending on ALMP measured as a share of GDP is relatively low (during the entire period 1993–2003 the average remained at around 0.5 per cent). However, there is a positive trend that indicates that improvement is in progress (figure 3.7). During the period 1993–97 the average ratio of spending on ALMP to GDP was 0.16 per cent; for the period 1998–2000 it was 0.27 per cent and for 2001–05 it increased to 0.48 per cent. The ratios of GDP spending on ALMP to the unemployment rate (registered unemployed) were as follows: 1993–97, 0.012; 1998–2000, 0.018; 2001–03, 0.026. These results show that more and more resources were allocated to ALMP over time.

How high or low is the spending on ALMP? The answer to this question is to be sought through comparative analysis with other countries. In comparison with the

Figure 3.7 Spending on ALMP as a percentage of GDP, Bulgaria, 1993–2005

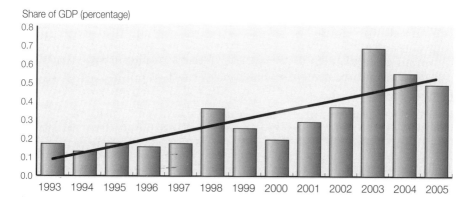

Source: Statistical Yearbook and annual reports of the National Employment Agency.

Figure 3.8 Participants in ALMP as a percentage of total registered unemployed,
Bulgaria, 1995–2003

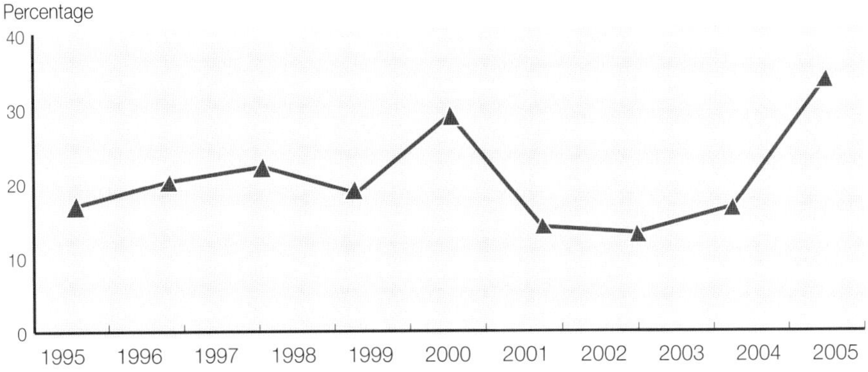

Percentage

Source: National Employment Agency.

CEE countries, Bulgaria spent less on ALMP per unemployed person[12] than Hungary,
Poland or Slovenia. The difference was even greater (a factor of more than five) in
comparison with the average EU15 level of 0.16 for the period 1991–2003.
Consequently, Bulgarian spending on ALMP can be regarded as low.

The second parameter of the ALMP – coverage – varied in parallel with the spending. As illustrated in figure 3.8, the number of ALMP participants showed a tendency to
increase. During the period 1995–97, 19.7 per cent of registered unemployed were covered by ALMP. This share increased to 20.4 per cent in the period 1998–2000 and to
21.1 per cent in 2001–03. There was an especially marked broadening of coverage in
2003, when the share of participants reached 33.8 per cent of total unemployed. In spite
of this positive development, the coverage of ALMP is relatively low. Almost four-fifths
of the registered unemployed were not involved in active measures on the labour market.

On the basis of the characteristics of ALMP presented above, their linkage with
the EPL is similar to the linkage between EPL and PLMP: moderate EPL strictness
corresponds to a low level of ALMP. Relatively easy dismissal of workers is not
sufficiently compensated by active policies in favour of a return to employment.

On the basis of the above relationships among EPL and ALMP and PLMP, the
following summary of the linkage between EPL and LMP can be made:

• The moderate protection of employment in Bulgaria is not compensated by the
  relatively low protection of the unemployed in terms of the coverage of
  unemployment benefits or measures and programmes for re-employment.

• There has been a tendency for LMP to improve, particularly over the period
  2001–03. This is expressed in the enlargement of the coverage and in the

---

[12] Ratio of GDP spending on ALMP to the unemployment rate of registered unemployed.

increase in spending (especially in 2003). The effect of such policies is clearly visible in rising employment and declining unemployment. On the other hand, the results from the process of activation of social protection confirm the thesis of a search for balance between flexibility and security. In the case of the Bulgarian labour market this means an increase in the level of LMP.

Linkage between EPL, LMP and social protection of inactive people of working age

The social protection of inactive people of working age is not an element of LMP. However, there is a direct connection between the two as regards participation in the labour market. This relationship is very important in Bulgaria because of the relatively high percentage of discouraged workers (12 per cent of the total inactive population) and the low participation rate. Strong social protection of inactive people of working age creates behaviour that does not motivate people to participate in the labour market. Thus a higher level of protection for inactive people than that offered by LMP would be expected to lead to a decline in labour activity.

In fact, social benefit is significantly lower than unemployment benefit in Bulgaria. The maximum amount of social benefit is equal to the difference between actual income and the guaranteed minimum income (in 2003 the minimum income was BGN 40 per month and the average unemployment benefit BGN 97.6). Moreover, spending on social assistance for inactive persons as a share of GDP is lower than spending on unemployment benefits – the former represents 0.3 per cent of GDP, the latter 0.4 per cent – while the group of inactive people receiving social assistance is twice as large as the number of unemployed receiving unemployment benefits.

These comparisons show that the social protection of the inactive population of working age can be assessed as modest, and lower than the protection of unemployed. In this sense the linkage between EPL, LMP and social protection of the inactive can be said to be decreasing.

Linkage between EPL and wage flexibility

Deregulation of the labour market in the context of lowering employment protection requires greater flexibility of wages. If we define flexibility as the possibility to react to change, wage flexibility can be evaluated using different basic relationships. In this analysis the conclusions concerning wage flexibility in Bulgaria are based on the reaction of wages following changes in productivity and unemployment.

The wage dynamic and labour productivity (as GDP per worker) are to a considerable extent unconnected and this is expressed by the substantial lag shown by movements in real wages. Productivity increased by about 19 per cent between 1991 and 2003, while the real wage declined by more than half. The gap between productivity and the real wage has shown a tendency to widen. This is a result of the fact that growth in real wage rates in most of the years was lower than in productivity.

Figure 3.9 Phillips curve showing the relationship between the unemployment rate and the nominal wage growth rate, Bulgaria, 1991–2003

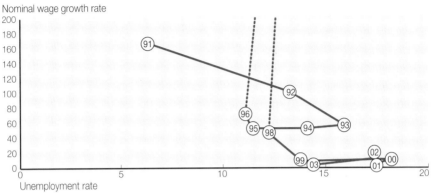

Note: As a result of extremely high inflation, the nominal wage rate in 1997 was 859.7%. This value has not been plotted.

Source: Authors' calculations based on data from the National Employment Agency and Statistical Yearbook.

Only in a few years did the growth rate of real wages exceed that of productivity. The conclusion arising from these disparities is that wage rates have low adaptive power to the changes in productivity.

The estimation of the linkage between wages and unemployment is based on an evaluation of the Phillips curve and on the methodology for calculating the wage rigidity index proposed by Layard, Nickell and Jackman (1991). As we can see from figure 3.9, there are two periods during which the Phillips curve for Bulgaria is almost horizontal. The first is from 1993 to 1996, and the second is the period from 1999 to 2003. This horizontal shape of the Phillips curve indicates a weak connection between growth rates in nominal wages and the unemployment rate. During these periods the sharp decrease in unemployment did not lead to significant changes in nominal wages. The shift of the curve towards the low nominal wage growth rates is connected with the attainment of macroeconomic stability.

The estimation of the real wage rigidity index[13] for the period 1991–2003 confirms the low flexibility of real wages. The value of the real wage rigidity index is 5.0 and is very high compared with estimates for other countries.

On the basis of the above analysis, it can be concluded that wage flexibility in Bulgaria is low. The reason for this low flexibility is the high degree of state intervention

---

[13] Real wage rigidity index was calculated on the estimation of the following equation:

$DLRW_t = -0.055 - 0.262 \, DLUMR_t + 0.0146 \, DLUMR_{t-1} + 2.035 \, DLPROD_t + -0.199 \, D3$, where $DLRW_t$ = changes in log of real wages, $DLUMR_t$ = changes in log of unemployment rate, $DLPROD_t$ = changes in log of productivity, D3 = dummy variable. The statistical estimation of the parameters is acceptable. The standard errors of the parameters are significant at 95 per cent, with exception of the variable $DLUMR_{t-1}$. Adjusted R^2 is 0.71 and DW statistic is 1.91.

in the wage determination process in the public sector. Despite the changes in the applied regulation mechanisms aimed at the reduction of the restrictions on wages, part of the monopolistic state-enterprise sector continues to apply some form of restriction. The linkage between moderate EPL strictness and low wage flexibility should therefore be interpreted taking into account the prevailing regulation mechanisms.

Linkage between collective bargaining and income security

Collective bargaining as an institutional form of income protection for insiders can be expected to play a decisive role in the wage negotiation process. In the case of Bulgaria the trade unions do not successfully perform this function. As a result, real wages have been weakly protected from inflation. During the entire period, real wages declined significantly. This erosion of real wages does not correspond to the extent of collective wage bargaining coverage, which implies that the trade unions, influence on the wage bargaining process is decreasing.

There is also a low degree of income protection for workers paid the minimum wage. The amount of the minimum wage in relation to the average wage is relatively low, and the replacement ratio of the minimum wage is between 35 per cent and 38 per cent. This indicates a higher level of job insecurity for workers hired on the minimum wage. This also increases the likelihood of replacement of workers by outsiders.

3.4.2 Effects of reforms on linkages

The impact of legislative and policy reforms on the linkages can be analysed from three standpoints: the effects of changes in the legislation; the effects of changes in LMP; and the effects of changes in social policy.

The effects of changes in EPL

The changes in Bulgarian labour legislation during the 1990s in the direction of reducing the strictness of EPL had a strong influence on labour market outcomes and labour market policies. In macroeconomic terms the effects of the linkage between moderate EPL strictness and low LMP were expressed in decreasing employment and high unemployment. A tendency for this policy mix to alter emerged after 2002, as social protection increased through the strengthening of ALMP. As was mentioned in the analysis of the labour market linkages in the previous section, the changes have mainly concerned the coverage and spending on ALMP. This process could be interpreted as seeking a better balance between EPL strictness and LMP.

The effects of changes in LMP

The changes in LMP (active and passive) carried out after 2000 have had a direct effect on the levels of employment and unemployment. PLMP measured as the amount of spending as a share of GDP shows a downward trend, with the share declining by 0.3 percentage points. This is the result of a decrease in the number of unemployed receiving unemployment benefits. Consequently, the changes in spending on PLMP have not led to increased income security for the unemployed.

There has been a cardinal change in the links between ALMP and labour market outcomes as a result of the changes in ALMP after 2000. The positive effect on the link with employment is expressed by a parallel increase in spending on active labour market measures as a proportion of GDP (an increase of 0.2 percentage points between 2000 and 2003) and in the number of employees (a rise of 0.4 per cent over the same period). The linkage with unemployment also changed significantly, with ALMP contributing to a decline in the number of unemployed.

The effects of changes in social protection

The changes in social policy during the period after 2000 cannot be regarded as significant. Although there have been some changes in eligibility rules, these have been minor. Despite this, the number of inactive social assistance recipients of working age increased by 5.8 per cent in 2002 and fell by 20 per cent in 2003. This reduction is primarily due to the decreasing number of unemployed. Furthermore, the level of social assistance remains very low. These facts suggest that after 2000 there was no substantial improvement in the social protection of the inactive population, so we cannot expect a major influence on the linkages.

The changes in income policy as part of the income protection measures during the period after 2000, on the other hand, have had a major influence on the linkages. These changes mainly concern workers hired at the minimum wage. Between 2000 and 2003 the minimum wage increased by nearly 65 per cent, thus increasing the protection of these workers. Overall social protection has tended to improve as a result. However, this cannot be interpreted as an important change in the linkage between EPL and social protection. The link between low EPL and low social security remains, despite the small improvement in social policy.

3.5 POLICY CONCLUSIONS

3.5.1 Labour market flexibility, job protection and income security

The existing, relatively high degree of flexibility as a characteristic of the present labour market is supported by the following conclusions of the study:

- There have been intensive structural changes in employment, reflecting the reshaping of the economic structure as a result of the internal reforms and external shocks.

- There has also been significant labour turnover as a reflection of labour reallocation between sectors and branches and between activity and inactivity.

- Labour market flexibility is evident in the high dynamics of its labour flows, which represent the movement of the labour force between employment, unemployment and inactivity, determined by both economic conditions and personal choice.

- The changes in the pattern of employment by forms of ownership have been significant. The private sector has played an important role in increasing labour market flexibility by providing opportunities for part-time employment, self-employment, employment under temporary contracts and multiple-job holding.

- The changes in the labour legislation on the one hand reduce the barriers to firing and hiring of workers, and limit employers' obligations with regard to job security and income protection. On the other, the regulations relating to such issues as collective bargaining, the various types of contracts, the flexibility of working time, the lengthening of the notice period in case of mass redundancies, and the efforts at improving control over working conditions, contributed greater order and protection of workers' rights.

- Job stability depends entirely on employers and on the business cycle, since there are no direct protective measures for either business or employment. Incentives for maintaining employment exist within the active labour market programmes inasmuch as employers who participate in the programmes and benefit from them are obliged under the programme to preserve employment.

- Income security is also limited under the government's commitments to preserving the minimum income level and the minimum wage. Additional preservation of incomes is provided by the social insurance system (through the minimum insurance thresholds and unemployment benefits introduced) and by the social assistance system (through the minimum guaranteed income and certain social assistance schemes).

- In general, the relatively high degree of labour market flexibility is accompanied by relatively low employment stability and income protection. In Bulgaria, there is a complementarity between employment protection and income security at a low level.

- More positive indications appear in regard to the relation between employment protection and labour market policy. The interaction between employment protection and labour market policy points to an absence of significant changes regarding employment termination, but there is progress regarding access to labour market programmes for both employed and jobless persons.

3.5.2 The role of workers' and employers' labour market institutions

In the process of seeking a balance between employment protection and social security, the main role is played by the trade unions and the employers' organizations. They obviously represent different positions but in the process of negotiations there should be areas in which a compromise is possible. The viewpoints of the trade unions and the employers' organizations regarding the flexibility/security problem are summarized below.

The trade unions' point of view

- Labour market legislation is liberalized to a degree that ensures the relatively high flexibility of the labour market. Further liberalization is not acceptable because it is likely to lead to reduced employment security.

- The Bulgarian labour market is characterized by high flexibility and low security. The low security is related to income security of workers, to uncoupling from productivity, payment delays, low social insurance security and so on.

- The changes in labour legislation should concern the following aspects:
  - increasing income security by implementing the wage guarantee fund;[14]
  - increasing employment security.

- Ways of increasing labour market flexibility could be sought through the improvement of internal (enterprise) flexibility by increasing labour flexibility, wage flexibility, working-time flexibility and part-time remuneration.

- A balance should be struck between deregulation and workers' security. This balance can be achieved by regulation of working time and the introduction of standard contracts. The trade unions regard the deregulation of permanent employment contracts as inappropriate. The present legislation contains broad possibilities for fixed- or short-term contracts. Further deregulation would mean lowering employment protection and, in combination with the low level of workers' security, would be likely to lead to mass redundancies.

- The procedures for coordination and consultation at national, sectoral, local and enterprise level on the issues of flexibility–security should be strengthened. In the framework of the existing labour legislation, social dialogue can solve the problems of security and flexibility and can be used to find an appropriate balance.

- With regard to increasing the respect for labour legislation, monitoring of employers should be improved and intensified.

---

[14] The fund was established in 2004 to ensure workers' earnings in case of employer insolvency.

The employers' organizations' point of view

- The labour legislation should move towards greater freedom for micro-enterprises to allow them to hire workers on more flexible contracts. This would increase the freedom of employers to operate with the workforce in accordance with their financial possibilities and business plans.

- Income security should be improved by increasing minimum incomes in relation to the average wage. The employers are against increasing the minimum wage because it will narrow the wage differential in enterprises and will not stimulate initiative on the part of the workers.

- Privatization contracts should not include job protection. This runs counter to economic efficiency and reduces labour market flexibility.

- Employers see the means to increase labour market flexibility through a reduction in the employment protection legislation and the negotiation of more flexible forms of remuneration and hiring.

The views of trade unions and employers' organizations on how to seek a balance between flexibility and security differ considerably. Nevertheless, several 'matching points' could be found which might be considered as a basis for further negotiations aimed at achieving this balance. These points are:

- social dialogue is a good instrument for agreements,

- internal flexibility can be increased by raising labour flexibility, wage flexibility, working-time flexibility, part-time remuneration and so forth;

- income security could be increased by the establishment of the wage guarantee fund.

3.5.3 The recommended type of labour market regulation

The type of labour market regulation appropriate for an economy depends on the relationship between the national labour market legislation and the social partners. Social dialogue in Bulgaria needs further development at all levels.

Improved balance between labour market flexibility and security *at enterprise level* implies more income and social security for workers. This means that wage bargaining should take into account labour productivity as well as the existing system of protection of wages against inflation. With regard to increasing social protection of workers, trade unions should insist on insurance higher than the minimum thresholds currently laid down.

The state supervision of compliance with the labour legislation should be combined with strengthened support for employers and workers in implementing it, and enlarging their participation in drafting and enforcing various regulations. New institutions such as labour courts and arbitration and mediation structures could promote rapid settlement of disputes and claims.

Increasing the adaptability of the labour force under the continuing economic reforms needs further state intervention via active labour market policies ensuring easier access to training and qualification for workers. The vocational education and training system is being reformed and state education standards for the acquisition of skills and qualifications are being developed. However, further efforts are needed to identify the real needs of vocational education and training so as to make the matching process more effective.

The relatively large numbers of the labour force who are inactive should be involved more actively in labour market programmes and schemes, thus increasing their opportunity for reintegration into the workforce.

CROATIA

4

Sanja Crnković-Pozaić *

4.1 INTRODUCTION

The labour market in Croatia is going through a period of fundamental change. Reform of the labour legislation, reduction of the fiscal burden, institutional capacity building, and first attempts at facilitating better social dialogue and improving competency in the design of efficient policy measures have all been under way simultaneously, making considerable alterations to the system.

These changes are happening at a time of falling registered unemployment and labour force survey (LFS) unemployment, and a cautious but sustained increase in employment. The positive macroeconomic environment can largely be attributed to growth in industrial production, tourism and rising consumption, and the increasing importance of investment expenditure. A considerable share of the latter is government investment in infrastructure, namely roads and housing construction.

The Croatian labour market is segmented and relatively undeveloped, with a low level of spatial and intersectoral labour mobility but an increasing turnover of both labour and jobs. It has a relatively inflexible formal economy which is regulated by national legislation, and a flexible informal economy, part of which is legal but unregistered and the other part both unregistered and illegal. The two economies are interlinked, as are their reactions to policy measures: as rigidity increases and the number of formal jobs falls, more informal activities are created.

4.1.1 Historical data

Long-term movements of employment and unemployment in Croatia show the well-known characteristics of a transitional economy, with some specific features relating

---

* Former Director of the Croatian Employment Service.

Figure 4.1 Annual change in employment, unemployment and the labour force,
Croatia, 1963–2005 (thousands)

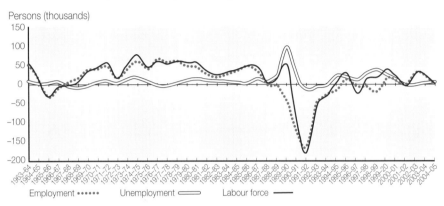

Source:Author's calculations based on CES and Croatian Bureau of Statistics.

to the armed conflict and its aftermath. Figure 4.1 shows the trends in major labour market movements in Croatia over the last 40 years.

During the socialist period, employment grew steadily with oscillations linked to the liberalization reforms of the 1960s and the oil crises in the 1970s. Unemployment did not seem to be related to the movements in employment to any large extent. In fact, increases in employment were usually accompanied by increases in unemployment as the labour force grew, fuelled by new job opportunities.[1] It is interesting to note that it was at the end of the 1980s that employment began to fall and unemployment to rise, a trend only deepened by the transition and the war. Former Yugoslavia was by this stage experiencing a deep recession, which had lasted some time, and the consequences of this probably contributed to the build-up of tension in the country.[2]

Activity rates in Croatia have historically been low and they still remain so by European standards. In the 1970s the activity rate was 54 per cent, in the 1980s it was 46 per cent and in the 1990s it was down to 45 per cent. These figures understate the actual rate due to problems of measurement;[3] the more representative rate from the LFS in the first half of 2005 was 49.9 per cent, with 57.3 per cent for men and

---

[1] Croatia had a long-term mismatch between labour demand and supply which was evident in its relatively low participation rates. This meant that the potential labour force was inactive due to slack demand for labour and tended to become active in periods of stronger job creation. Such increases in the labour force were evident in the growth of both employment and open unemployment, which explains why these two groups tended to show simultaneous increase.

[2] One of the causes of the conflict in Yugoslavia was the weakening economic position of the two republics which had contributed most to the GDP of the country, namely Slovenia and Croatia. Most of the other republics of the federation were net recipients of transfers through a system of support and their position became increasingly volatile without this.

[3] The coverage by official sources of statistics of all economic activities of the population was inadequate in the socialist period because it measured only employment in the socialist sector. When large firms started to go bankrupt their

Figure 4.2 Biannual employment figures from establishment data and the LFS, Croatia, 1996–2005 (thousands)

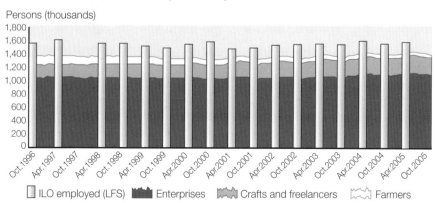

Persons (thousands)

☐ ILO employed (LFS)   ▪▪▪ Enterprises   ▨▨ Crafts and freelancers   ⟨⟩ Farmers

Source: LFS 1996–2005, Priopćenja, Croatian Bureau of Statistics.

43.3 per cent for women. The employment rate is also relatively low at 43.3 per cent (50.2 for men and 37.3 for women) but is slowly increasing.

If we look at employment trends over the transition period, they tend to show very different, if not divergent, trends, depending on their source. As we can see from figure 4.2, LFS data show a consistently higher level of employment than establishment sources. The difference can be attributed partly to the fact that the latter cover only persons with labour contracts, farmers and craftsmen, while the LFS covers all types of economic activity within the United Nations production boundary, which includes own-account workers, family workers as well as working pensioners and the working 'unemployed'. On the other hand, the establishment sources, which depend on a monthly survey of all bigger enterprises and an underrepresented number of small and medium enterprises, overestimate job loss and underestimate job creation. Certain corrections were made to the sample recently, but comparisons with administrative sources (Croatian Bureau of Pension Insurance and the Croatian Bureau of Health Insurance) show a higher level of employment in the formal economy.[4]

---

overrepresentation in the samples used showed a more drastic fall in employment than actually took place because there were no instruments in place to measure increases in employment in the sector of small and medium enterprises. These problems were gradually improved upon, but the labour force survey remains the only source that gives an indication of the actual scope of economic activity. However, even this source shows relatively low activity rates as labour force reserves remain high.

[4] The two sources of administrative data also have their problems. For example, the Croatian Bureau of Pension Insurance has a certain number of insurees who are on payrolls of enterprises in the previously occupied areas in eastern Slavonia but who have not worked since the beginning of the occupation. There are also persons who are able to pay for extended pension insurance although they are not employed. Substantial adjustments and improvement of establishment sources in the Bureau of Statistics are planned for the near future.

Figure 4.3 Registered and LFS unemployment, Croatia, 1988–2006 (thousands)

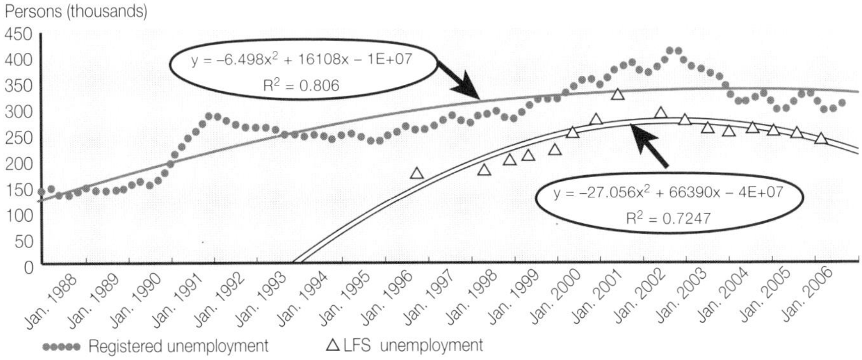

Persons (thousands)

$y = -6.498x^2 + 16108x - 1E+07$
$R^2 = 0.806$

$y = -27.056x^2 + 66390x - 4E+07$
$R^2 = 0.7247$

•••• Registered unemployment   △ LFS unemployment

Source: CES, LFS various years, Croatian Bureau of Statistics.

On the other hand, registered unemployment as published by the Croatian Employment Service (CES) and LFS unemployment are convergent through time. Analyses of the LFS data capture those persons registered as unemployed at the employment office who remain registered while working on short-term contracts, in the informal economy and in agriculture as a family worker. Up until the introduction of the new Job Placement and Unemployment Insurance Act in 2002 there were no provisions for monitoring the behaviour of the unemployed regarding job search and availability for work, which, together with absence of work, represent the international standard for definition of unemployment status.

Figure 4.4 shows a time series of unemployment figures from the register of the employment service and the LFS. The sharp increase in registered unemployment is reflected in the unemployment dynamics from the LFS, but the level itself is consistently lower.

In the second half of 2004, 7.5 per cent or 17,700 of the registered unemployed were actually employed according to ILO criteria, representing 1.1 per cent of total employment. A further 44,900 or 14.9 per cent of the registered unemployed were not looking for work, 7.9 per cent were not available for work and 3.9 per cent did not even want to work (down from 6.5 per cent in 2002). On the other hand, there were 32,000 workers who were unemployed according to ILO criteria but not registered with the employment service. The total difference between the two unemployment counts in 2004 was 67,000, down from 116,000 in 2002. Since the introduction of the new Law on Job Placement and Unemployment Insurance, the employment service monitors active job search, availability for work and the incidence of employment. This practice has resulted in an increasing number of the registered unemployed being taken off the register, mostly because they have worked in the previous month.[5]

---

[5] CES exchanges data with Regos, an institution responsible for monitoring the payments of contributions which are now levied on all types of contracts except student contracts and authors' contributions.

Figure 4.4 Average monthly employment 2000–04 and monthly employment 2005,
Croatia (thousands)

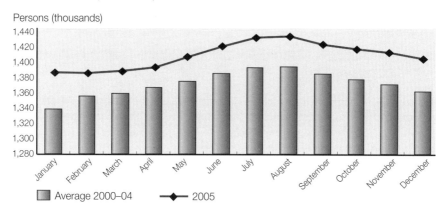

Source: CBS, establishment sources.

As we can see in figure 4.4, the tendency is for employment to have increased substantially in 2005 in relation to the five-year average. This is a good sign and it is mirrored in the increasing numbers who are employed from the unemployment register. Although outflows from registered unemployment have been greater than the inflows since spring 2002, the number moving from the register to employment has exceeded the number of new entrants to unemployment only during the summer months, when seasonal employment growth dominates. For a very long time, separations from the register were split between employment and inactivity or informal employment, and flows into inactivity would dominate when job creation was low in the formal economy.

The exits from the register other than to employment have recently been attributed to the new law on job placement. Since its implementation, around 800 (0.2 per cent) persons per month have been taken off the register either because of earnings higher than the maximum legal amount, failure to search for work actively or unavailability for work. In the summer months of 2003, this figure was up to more than 4,500 thousand due mostly to short-term contract work in the tourist season.

One of the concerns linked to the implementation of the new legislation is that some labour market activities are expected to move outside the ambit of the public employment service. Since the declaration of vacancies became voluntary (it used to be mandatory for employers), there has been a dramatic decrease in jobs available to the employment service. This initial decline is expected to recover but it will have to launch a major marketing effort and offer employers a higher quality of service.

In summary, the transitional labour market has specific features which should be taken into account when making comparisons with developed countries. Informal employment provides a buffer for inadequate job creation in the formal economy but most income support, unemployment and social benefits are linked to formal unemployment status. This makes the de facto living standard higher than can be interpreted from official statistics. Actual employment is understated while unemployment is overstated, with implications for the way in which corrective mechanisms need to be applied.

4.2 LABOUR MARKET FLEXIBILITY AND EMPLOYMENT STABILITY

The stability and flexibility of the labour force can be measured by considering formal and informal employment relationships, workers' wages and benefits, contract duration and job tenure. Multiple-job holding is also examined here as an indicator of the need to augment insufficient earnings.

4.2.1 Formal and informal employment relationships

Formal employment is always covered by labour contract. While contracts can be permanent or temporary, according to CES data more than 75 per cent of all new labour contracts are now temporary. In this way, employers guard themselves against costs related to dismissing workers with contracts without limit of time, i.e. severance payments and procedures related to proving violation of responsibility or inability to fulfil the requirements of the job.

The Labour Law (art. 10) states that a worker can only work on a temporary contract on assignments that are by their nature temporary, and cannot continue on such a contract for longer than three years. Moreover, there must be a break of at least six months between the end of one temporary contract and the start of another.

Short-term contracts should only be resorted to if the nature of the job is a once-off activity that is not linked to normal business processes. This type of contract is legal and, following the introduction of the Law on Mandatory Contributions, provides more social security for the worker, since the employer has to pay mandatory health and pension insurance. The only insurance that short-term contract workers do not have is that related to unemployment benefits. The reason behind not extending this type of protection is the belief that temporary workers would be facing moral hazard and intentionally resorting to unemployment spells once they had worked for a sufficient period and become eligible for unemployment benefit. Short-term contracts are not covered by any other rights guaranteed under the Labour Law.

Providers of artistic or intellectual services, such as research analysts, writers, film makers, dancers, architects and designers, may use contracts exempted from the Law on Mandatory Contributions, mainly due to the strong lobbying by the workers concerned.[6]

---

[6] Most research institutions, for example, subsist partly on projects run on 'authors' contributions'. Often, rather than being employed, the authors are paid for their output (articles, research, consultancy) and are only liable for personal income tax on this fee. Self-employed 'authors' such as artists or freelance journalists are often insured through their professional associations.

Table 4.1   Formal activity status of the employed, Croatia, 2002 and 2004
(numbers and percentages)

	2002		2004	
	Numbers	%	Numbers	%
Labour force	1 533 655	100	1 542 438	100
In work[1]	1 400 392	91.3	1 452 297	94.2
Formally inactive[2]	96 837	6.3	72 434	4.7
Unemployed[3]	36 426	2.4	17 707	1.1

Notes: [1] Employees, self-employed, agricultural workers, family workers, contract and own-account workers. [2] Pensioners, students and housewives. [3] Registered and non-registered unemployed.

Source: LFS.

The cheapest legal employment contract is a students' or pupils' contract. Free of tax and contributions, the only costs associated with this contract are those of mediation, payable to the franchised job placement services in universities or secondary schools dealing with this category of worker. Technically, only regular students are allowed to work but sometimes students waive their right in favour of non-students for a fee, though this is not a very widespread phenomenon.

All other types of work not covered by a labour contract are illegal but nonetheless substantial. Table 4.1 shows the various activity statuses of the employed in the second half of 2002 and in 2004. In 2002, out of the 1.5 million workers defined as employed according to ILO criteria, 91.3 per cent declared themselves to be working, 6.3 per cent were working but were pupils, students, housewives, pensioners and therefore 'inactive', and 2.4 per cent were 'unemployed'. This implies that 8.7 per cent of the workforce in 2002 and 5.8 per cent in 2004 do not feature in the employment statistics from establishment sources. They represent the legal but unregistered or illegal employment in Croatia. There were in all 133,300 individuals working in the informal economy in 2002 and 89,517 in 2004. This has to be considered as only a smaller, measurable share of the actual informal economy.

4.2.2   Wages and benefits

The degree of security available to workers on the labour market can be measured by the types of rights and benefits that the employed enjoy. Table 4.2 shows that 77 per cent of workers in 2002 received wages or salaries and the full package of insurance guaranteed under the Labour Law, including health insurance, pension insurance and unemployment insurance, and this share increased to 85.4 per cent in 2004. The remaining 23 per cent and 15.6 per cent respectively only had partial benefits, which

Table 4.2   Worker remuneration and benefits, by employment status, Croatia, 2002
and 2004

	2002		2004	
	In work	% receiving remuneration and full social security contributions	In work	% receiving remuneration and full social security contributions
All workers	1 533 657	77.0	1 542 439	85.4
All employees	1 179 497	89.2	1 189 380	98.1
Private sector employees	611 337	88.1	658 399	96.9
Public sector employees	535 063	90.7	510 354	99.6
Mixed sector employees	33 098	87.9	20 627	98.8
Self-employed and family workers	313 206	40.1	321 077	46.1
Short-term contract and own account workers	40 953	5.0	31 982	8.9

Source: LFS.

means that they were missing any one of the abovementioned insurances or that they had not received any wages.

The degree of security in the public sector is greater than in the private sector (respectively 99.6 per cent and 96.9 per cent coverage by full benefits), but both sectors have significantly improved in this respect since 2002. The share of stable returns from work (wages plus benefits) is lowest for persons working on short-term contracts, own-account workers (8.9 per cent in 2004 in relation to 5 per cent coverage in 2002) and the self-employed (46.1 per cent coverage, up from 40.1 per cent in 2002). Since health insurance is a constitutional right for Croatian citizens, eligibility for this type of insurance is not restricted to those in an employment relationship.[7] Although some interviewees declare that they have no health insurance through work, this does not necessarily mean that they are without it.

Pension insurance, on the other hand, has been designed with a strong bias toward the full-time job relationship, with all other forms of part-time work recalculated to the full-time equivalents. The result is that individuals working part time have had to have more years of service in order to receive a full pension, regardless of their contributions. This is a systemic rigidity that has now been rectified in line with the more flexible legislation on mandatory contributions for work that is not full time and permanent. Up until these amendments became

---

[7] Health insurance can be claimed through a working member of family or through the local authorities if there are no working family members.

operational, there was a clear bias in the system against atypical forms of work in the social insurance system. Legislative flexibility notwithstanding, the share of flexible forms of work remains relatively low.

4.2.3 Duration of contract

Another element of security on the labour market is the type of contract by duration offered to workers. Table 4.3 shows the four usual types of contracts found on the Croatian labour market in 1997, 2002 and 2004. A very high share of contracts without limit of time indicates that the employment relationship still enjoys a high degree of security, as in most other European countries (Auer and Cazes, 2003). The 88.3 per cent share of contracts without limit of time in 1997 decreased very slightly to 87.6 per cent in the second half of 2004, but the share of fixed-term contracts has increased from 6.7 per cent to 10.3 per cent. This indicates a tendency which has been fuelled by employers offering new personnel fixed-term contracts. Up until the mid 1990s more than 50 per cent of contracts for new posts were permanent. This share went down to just over 20 per cent in 2004, with a tendency to fall to just over 10 per cent in the tourist season when most of the hiring is temporary.

The duration of fixed-term contracts is also an interesting indicator of the stability of the employment relationship. There has been an increase in fixed-term contracts, as already shown above, but there is a parallel tendency for fixed-term contracts to be of shorter duration.

In table 4.4 the number of contracts of one to five months has gone up from 30,600 in 1997 to 82,000 in 2004, increasing their share in total fixed-term contracts from 20.3 per cent to 54.9 per cent. At the same time both the 6–12 month contracts and the

Table 4.3   Types of contract by duration, numbers and percentage of total employment, Croatia, 1997, 2002 and 2004

	1997		2002		2004	
	Number of contracts	% of total	Number of contracts	% of total	Number of contracts	% of total
Contracts without limit of time	1 147 803	88.3	1 092 040	87.5	1 071 707	87.6
Fixed-term contracts	87 416	6.7	121 161	9.7	125 498	10.3
Seasonal contracts (also fixed-term)	25 948	2.0	16 034	1.3	15 582	1.3
Short-term contracts	38 107	2.9	18 905	1.5	10 170	0.8
Total	1 299 274	100.0	1 248 140	100.0	1 222 957	100.0

Note: Only employees and family workers are included.

Source: Author's calculations based on LFS and CBS data.

Table 4.4   Duration of fixed-term contracts, numbers and percentage of total
fixed-term employment, Croatia, 1997, 2002 and 2004

Duration	1997		2002/2		2004/2	
	Numbers	%	Numbers	%	Numbers	%
Less than 1 month	4 402	2.9	4 851	3.1	3 118	2.1
1–5 months	30 678	20.3	80 046	51.6	81 762	54.9
6–12 months	31 773	21.0	24 406	15.7	26 305	17.7
Longer than 12 months	22 934	15.1	13 830	8.9	14 176	9.5
As required	61 685	40.7	32 109	20.7	23 713	15.9
Totals	151 472	100.0	155 242	100.0	149 074	100.0

Sources: LFS, 1997, 2002/2, 2004/2, CBS; author's calculations.

longer-term contracts have reduced their share so that in 2004 only 9.5 per cent of the contracts were of a duration of more than 12 months. There has also been a steep reduction in open-ended contracts whose duration depended on the requirements of the job, from 40.7 per cent to 15.9 per cent.

These figures indicate an increasing number of temporary jobs on the market but also a worsening position of workers competing for jobs. A higher turnover of workers is also apparent on the unemployment register as individuals register several times a year between short, temporary jobs, usually on fixed-term contracts. The Law on Job Placement and Unemployment Insurance has recognized this tendency and made access to benefits easier for those who work predominantly on fixed-term contracts. While previously individuals had to work for at least 12 months over a period of 24 months if they wanted to claim benefit, they are now eligible after only 9 months worked over any length of time.

The position of short-term contract workers is worse than that of workers with normal fixed-term contracts. Although they do have access to pension and health insurance, they have no unemployment insurance and can therefore never claim unemployment benefit.

4.2.4   Job tenure

Permanence of contracts, although an indication of intent by the employer at the beginning of the work relationship, is no safeguard against dismissals. Most of the 800,000 and more workers who lost their jobs during transition had contracts without limit of time. It is therefore important to look at the duration of employment with the same employer to see the actual tendencies that are very much linked to the state of the economy and other factors that influence enterprise activity. Each enterprise has its core workforce which guarantees a stable production capacity; other workers are more or less temporary.

Figure 4.5 Distribution of the duration of employment with current employer, Croatia, 1998, 2002 and 2004

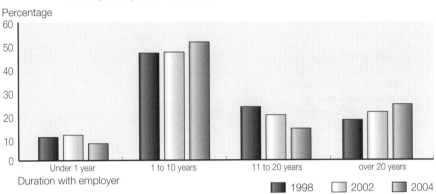

Source: LFS, 1998–2004.

Of those in employment in 2004, 80.6 per cent took up their job at the beginning of the 1990s and 13.9 per cent did so over the course of 2004. Figure 4.5 shows employment duration for employees in the period 1998 to 2004. The main tendencies in the duration of employment are reflected in this chart: almost half of the employees had been with their employer for less than ten years and their share increases slightly over time.

The share of employees with 11 to 20 years of service has decreased in this period from 23.6 per cent to 20.3 per cent. Tendencies in the opposite direction can be found in the categories of workers at both ends of the spectrum: the share of those with less than a year and those with more than 20 years of service is increasing. The rising share of individuals with more than 20 years of service is possibly a demographic phenomenon due to the baby boom generation. The dominance of older workers in the labour force is reflected in the age structure of workers joining the register from firms in restructuring (31 per cent of the registered unemployed in December 2003 were older than 45 years of age).

Generally speaking there is no great distinction between men and women regarding the duration of employment, as can be seen from figure 4.6. The share of employed men with up to 15 years of service is slightly greater than that of women, while the opposite is true of tenure from 20 to 25 years, where the share of women is slightly higher. The earlier retirement age of women is reflected in their lower share in the over-30-year tenure. When this information is linked to the characteristics of unemployment by sex, we see that men were more prone to the risk of unemployment at the beginning of the transition and during the war. Some of these men are either still registered unemployed or have most probably left the labour force, which is reflected in their lower share of 15–20-year tenures. Well over half of both employed men (63.7 per cent) and women (60.1 per cent) found their

Flexicurity

Figure 4.6 Distribution of the duration of employment with current employer by sex, Croatia, 2002/03

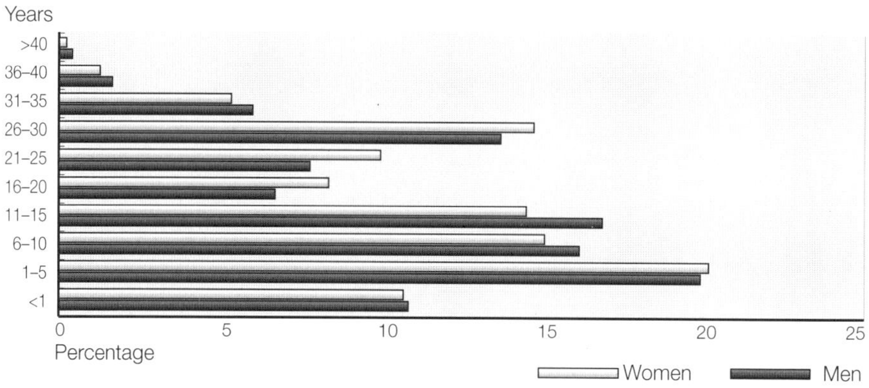

Years

Source: LFS, 2002/2, CBS, 2003; author's calculations.

job after the beginning of the transition. If we include the five years prior to transition we can see that 70.4 per cent of male and 68.5 per cent of female employment began over the last 20 years.

Some additional insights into gender issues concerning employment can be seen in figures 4.7 and 4.8, where duration of employment is linked to average age and earnings for men and women.

There are gender differences in the relationship between wages and job tenure. As can be seen in figure 4.7, men, on average, earn more than women at all employment duration levels, while the tenure-based earnings curve is more pronounced for

Figure 4.7 Average wage by sex and job tenure, Croatia, 2004

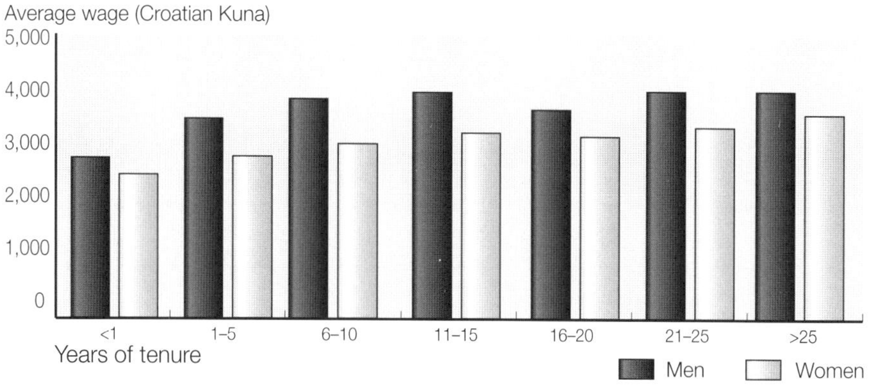

Source: LFS, 20042/2, CBS.

104

Figure 4.8 Average wage by sex and age, Croatia, 2004

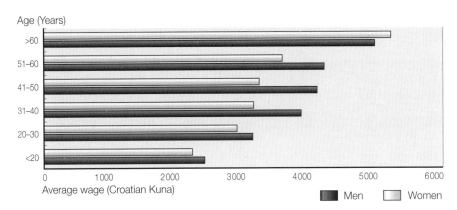

Source: LFS, 2004/2, CBS.

women than for men. Age-related wages also show that women are in a relatively worse position, as can be seen in figure 4.8. The figure shows that in all age groups men have higher average wages than women except in the oldest age group (which is under the influence of atypical high wages for a group of older women on the one hand and a very small sample as most women retire before the age of 60). The age-related earnings curve is steeper for men, showing that even though average wages increase with age for both sexes, they do so more noticeably for men than for women. The average age of the employed is rather high, at about 39 years of age for both sexes. Even employees with less than a year of service have an average age of around 30 years, which reflects the difficulties the young are facing when entering the labour market.

This analysis has shown that gender differences are considerable on the labour market as far as net earnings are concerned, though it has not been shown that the differences in job tenure are that large.

4.2.5 Multiple-job holding

A comparison of average earnings per month and the relatively high costs of living in Croatia indicate that some workers and indeed many other groups of the working-age population such as the registered unemployed have to work just in order to make ends meet. Table 4.5 shows the incidence of multiple-job holding in 1998 and 2002 by employment status, hours of work and regularity.

There is a clear decrease in multiple-job holding over the period, from 4.6 per cent to 2.9 per cent of total employment, but the regularity characteristics have not changed significantly, with about half of such workers having regular additional jobs, one-third working occasionally and about one-fifth seasonally.

Table 4.5   Characteristics of multiple-job holding, numbers and percentages of total employment, Croatia, 1998 and 2002

	1998		2002	
	Numbers	%	Numbers	%
Total employment	1 549 237	100	1 533 657	100
Multiple-job holders	72 008	4.6	44 807	2.9
Regularity				
Regular multiple-job holders	33 909	47.1	22 289	49.7
Seasonal	14 204	19.7	9 265	20.7
Occasional	23 895	33.2	13 254	29.6
Additional hours of work per month				
1–10	31 830	44.2	16 929	38.0
11–20	23 659	32.9	18 639	41.8
20+	16 519	22.9	8 984	20.2
Employment status				
Public sector employee	38 523	53.5	19 111	42.7
Private sector employee	21 159	29.4	19 552	43.6
Mixed sector employee	4 639	6.4	1 210	2.7
Agricultural worker	3 369	4.7	1 682	3.8
Family worker	1 688	2.3	716	1.6
Craftsperson	1 359	1.9	941	2.1
Owner of enterprise	1039	1.4	631	1.4
Own account worker	232	0.3	238	0.5
Freelance worker	0	0	188	0.4

Sources: LFS, 1998, 2002/2, CBS; author's calculations.

In terms of hours of work, the duration of additional work has increased so that in 2002 most of the workers concerned worked between 11 and 20 additional hours a week while the share of those working an additional 1 to 10 hours declined.

The distribution of employment status among multiple-job holders shows that those who already have an above-average, stable job and regular earnings represent the highest share of multiple-job holders, namely public sector employees with 42.7 per cent and private sector employees with a 43.6 per cent share. The most likely reason for this is that employees per se have more or less fixed working hours, which makes it possible to allocate free time to additional economic activities. By contrast, those categories which may be in greater need of additional earnings are already putting in more than the average number of working hours doing their principal jobs and have little time remaining for additional work.

4.2.6 Summary

The flexibility of the labour force has been examined by considering five different indicators. First, the structure of employment was looked at in terms of formal and informal employment status. About 6 to 10 per cent of the employed were not supposed to be working, being pensioners, informal workers, unemployed, and so on.

The second indicator concerned wages and benefits by employment status, and 32 per cent of all employed were found to have received only partial benefits or to have not had wages paid in the reference period. Typically those employed in the informal economy were in a worse position, along with workers on short-term contracts and own-account workers, with the highest percentages of partial benefits.

The third indicator relates to the types of contract concluded on the labour market. Although employees were found predominantly to hold contracts without limit of time, only 15–20 per cent of the new entrants on the labour market managed to acquire such a contract, while others held either fixed-term or short-term contracts. If this trend continues, the share of employees holding contracts without limit of time will rapidly decrease. The reason why the share of contracts without limit of time has decreased very little from 1997 is the fact that although many fixed-term jobs are created over the year, especially during the summer season, most of these jobs are gone again and these changes cancel one another out when yearly averages are looked at. It is likely that the tightening of the Labour Law provisions on fixed-term contracts may make it more difficult for employers to use this type of contract for permanent types of jobs.

The fourth indicator was job tenure with the present employer and this particular job characteristic was looked at by age, gender and sector of ownership, i.e. status in employment. The findings point to a situation in which 65 per cent of the employed had found their present employment since the beginning of the transition. However, the average age of the working population is about 40 years for both men and women, indicating that the young are at a distinct disadvantage on entering the labour market. Gender issues do not seem to be very important in the duration of employment and women seem to dominate among those with longer tenures. However, women earn less at all tenure levels and years of service. The gender wage gap[8] starts at 0.3 per cent in favour of women under one year of tenure but then widens in favour of men. The biggest difference is found at the tenure level of 11–15 years, when wages are on average 40 per cent higher for men. Thereafter the gap is smaller, narrowing to 18 per cent in favour of men at 25 years of tenure and above.

---

[8] The data in figure 4.7 refer only to employees. There is quite a large non-response to earnings-related questions and estimates might be slightly less rigorous.

Multiple-job holding as an indicator of the need to supplement income from the main job in order to earn enough to live on has shown that this activity is on the decline and that the persons who take part are predominantly those who already have better paid jobs either in the private or the public sectors and not necessarily in the informal economy.

In summary, the basic hypothesis that more flexible types of work which are typically characterized by frequent changes of job, partial benefits and inadequate social security and shorter job tenure sometimes occur in the formal economy, especially in the private formal sector, but are much more characteristic of the informal economy. These findings confirm the hypothesis that the two segments of the labour market have very different work characteristics and that one is much more precarious than the other.

4.3 LABOUR MARKET FLEXIBILITY AND INCOME SECURITY

One of the important features of a flexible labour market is a well-interlinked system of employment and social protection. If employment protection is reduced, this loss of security must be replaced by similar levels in the area of social security. In the welfare state paradigm there was a high level of social protection across the board, mostly of the passive kind. There was an income support system which ensured a high wage-replacement rate, as well as active labour market measures which increased the chances of redeployment for some groups. Although most systems had a certain amount of targeted employment protection as well as passive and active labour market measures and policies, these legal provisions were not considered part and parcel of one system. For example, employment protection is ensured through the Labour Law while active labour market policies are part of the Law on Job Placement and Unemployment Insurance; all other aspects of protection are covered by other specific types of legislation concerning insurance. Although care is taken that no one falls out of the social welfare net by making interlinkages across legislation, social policy has rarely succeeded in efficiently streamlining legislation linked to the labour market.

What has changed in the thinking and practice in this area is that individuals are now expected to take responsibility for their own lives, that the drive for competitiveness means that enterprises need to be relieved of the burden of social security in order for them to thrive and expand, and that the Government has to take over some of the costs of labour market restructuring from the employers. Access to benefits thus becomes contingent on individual behaviour, labour market policy becomes much better targeted at those groups who are in danger of becoming long-term unemployed, and the costs of severance payments and notice periods have partly been taken over by the Government and transferred to recipients as upgrades in the level and duration of their unemployment benefits. However, if access to benefits is not equal for everyone, the whole mechanism will be inefficient and not yield the required trade-off effects.

4.3.1 Legislative reforms and labour market flexibility

Prior to transition the labour market was very well defined, the main actors being large enterprises which employed most of the new entrants on the labour market over and above their actual needs. Unemployment was relatively low and most of it was due to queuing at the entrance to the labour market by young, first-time jobseekers. Unemployment rates were traditionally higher for women than for men. Labour hoarding varied from 15 to 30 per cent, depending on the economic sector, and labour productivity was low on average. The changes in legislation during the early part of transition did not dramatically change the rules defining behaviour on the labour market. It is only the recent changes in legislation that have taken a radical turn, and these are a first step towards a more flexible labour market.

The Labour Law

The new Labour Law was first implemented in January 2004 and was the subject of much debate, negotiation and conflict during the drafting period. Croatia had previously had one of the most rigid legislative frameworks in Europe in terms of the length of notice periods, size of severance payments and pockets of very highly protected workers in the public sector. The shift towards greater flexibility has been only partially achieved and has involved many compromises. The end-effect has been a hybrid situation, in which not all types of work have been defined as employment and as such are not covered by the Labour Law. For example, the Job Placement and Unemployment Insurance Act defines unemployment status clearly according to ILO criteria (with small adjustments regarding hours of work) but the Labour Law still defines employment in terms of the labour contract so that no other types of work enter the employment count (for example, short-term contracts and student contracts are excluded). Some of the more important changes concerning only contracts without limit of time are set out below.

Notice periods (Labour Law, art. 113)

Notice periods are related to specific years of service for contracts without limit of time, and are divided into six categories of length of service. Regular separation brings with it a notice of between two weeks (for under one year of service) and three months (for more than 20 years of service). For workers who have spent more than 20 years with their employer, notice periods are extended for two more weeks if the worker is older than 50, and for a month if the worker is older than 55. As discussed earlier, 322,000 workers have more than 20 years of service. If the dismissal is the fault of the worker, the notice period is halved.

Severance payments (Labour Law, arts. 118 and 119)

Notice which is given after at least two years of service with the present employer and which is not the worker's fault needs to be accompanied by a severance payment. Average net earnings received over the last three months of work determine the level of the severance payments. This level cannot be lower than one-third of these earnings and cannot be higher than six months' earnings, except in the case of specific alternative arrangements contained in collective agreements or definite statutes.

Redundancies

Mass redundancies have been redefined. An employer who intends to dismiss 20 or more workers needs to put forward a redundancy programme within 90 days of the intended redundancy. In the course of drawing up the social plan the employer is required to consult the works council and the regional employment service.

On the whole, the main effect of the new changes will be a reduction in the separation costs borne by the employer, which were previously considerable. Also, the speed at which turnover of personnel is possible has been increased, and this again is a very important cost saver and gives a boost to structural change. Another break-through that has been achieved is recognition by the social partners of the direction of change of the laws regulating the labour market and the necessity to compensate the loss of job security with social rights during unemployment. The trade-off for the loss of benefits linked to employment has been secured by greater rights of the unemployed in the form of higher unemployment benefits of longer duration, plus a one-off lump sum which goes to the potentially hard-to-place, i.e. those persons with long years of service and/or an age constraint. A further step is needed to connect the legislative solutions with conscious policies to back up employability with real chances for individuals to re-enter the labour market.

The Job Placement and Unemployment Insurance Act

This law was passed in 2001 and involves some of the most fundamental changes in legislation concerning the functioning of the labour market. Its main aims are to:

- introduce international standards into the definition of unemployment based on ILO methodology;

- encourage competitive job placement;

- reduce red tape, especially that affecting employers;

- motivate the unemployed in active job search;

- pave the way for information technologies; and

- create more responsibility in the management system.

International standards were introduced in a way appropriate for the Croatian labour market. The need for unemployed persons to show active job search, availability for work and absence of work in order to be eligible for unemployment benefit was dealt with by integrating these activities with the business processes of the public employment service. For example, the steps that a person needs to take to demonstrate they are actively looking for work are those also necessary for successful job placement. This includes in-depth interviews (up to three) during which a detailed work profile is defined and a 'professional plan' drawn up. This process can have one of three outcomes. If a person has skills that are needed on the labour market, a process of monitored job search is initiated. If there are various impediments to placement, which can range from lack of job-search skills to lack of employability due to redundant skills, the unemployed person enters into the process of preparation for employment. This can include attendance at job-search, self-assessment and activation workshops, in-job training or a change of occupation. The third outcome is self-employment, which is a solution for 5–7 per cent of the unemployed, who are either already active in the informal economy or have the makings of a successful entrepreneur. Most of these processes are defined through application decrees or operating instructions in the public employment service.

The verification of availability for work involves a statement of two hours in the day during which the unemployed person volunteers to be available to the staff of the employment service.

The criteria of absence of work, on the other hand, have been interpreted in a specific way in Croatia. Unemployed persons are allowed to earn up to the maximum unemployment benefit without being taken off the register. The incidence of such earnings is checked monthly by the institution responsible for monitoring the payment of mandatory contributions. On average, about 2,000 unemployed persons have been earning more than the maximum amount allowed, but in August 2003 this count was more than 4,500. The rationale behind this approach was that the unemployed should not be discouraged from working, though a limit needed to be set above which these economically active persons would be considered as employed. This practice has demonstrated that a large number of the registered unemployed are in work, although many have earnings below the threshold allowed.

With regard to competition in job placement, several new domestic and international private employment agencies have been registered since the law came into force. Some specialize in job placement for highly educated individuals looking for jobs in management or in the domain of information technology, while other agencies focus mostly on short-term jobs.

The reduction of red tape affecting employers was initiated in several ways. First, employers are no longer under any obligation to declare vacancies to the public employment service and many refrained from doing so as soon as they could. This presents a real challenge for the employment service and unless the public employment service continues to increase its capacity to anticipate employers' needs and provide specialist support for labour market services, the private sector is bound to be more efficient and effective in filling its job vacancies.

Insurance of Workers' Arrears in Bankruptcies Act

The question of insuring workers' earnings arrears is an important piece of legislation linked to the general bankruptcy legislation. The law has been designed to protect workers' entitlement to various types of income that should have been paid in the three months prior to the bankruptcy. Types of income which are covered by this mechanism are: wages, contributions for compulsory insurance, wages that should have been paid in times of sickness, annual leave, severance payments in the event of dismissal, compensation for professional risks (accidents at work and occupation-related illnesses). Compensation for these forgone rights will be partial: the insurance covers refunds linked to the minimum wage or a certain percentage thereof. Arrears will be paid not only to those who are employed at the time of the bankruptcy but also to those who were employed in the three months prior to the bankruptcy and have submitted their request within 30 days of the declaration of bankruptcy. The guarantor for the arrears is the Employment and Development Fund and the requests for payment of arrears are submitted through the offices of the employment service.

This legislation will reduce the risk of financial loss to the workers resulting from adverse business developments, in line with EU guidelines regulating this field (Council Directives 80/987/EEC and 2002/74/EEC).

Pension Insurance Act

The aim of legislative changes regarding pension insurance was to bring workers' rights in line with more flexible types of work, especially part-time and occasional work. Previously, all types of work that were not full time had very difficult access to pension insurance rights. All hours of work below the full-time level used to be converted to full-time equivalents and this made it impossible to reach the minimum period of service needed to be eligible for an old-age pension. Now, men have access to an old-age pension from the age of 65 (60 in the case of women) if they have worked for at least 15 years, regardless of the hours of work. A special algorithm will be used to calculate the level of pension, which will, of course, be lower than the pension for full-time workers.

4.3.2 The role of the social partners

The most direct influence of the social partners on employment policy is through the Governing Council of the Croatian Employment Service and through Advisory Committees in regional employment offices.

Under the Job Placement and Unemployment Insurance Act, the Governing Council has a tripartite structure: three representatives are nominated by the Ministry of Economy, Labour and Entrepreneurship, and three trade union representatives and three employers' representatives are nominated by the members of the Economic and Social Council.[9]

---

[9] The Economic and Social Council is a tripartite body whose role is to promote discussion and cooperation between the social partners on important issues such as legislation, policy, institutions and other matters of interest. Major government decisions, policy and actions should be discussed at the Council with the social partners.

The Advisory Committees have to be set up in the regional offices of the employment service. The directors of these offices are obliged to consult the Advisory Committee before reaching any decisions which may influence the position of the unemployed, especially decisions relating to active labour market measures. A recent analysis of the functioning of these bodies has shown that the bodies that have been constituted meet rarely, on average once a year: moreover there is often a lack of interest of some members, which makes it difficult to organize meetings. One of the main reasons given for the lack of activity is the top–down way in which active labour market measures are designed and the lack of influence at local level regarding the way mass redundancies are conducted.

The medium-term plans concerning the functioning of the public employment service may help strengthen the importance of Advisory Councils, first through the development of partnerships. Formally and institutionally, the social partners are in a position to influence social policy, but in fact many of the decisions are drawn up in government circles and then discussed with social partners in various forums such as the Government Committee for Monitoring ALMP Measures, the Government Department for Social Partnership, the Governing Council of the Croatian Employment Service and the Economic and Social Council, all of which have a tripartite structure. The main problem with interaction is the divergent interpretations of the labour market among the social partners and the uneven capacity to address its challenges, which means that many arguments are essentially political. Recently, much research has been done on the Croatian labour market and these findings will be discussed in the social partners' arena too.

The new National Action Plan for Employment, accepted by the Government in 2004, was designed with participation from trade unions and employers' representatives. However, the annual action plan for 2006 was an intrasectoral activity, drawn up without much participation.

Another problem influencing the efficiency of social dialogue is the lack of agreement on most issues among the various trade union confederations. Consensus is difficult to achieve and there is also lack of accord among the small number of employers' associations.

Trade unions

It is estimated that 40 to 45 per cent of the employed are members of one of the existing unions. At the beginning of the 1990s, in the socialist period, union density was 92 per cent. During the past decade, a drastic decline in employment from 1.9 to 1.3 million and an increase in the number of pensioners from 600,000 to 1.1 million have transformed the structure of employment. New job creation has almost exclusively been in the SME sector, which has no tradition of unionization.

According to the Labour Law, a trade union can be registered by at least ten employees and a confederation can be made up of at least two trade unions, which means that 20 people can constitute a confederation. In the wake of this legislation, many small unions competed with each other for members, fragmenting the trade union movement. Workers were thus less inclined to join a union, with the result that the majority did so only in reaction to an abuse of their rights at work by their employer.

There is no law in Croatia on the minimum level of representation of unions, but there is a 1999 law on Electing Candidates from Trade Unions to Tripartite Bodies at national level. To be eligible for representation on the Economic and Social Council, a trade union confederation must be registered with the Registry of the Ministry of Economy, Labour and Entrepreneurship, have at least 15,000 members, be financed by at least five individual unions, have organizations in 11 out of 21 counties, have democratic representation mechanisms, and have signed at least three collective agreements at national level over the previous two years.

There are five such confederations in Croatia. The biggest are the Union of Independent Unions (SSSH) with 65 per cent of the total number of unionized employees, the Trade Union of Public Employees with 10.5 per cent, the Independent Croatian Trade Unions (NHS) with 9.2 per cent, the Croatian Trade Union Organization (HUS) with 7.4 per cent and the Organization of Workers' Trade Unions (URSH) with 7.1 per cent.

Employers' associations

The Croatian Chamber of Commerce is an organization which represents employers and which is financed through a mandatory contribution based on gross wages. Apart from this organization, there are voluntary employers' organizations: the Croatian Association of Employers (HUP), the Organization of Employers in the Wood Processing and Paper Industry, the Union of Independent Employers' Organizations (SNUP) and others. Unlike the trade unions, an employers' association need not show a certain level of representativeness in order to participate in the Economic and Social Council, and HUP is currently the only member of this Council.

It is not publicly known how many employers participate in HUP, but it is said to represent 5,000 employers in 23 sector organizations, employing more than 300,000 workers. Territorially, it covers Osijek, Rijeka, Split and Zagreb. Other organizations have tried to become members of the Economic and Social Council but with little success.

Rigidity of legislation and workers' protection

Unlike most employers, members of the Government and certain experts, the trade unions do not believe that Croatian workers are overprotected. As far as protection mechanisms are concerned – notice of dismissal, notice periods, severance payments, group notices – they claim that Croatian workers have similar levels of protection to their European counterparts. However, where workers' rights during court cases and job loss are concerned, European workers enjoy much better protection. This is especially apparent in terms of the level and duration of unemployment benefit. After seven years at the same level, the benefit was raised from HRK 900–1,000 to 25.1 per cent of the average wage and the duration of benefit was linked to the number of years spent in work. Individuals who have worked for more than 20 years can claim benefit for a period of 390 days, those who have worked for 15 years can claim for 364 days and others with fewer years of work for 312 days. Women who have worked for more than 25 years and men who have worked for more than 30 years can claim benefit until retirement age or redeployment. The benefits of re-registering unemployed are calculated with respect to the years in work since the last claim.

The second feature considered unacceptable by the trade unions is the benefit coverage of the unemployed, which is low at 18–20 per cent.

Furthermore, the Croatian courts are very inefficient and workers' lawsuits compete with all other court cases, so that it may take years before a judgment is handed down. The capacity of the labour inspectorate for monitoring and imposing penalties is low and the number of inspectors too small to exert a meaningful influence on the employers.

New jobs that are created are often badly paid, unregistered, uncertain and very rarely permanent. There are still about 45,000 workers in Croatia who work without pay. Likewise, Croatia has still not ratified the Protection of Workers' Claims (Employer's Insolvency) Convention, 1992 (No. 173), which has been a longstanding demand of the trade unions. Recently, a similar law has been introduced which guarantees the reimbursement of workers' unpaid wages following a bankruptcy. According to the Penal Code the failure to pay wages is an offence punishable by fines or a jail sentence like any other crime. The Association of Croatian Employers is very much against this ruling but it remains unchanged.

The trade unions all agree that the way to increase worker protection is to promote collective agreements at all levels and to develop social partnership at national and local levels. It is considered particularly important to develop bipartite social dialogue between employers and trade unions at sectoral level. As a barrier to achieving this, the trade unions point to the lack of mutual trust between existing social partners, which results in the issuing of declarations but no real improvement in relations.

The following is the list of suggestions that the trade unions consider important to improve the position and security of workers:

- increase the number of labour inspectors and extend their mandate beyond reporting incidents, allowing them to impose penalties on employers who are breaking the Labour Code;

- enable trade unions to take employers who do not abide by collective agreements to court on behalf of all the workers they represent, since individuals often lack the courage to do so on their own, despite legal support, counselling and representation in court from the trade union;

- introduce workers' representation on labour tribunals and an efficient process of arbitration preceding court cases;

- give greater power to works councils and require smaller firms to introduce them since most often workers' rights are not respected in firms with fewer than 20 workers;

- increase the minimum number of workers' representatives in works councils depending on size. For example, for firms with 20–75 workers only one person can represent workers' interests, which is not enough.

The trade unions consider the link between the high level of social protection and the barriers to job creation to be too simplistic to form the basis for changes in employment policy. They consider the present stalemate in job creation to be attributable to other reasons since the level of social protection in Croatia is not presently such that it could be detrimental. Sluggish development is more attributable to incomplete privatization, incompetent and overpaid managers, production oriented towards the domestic market instead of exports, and in the case of many enterprises low productivity and lack of competitiveness. The trade unions consider the cost of labour to be one of the factors of competitiveness but by no means the only one. They point out that the success of many Croatian innovators in international exhibitions has not been exploited as a source of competitive advantage in the economy, that new technologies are not being introduced, that little money is channelled into research and development and that investment in human resources is very limited. They also suggest a series of changes that could increase competitiveness:

- reform the education system in preparation for developing a knowledge-based society (regular school, vocational education and training, and adult education);

- permit the participation of social partners in most decision-making processes at all levels;

- stimulate further small and medium enterprises;

- use tax rebates for employers and workers who invest in education;

- promote information technologies and their implementation;

- reduce the costs of the public sector and increase its effectiveness;

- invest in infrastructure and improve the transport linkages inside Croatia as well as the major trade routes;

- improve the justice system and make it more accountable.

The employers, on the other hand, take the view that there is not enough flexibility on the labour market in Croatia and that the legislative changes have stopped short of introducing the necessary level of deregulation. Some of the criticisms are the following:

- The rules surrounding fixed-duration labour contracts are too strict.

- Part-time working hours are not paid *pro rata*.

- The coverage of collective agreements and individual labour contracts, and the application of the principle of applying those rules most favourable to the worker, undermines much of the deregulation achieved so far.

- Although there has been a reduction in minimum notice periods and severance pay, notice periods can be interrupted by justifiable absences from work (such as maternity leave or sick leave), and severance pay is still payable in case of injury at work or occupational disease and to those workers who unjustifiably refuse alternative employment.

- Flexibility in terms of hours and levels of staffing is hampered by the high level of protection relating to workers with family responsibilities.

- Joint decision-making through works councils requires employers to consult before dismissing certain categories of workers.

On the basis of these arguments the employers' associations take the position that workers are still overprotected and that employers still need more room to make business-related decisions.

4.4   POLICY RECOMMENDATIONS: ADDRESSING THE CHALLENGE

In a global market, enterprises find themselves in more turbulent competitive conditions and their survival has become more uncertain. Adjust or die is the creed today and this has brought with it pressure for more flexibility on the labour market – the shouldering of insecurity is being diverted from enterprises to workers. Not surprisingly, in a world where the tradition of workers' rights has deep roots (in both socialist and capitalist European economies), there is huge opposition to this process. The question is: can workers be protected when their enterprises are exposed to competition? National legislation, workers' organizations and human rights organizations, both international and national, have defined very high standards for individual rights in life and at work. How can these laudable goals be achieved in a national and a European setting? One of the worse effects of globalization is the deepening of the rift between the skilled, who have learning opportunities in and outside work especially in technologically developed sectors, and those without skills and little opportunity for acquiring them.

Competitiveness today depends mostly on the quality of the labour input, its innovativeness, ingenuity and joint vision. On the other hand, community development in both economic and social terms is a prerequisite for sustainable economic growth. Fast growth without an improvement in the quality of life for the majority can have high social costs, creating barriers to further growth. In such a complex setting, can the drive for flexibility be the answer?

Under the former Soviet system, job security was total, and the countries concerned provide an example of how a lack of competition and the 'security' that goes with it can lead to stagnation. The transition countries now have a high level of flexibility in their informal economies, but there is very little evidence of a level of performance that outstrips that in the formal economy. In fact it is usually economic activity which workers resort to in the absence of a better solution in formal employment, with lower productivity levels.

Policy options are needed to reduce the labour market segmentation which arises from these differences in the working environment in transition countries. In order to achieve this, the labour legislation in the formal economy needs to be deregulated, and informal economic activities should be legitimized and/or squeezed out. This has to be done in such a way that all types of work ensure the same levels of social security, which can only come about through interventions in the tax system, labour legislation and social security arrangements. Under conditions of abundant labour, the behaviour of employers is such that many workers lack basic insurance, wages are not guaranteed and decent remuneration for work is often absent. Once the labour legislation has put all types of work on an equal footing, labour inspectorates need to be more widely present with the power of authority to close those establishments that employ people without registering them for mandatory social insurances. The dichotomy between permanent and fixed-term contracts should be abolished and all contracts made permanent, but the ease with which they can be terminated and the costs associated therewith should be further reduced. Rather than having the system officially condone moonlighting, the level of social protection for the unemployed should be sufficient to allow individuals to live adequately on unemployment benefit.

Croatia has made very important changes in its legislation, which move towards equalizing the position of all who work. Issues of social security have also been solved in this way, as all individuals working on short-term contracts who were previously denied access to social security are now eligible. However, there are still some weaknesses in the legal protection of workers, large arrears in work-related lawsuits, a weak labour inspectorate and weak trade union activity in the private sector and in the informal economy. Certain advances have been achieved in the new law regulating workers' arrears prior to bankruptcies, and it is clear that more pressure will have to be applied to employers in order to secure more efficient protection of workers' rights. At the same time, notice periods, severance payments and other costs of mobility need to be traded off with longer – and, in time, higher – unemployment benefits. If the benefit is not high enough to cover the simple cost of living, informal markets will have to supply the difference and this will feed the informal economy. This vicious circle must be broken at the point, if it is ever reached, when more jobs are being created and formal employment becomes a realistic alternative for the unemployed. There is no third way.

The link between employability, security and income also needs to be looked at in terms of policy recommendations. Today, security can no longer be linked to the preservation of existing jobs at all costs. Mobility is good for development and it should be promoted, especially in periods of rapid structural change. The main source of stability as well as income potential stems from employability rather than protection through a rigid legal framework, trade unions and worker-oriented labour courts. Adapting enterprises to new circumstances with a reduction of the workforce is not something that enterprises do because they are habitual law-breakers but rather because they try to adapt in the short term in order to keep the company alive.

4.4.1 The role of active labour market policies in job security

Policies to facilitate restructuring in flexible labour markets should include:

*   Creating mobility or redeployment centres for pending large-scale redundancies, whose aim is to put back into work those workers who are about to lose their jobs

*   Identifying potential long-term unemployed and helping them regain competencies which are in demand on the labour market

*   Placing very high importance on the activation principle which requires more individualized or group-oriented services in the public employment service

*   Introducing the workfare principles for persons who use the social welfare system such that they receive training during their community-based work

*   Developing public–private partnerships which will facilitate networking of all stakeholders in the area of employment, development and education

*   Introducing effective mechanisms for giving support to jobseekers in their job search and career guidance.

4.4.2 Roles of individuals, companies, social partners, labour market institutions and the State in a changing labour market

Individuals

The role of the individual in seeking and finding work has become much greater now that information sources have become open to all those who care to look. The era of state paternalism is over and individual responsibility has become the norm, especially among the unfortunate who are out of work.

Companies

In the business world today a paradigmatic shift is becoming visible. Corruption and cut-throat competition have characterized the biggest enterprises and questions of ethics are beginning to be asked once again. People are becoming a key competitive advantage and this trend will slowly push out those companies not capable of mobilizing motivated, capable and creative employees. As such, these workers will be in a good position on the labour market and will easily find new jobs.

Social partners

The present role of the trade unions is to slow down or stop the process of reform on the labour market. This will have to change in view of the need to provide equal standards of protection for all workers and not just some of them. The real challenge is how to provide protection for the informal economy worker rather than how to further increase the level of protection for workers in the already highly protected public sector. The second biggest challenge is to focus on training as an obligation of the employer and to introduce this element into the labour legislation as well as in the delivery of support and services to employees.

Labour market institutions

Both public and private institutions such as job agencies and the public employment service need to work together to increase the accessibility of information. Further, the employment service must build competencies for early identification of potentially excluded categories and cooperate more closely with the social welfare system, non-governmental organizations and all those who have an interest in the same target population. The employment service might be expected to orient itself in the future towards more involvement in development initiatives on the one hand and setting up community works on the other.

The State

The role of the State should be reduced to implementing macroeconomic policies that provide a stable and predictable environment and to providing services to citizens, companies and other organizations with a minimum of bureaucracy. The fiscal system must promote the value of work and it should have the widest possible base. Support to start-ups and an enabling environment for entrepreneurship is essential. However, the biggest obligation of the State is to invest in a good education system and support scientific research. A crucial feature is an up-to-date adult education system capable of providing the skills needed on the labour market. Also, a sophisticated system of labour market data collection from enterprises, educational establishments, employment services and the government needs to be set up in such a way that a good information system starts to develop.

Worker security based on maintaining all jobs at all costs is a stance which will create problems for a small open economy striving for global competitiveness. The key to security on the labour market is through training, personal development and activation.

HUNGARY

5

János Köllő and Beáta Nacsa[*]

5.1   INTRODUCTION

Hungary entered transition with a highly flexible labour market relative to the other former socialist countries. After the market-oriented reforms of 1968, employers were restrained in wage setting only indirectly by progressive taxes on the firm's wage increment, and were free to adjust employment provided they did not engage in politically harmful mass dismissals. Workers were allowed to change employer without administrative restrictions, which was reflected in relatively high rates of labour turnover throughout the 1970s and 1980s (over 15 per cent per annum). The immediate pre-transition period brought about further liberalization, including the gradual abolition of wage controls; the removal of political constraints on mass redundancies; and the establishment of a series of institutions fostering firm entry and exit.

Fifteen years on, comparative research based on institutional rankings and scores continues to suggest that the Hungarian regulations are highly flexible, and definitely the least restrictive within the former Soviet bloc (see, inter alia, Cazes and Nesporova, 2003, p. 120; Riboud et al., 2002; Rutkowski et al., 2005). Furthermore, as will be shown later, everyday practices are not always as strongly regulated as readers of the Labour Code and the Employment Act might think.

At the same time, Hungary's employment ratio is one of the lowest (and its male labour force participation ratio is the single lowest) within the OECD. While the Hungarian labour market is quite flexible, it is also surprisingly small. The huge gap between the country's employment ratio and that of the EU is mostly accounted for by a multitude of prime-age adults completely withdrawn from the labour market. A high proportion of these workers left employment 15 years ago and will presumably never return to the labour market. Further withdrawal was encouraged by permissive

---

*Institute of Economics, Budapest.

121

retirement policies, a generous childcare scheme, and a sizeable informal economy providing shelter for those who were either pushed out of employment or who chose to leave the labour market permanently or for protracted periods.

Given the patterns of non-employment, improved labour market institutions, taken in the narrow sense, may not promise remarkable employment growth. Employment policies can be efficient if they address the problem of lasting inactivity, and reconsider the institutions that encourage permanent exit from the labour market. Understanding the motives of exit and assessing the contribution of the current welfare system seem to us more important tasks than reinforcing Hungary's leading position in the East European 'flexibility contest'.

This chapter is organized in six sections. Section 5.2 gives a brief overview of the basic facts, while section 5.3 introduces the most important institutions conditioning wage setting, hiring, firing, and other aspects of the employment relationship. Section 5.4 turns to the flexibility issue itself by reviewing the existing evidence on wage responsiveness, demand elasticity, adjustment costs, and worker and job mobility. Section 5.5 gives a brief overview of institutions and conditions encouraging permanent withdrawal from the labour market, and section 5.6 concludes.

5.2 THE BASIC FACTS

5.2.1 Employment and participation

Comparative data (table 5.1) suggest that the Hungarian labour market performs poorly in international comparison. The employment rate for Hungarian men is among the lowest in Europe (together with Poland and Slovakia) while their

Table 5.1 Employment–population and participation–population ratios by age, Hungary, 2002 (percentages)

	Male				Female			
	Employment by age group		Participation by age group		Employment by age group		Participation by age group	
	15–64 years	25–54 years	15–64 years	25–54 years	15–64 years	25–54 years	15–64 years	25–54 years
EU minimum	68.1	84.0	72.6	90.0	42.0	54.0	47.9	60.3
EU maximum	82.9	94.2	88.9	96.6	73.9	82.4	77.1	85.6
EU mean	72.9	86.7	78.5	92.3	55.7	73.2	61.0	73.2
Visegrad-4 mean[1]	64.2	80.6	73.3	90.1	51.2	68.4	59.4	77.8
Hungary	62.9	79.7	67.1	84.3	49.8	66.5	52.7	69.9

Note: [1] Czech Republic, Hungary, Poland and Slovakia, unweighted mean.

Source: OECD, 2003.

participation rate is the single lowest within the OECD. Female employment and participation compare favourably to Southern but not to Western, Northern or Central Europe. These patterns continue to hold after the effect of Hungary's relatively low retirement age (recently increased from 60 to 62 for men and from 55 to 58 for women) is controlled for.

5.2.2 Inactivity versus unemployment

As suggested by a comparison of the employment and participation figures in table 5.1, the Hungarian non-employed are much more likely to be inactive, as opposed to unemployed, than their counterparts East and West. The bias for inactivity within prime-age non-employment is a relatively new feature. The proportion of active jobseekers within non-employment fell from nearly one-third in 1992 to one-sixth in 2001. In relative terms the trends were similar for men and women: nearly half of the non-employed prime-age males were searching for work in 1992 as opposed to a quarter in 2001, while prime-age women's search intensity fell from 20 to 10 per cent. However, in absolute terms male search intensity fell by 25 percentage points as opposed to only 10 percentage points for women.

Table 5.2 Non-employment and unemployment at age 25–54 by status, Hungary, 1993 and 2001 (percentages)

	Male		Female	
	1993	2001	1993	2001
Non-employment rate	**22.8**	**20.4**	**33.5**	**33.4**
Unemployment rate	**10.9**	**5.4**	**8.6**	**4.4**
Composition of the non-employed				
Retired	34.0	45.3	29.8	29.4
On childcare benefit	0.3	1.0	23.0	32.2
Other	65.7	53.7	47.2	38.4
Total	100.0	100.0	100.0	100.0
Search intensity (unemployed/non-employed)				
Retired	2.7	1.1	2.2	0.9
On childcare benefit	..	2.2	2.9	1.4
Other	64.0	40.8	36.8	22.4
Total	43.0	22.4	18.7	9.4

Note: Labour market status according to ILO–OECD definitions. .. = not available.

Source: LFS, April–June 1993 and 2001.

123

The patterns of change in the prime-age group are further examined in table 5.2, comprising data from the 1993 and 2001 April–June waves of the LFS (arbitrarily chosen for sake of illustration). While the rates of non-employment did not change significantly between 1993 and 2001, unemployment fell substantially via two channels. First, a growing proportion of prime-age men and women left the labour market in favour of a pension and/or childcare benefit and stopped searching for jobs (or vice versa). Second, search intensity fell substantially even among those not receiving a pension or childcare benefit, from 64.0 to 40.8 per cent for men and 36.8 to 22.4 per cent for women.

Alternative measures of willingness to work depict a similar picture. The combined proportion of those non-employed who searched for or simply 'wanted a job' amounted to 58.3 per cent in 1992. Their share dropped to 48.2 in 1995, 40.2 in 1998 and 42.1 in 2001.

5.2.3 The lasting effect of the transition shock

The employment gap between Western Europe and Central and Eastern Europe, including Hungary, partly results from a rude shock to the labour market at the onset of transition. This point is supported by figure 5.1 showing the distribution of the Hungarian non-employed population in October–December 2000 by the year its members were last employed. The actual distributions are compared to expectations in a steady state characterized by equal time-invarying flows to and from employment and constant exit-to-job hazards.

The deviations from the expectation were minor with respect to cohorts leaving employment before 1989 and after 1991. By contrast, the number of people losing jobs in 1989–91 and staying non-employed until the end of 2000 exceeded the expectation by 403,000 in all age groups and 147,000 in the age range 15–59 years. This compared to employment levels of 3,877,000 and 3,783,000, respectively. In relative terms, the 'bumps' above the expected values accounted for about 10 per cent and 4 per cent of aggregate employment in the respective age ranges. This was roughly equal to the gap between Hungary's employment ratio and the EU average (about 8 per cent in all age groups and 6 per cent in the prime-age range). The members of these cohorts are rather unlikely to return to employment, including those below the retirement age. Slightly less than two-thirds of the cohorts' prime-age members have already retired (63 per cent), with only 23 per cent reporting willingness to work, 5 per cent registered as unemployed and 4 per cent actively searching in the labour market.

5.2.4 Inequalities

Inequalities by region, education and ethnicity have been large in international comparison since the start of transition and do not seem to be diminishing. Regional unemployment differentials were decreasing in the 1990s but the trend was reversed as the western and central parts of the country started to recover from the transform-ational recession. Similarly, the differences between rural and urban settlements

Figure 5.1 The distribution of the non-employed population in 2000 by year of last employment, Hungary (thousands)

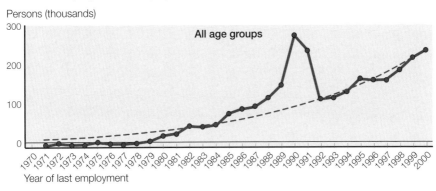

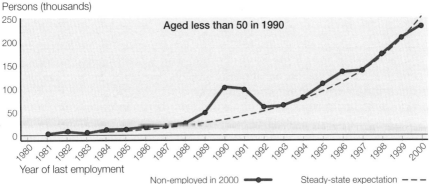

Note: Fourth quarter.

Source: LFS, 2000.

(except for Budapest) are on the rise, following a transitional period of diminishing inequality (Nagy, 2003).

Inequalities by education have also been large compared to Western market economies and continue to grow. This, in fact, is a common feature of transforming post-communist economies, as shown by the small descriptive regressions of table 5.3. The female unskilled employment ratios are lower by 7.5 per cent, and the male by 13.7 per cent, holding the gender-specific aggregate employment ratios and the population share of the unskilled constant. (The latter is thought of as a crude proxy of the median unskilled worker's position in the ability distribution, with higher shares predicting better position. It also controls for the weight of unskilled employment in determining aggregate employment.) Similar regressions using country dummies for the Central and Eastern European countries yield –8.0 and –9.8 per cent lower unskilled ratios for Hungary.

Table 5.3   Unskilled employment–population ratios in the OECD, 2002
(OLS regressions)

	Female		Male	
Aggregate employment ratio (gender-specific)	1.0316	7.02	1.3956	7.45
Fraction ISCED 0–2 (gender-specific)	0.2518	3.08	0.2141	7.74
Czech Republic, Hungary, Poland, Slovakia	–0.0747	2.06	–0.1374	3.75
Constant	–0.2564		–0.4938	
R^2	0.7684		0.8988	
Number of countries	30		30	

Notes: All data relate to people aged 25–64 years. t-values in the second and fourth columns, computed from Huber–White standard errors. Dependent variable: Employment ratio of people with ISCED 0–2 educational attainment (gender-specific).

Source: OECD, 2005.

The social group hit hardest by the transition was Hungary's sizeable Roma community, accounting for about 5 per cent of its population. Surveys conducted in 1993 and 2003 estimated Roma unemployment to exceed 50 per cent – a level high above what might be expected on the basis of the skill composition and spatial allocation of the Roma population (Havas et al., 2002).

5.3   FLEXIBILITY AND JOB SECURITY: THE INSTITUTIONAL BACKGROUND

This section looks at the most important institutions conditioning labour market flexibility and job security, that is, the response of wages and employment to the changing fortunes of businesses. The discussion is primarily based on repeated cross-sectional data from the Labour Force Survey (LFS) and the Wage Survey (WS). Four data sets will be particularly extensively used. The first one is the supplementary survey of the LFS in April–June 2001 (LFS–S), which included questions on wages and union membership. The second is a pair of surveys (NLC–EJS) conducted by the National Labour Centre (recently renamed the Employment Office) in 1994 and 2001. The surveys were targeted at recipients of unemployment benefits entering employment, and included questions about job characteristics and wages before and after unemployment. Third, we rely extensively on the 2000 October–December wave of the LFS – a database that was supplemented with regional and industry-wide information at the Institute of Economics of the Hungarian Academy of Sciences. Finally, we draw information from the 1998 wave of the Wage Survey (WS98), which was supplemented with information on collective wage agreements. Annex 5.1 presents a brief description of the data sets.

5.3.1 Wage setting

Hungary has a predominantly decentralized system of wage determination with relatively few workers covered by industry-wide bargaining or other types of agreements made outside the firm. Though a national tripartite body of interest reconciliation (Érdekegyeztetö Tanács, ÉT) has been in place since the early 1990s, it only formulates recommendations concerning average wage growth. According to the available institution-based statistics (Neumann, 2005), the proportion of employees covered by industry-wide wage agreements fell from nearly 30 per cent in 1992 to less than 10 per cent in 2002, while firm-level agreements covered 20 per cent in 1992 and dropped to less than 5 per cent in 2002. The combined upper-bound estimate of coverage (15 per cent) in 2001 lagged slightly behind survey-based estimates available for the same year. In the LFS–S, 22 per cent of employees reported that their wages were affected by collective agreements concluded inside or outside the firm. Coverage was relatively low at 32 per cent even among the workers of medium-sized and large firms (with 50 or more employees).

Both the institution-based and the survey-based indicators hint at substantially lower levels of unionization, and coverage by collective agreements, than do the expert estimates used in international comparative research. Several authors (including Cazes and Nesporova, 2003, p. 119; and Ederveen and Thissen, 2004, p. 26) rely on estimates of the ILO and the OECD which give figures as high as 60 per cent for union membership and over 70 per cent for coverage in the mid 1990s. The LFS–S, which provided the first more or less reliable data on the topic, suggests that 20 per cent of wage earners were union members, 37.5 per cent were employed at a unionized firm, and 22 per cent thought his or her wage was affected by some sort of collective wage agreement. For the private sector the respective figures were 15, 29 and 17 per cent.

Unlike the private sector, which is virtually unconstrained in wage setting, the public sector is subject to strict regulations by a wage grid that sets minimum and maximum salaries for public servants and minimum salaries for public sector employees. Kézdi (2002) showed that the wage grid is affected by market forces, in that more marketable skills are paid closer to competitive wage levels. Nevertheless the regulations bias the overall wage distribution and affect the rest of the labour market.[1]

5.3.2 Minimum wage

An effective national minimum wage was introduced in 1989 by the country's last communist government. The minimum relates to monthly pre-tax 'base wages' (earnings net of overtime pay, shift pay and bonuses), is legally binding, and covers all employment contracts. In 1990–98 adjustments were negotiated annually by ET,

---

[1] This was easy to observe in election years (1994, 1998, 2002) when spectacular wage hikes in the public sector were followed by private sector employers.

the national-level tripartite council, while in 1998–2002 the minimum wage was set unilaterally by the government. For part-timers, who account for 3.5 per cent of paid employment, the wage floor is proportionally lower but no other exceptions are made.

At its introduction the minimum wage amounted to 34 per cent of the average wage while in 2000 (just before two major hikes) it stood at 29 per cent, a level far below the European average but only marginally lower than that of Spain, the laggard within the EU. Despite its low Kaitz-index, Hungary's minimum wage was already effective in 2000. The proportion of workers paid 95–105 per cent of the minimum wage amounted to 5 per cent – a ratio similar to those reported for Austria, Belgium, Denmark, the Netherlands and the United States by Dolado et al. (1996).[2] Quite unexpectedly, Viktor Orbán's right-wing government nearly doubled the minimum wage in 2001 and 2002. The hikes raised the ratio of the minimum wage to the average wage to 39 and 43 per cent, respectively. By 2005 the ratio fell to 36 per cent, which lags behind the EU15 average by more than ten percentage points, equal to the ratio in the United States, but exceeds levels in Russia (20 per cent) or Spain (26 per cent).

5.3.3 Hiring: Types of employment contracts

As discussed in *Labour markets in transition* (Cazes and Nesporova, 2003), employment contracts are typically of indefinite duration in Central and Eastern Europe, and there has been little move towards alternative legal forms of the employment relationship. Similarly to many other analysts, the authors regard the dominance of indefinite contracts as an impediment to flexibility. The fact that over 90 per cent of the employment contracts in effect are open-ended seems to justify these concerns in the Hungarian case, too. However, these data relate to all workers in employment, many of whom will stay in their jobs until retirement without ever being considered for redundancy. Whether they have open-ended or fixed-term contracts makes little difference to their labour market flexibility. Departures from the state socialist legacy of 'lifelong' contracts is more important in the case of new hires and it seems that substantial changes have occurred in this respect. The available data suggest sharp differences in the typical legal form of ongoing versus new contracts. While only about 4 per cent of the ongoing contracts have been concluded for less than six months or a trial period, the respective shares exceed one-quarter with new hires and one-half with new hires from unemployment, as shown in table 5.4. The share of open-ended contracts amounted to 92.4 per cent with all workers, but only 67.8 per cent with new hires and 39.5 per cent with hires from unemployment in 2001.

In Köllő and Nacsa (2005) we present weak evidence that job termination rates differ by type of contract, with the difference being larger for short tenures.

---

[2] The data relate to firms employing 5 or more workers and the public sector. Authors' calculation using the WS.

Table 5.4   Employment contracts of all in employment and new hires, Hungary, April–June 2001 (percentages)

Type of contract	All employees April–June 2001	Employees hired in January–June 2001 (LFS–S)	UI recipients hired in April 2001 (NLC–EJS)
Indefinite duration	92.4	67.8	39.5
Fixed-term, > 6 months	3.1	5.0	9.6
Fixed-term, 2–6 months	2.6	10.9	9.2
Fixed-term, 1 month	0.6	2.4	7.2
Trial period	1.3	13.9	34.5
Total	100.0	100.0	100.0

Sources: LFS–S and NLC–EJC.

A potentially significant part of the difference may be accounted for by endogenous selection, but, with the recently available data at hand, we could not reject the assertion that open-ended contracts were detrimental to mobility.

5.3.4 Firing and severance pay regulations

Workers laid off for economic reasons after three or more years of tenure are eligible for severance payments ranging from one to six months' wages. Under random selection for redundancy and full compliance, the existing regulations would imply an eligibility ratio of 75 per cent and an average severance pay exceeding two months' wages. The actual incidence and sum of severance payments are far lower than that. The NLC–EJS of 1994 suggests that only 20 per cent of the interviewed who had been laid off received severance pay, with the mean payment amounting to 0.7 of a month's wage. In the repeated survey of 2001 only 5.7 per cent of those made redundant were paid severance amounting, on average, to 0.4 of a month's wage. Payment receipt is limited by a strong bias towards redundancies for groups ineligible for severance pay rather than non-compliance with the regulations. The strengthening bias towards ineligible workers may be partly explained by enterprises wanting to reduce their adjustment costs, but a number of other reasons may have similar effect, such as a more frequent incidence of temporary lay-offs (discussed below) and a growing share of the tertiary sector and small firms.

5.3.5 Part-time employment and other flexible forms

Part-time employment is a potentially important point of departure from the communist legacy of open-ended contracts fixing a monthly salary and an eight-hour workday. Despite liberal regulations, part-time employment has continued to have a marginal and declining share in the Hungarian labour market, a trend only broken by a temporary increase in 1997–98. The proportion of employees working part time has remained at almost zero in prime-age cohorts: slightly above 1 per cent with males and 3.5 per cent with females according to LFS data from 2002. The NLC–EJS of 1994 and 2001 suggested slightly higher shares for *unemployed* women entering employment. While only 0.9 and 1.2 per cent of the male unemployment insurance benefits recipients entered part-time jobs in 1994 and 2001, the respective shares were 4.2 and 6.8 per cent for females.[3] In section 5.5 we come back to possible supply-side explanations of low shares.

Information on other forms of flexible employment is scarce and predominantly anecdotal. Under socialism, rigidities were substantially reduced by formal and informal multiple-job holding; formal second jobs seem to have now disappeared completely from the Hungarian labour market. According to LFS data, the proportion of employees holding more than one job fell from 4.1 per cent in 1992 to only 1.7 per cent recently (Fazekas, 2002, p. 318). The figures are similar to those reported for the Czech Republic in 1999 and considerably lower than those of Poland and Croatia in 1998 (Cazes and Nesporova, 2003, p. 50). The scope for informal multiple-job holding and moonlighting has been substantially reduced by the development of the tertiary sector and elimination of shortages.

Many experts argue that disguising the employment relationship as a 'business contract' is an alternative technique widely used to achieve higher flexibility (and evade taxes). Since changes in the legislation in 2003, disguised employment contracts have been treated as tax fraud, and inspections by the tax authorities have revealed a multitude of such cases. Another illegal means of increasing flexibility is to combine a fixed salary, typically equal to the minimum wage (in 2004, 11 per cent of employees were paid 95–105 per cent of the minimum wage), and additional payments in cash. Given the nature of these transactions, straightforward evidence on the magnitudes is difficult to find.

5.3.6 Unemployment assistance

A minority of those jobless workers who decide to stay in the labour market are eligible for insurance-based unemployment benefits and/or means-tested social benefits. Several papers based on comparative research found that in the first few years of the transition period the value of the Hungarian benefit package – at that time made up of unemployment insurance (UI) and unemployment assistance (UA) – was rather high in international comparisons (Burda, 1993; Bardasi et al., 2001). As discussed in detail in Nagy (2001a), the generosity of both benefits was later considerably reduced. The share of unemployed workers receiving any kind of benefit dropped from 62 per cent in 1992 to only 34 per cent in 2000, and the ratio of mean UI benefit to the average wage fell from 39 to 26 per cent in the same period.

---

[3] The surveys set the limit of part-time employment at 36 hours.

The maximum duration of eligibility was also cut from 24 to 12 months in the case of UI, and from indefinitely to 24 months in the case of UA. Nagy demonstrates that the historical decrease in coverage and the benefit–average wage ratio was explained by the tightening of benefits rather than compositional changes of the UI stock. Further reforms followed in January and May 2000, which included the shortening of the maximum duration of UI from 12 to 9 months and a slight decrease in the replacement ratio, the abolition of UA, and provision of a means-tested, flat-rate social benefit (SB) for non-employed adults, irrespective of their previous work history. The benefit is administered and managed by local government and is conditional on registration in labour offices and participation in public works (PW). Local governments are authorized to call social benefit recipients to do public works at any time and for any duration. (At least 30 days of public work has been set as a precondition of receipt of social benefit, though, in practice, local authorities can choose to pay social benefit without creating publicly useful jobs.) Furthermore, the real estate property of social benefit recipients can be mortgaged in favour of the local government.[4] Participants in public works, typically involving street cleaning, road repair, park maintenance and other low-skill activities, are paid the minimum wage, which compares favourably to social benefit. Galasi and Nagy (2001b) found a major, two-digit fall in UA/SB receipt as a result of these reforms.

5.3.7 Active labour market policies

At the end of the 1990s, Hungary's per-gross domestic product (GDP) and per-unemployed expenditures on active labour market policies (ALMPs) were relatively high compared to other transition countries (except for Slovenia and Poland) but way below the average of the EU and the OECD (Cazes and Nesporova, 2003, p. 117; Ederveen and Thissen, 2004, p. 23). A slight increase in the share of ALMP in total expenditures since then has not fundamentally changed the picture. While outlays for benefits and administration dropped from 2.7 to 0.7 per cent of the GDP in 1992–2000, ALMP expenditures also declined from 0.4 to about 0.3 per cent (Frey, 2001, p. 78). Recently, close to two-thirds of the employment policy budget is spent on benefits and one-quarter laid out for ALMP, with the rest covering the expenses of labour offices. The combined number of benefit recipients and ALMP participants fell by 26 per cent in 1992–2000, while total expenditures were cut by 64 per cent and ALMP expenditures decreased by 36 per cent, suggesting a decline in expenditure per unemployed person. This is explained by several factors, including the tightening of benefits and move to cheaper ALMP measures: in 1992, 15.5 per cent of the unemployment budget was spent on 13.4 per cent participating in ALMP; in 2000, 28.2 per cent of the budget covered the costs of 37.3 per cent participating in active programmes.

---

[4] The mortgage becomes effective on the death of the SB recipient, i.e. the cumulated benefit paid to the recipient can be reclaimed from his or her heirs.

5.3.8 Pensions

Massive flows to early retirement during the transition had strong and lasting impacts on the Hungarian labour market. Early retirement was explicitly encouraged by the governments of the early transition period, with the result that in 1991–97 early retirement (as opposed to old-age and disability pensions) accounted for a high and growing share of total retirement: 23 per cent in 1991, 27 per cent in 1994, and 30 per cent in 1997.

Flows to both early retirement and disability pensions during the transition were strongly affected by conditions on the labour market. Köllő and Nacsa (2005) estimated how the probability of being on a pension was explained by personal characteristics and variables describing conditions in the regional labour market. The model interacted the person's age with the unemployment rate of his or her place of residence. The coefficients of the interactive terms captured how the share of retired persons varied with local labour market conditions at single years of age. The estimated parameters suggested tremendous regional differences in the probability of being retired before the general retirement age: five years prior to the mandatory age limit, 37 per cent of the men were already retired, with the estimated proportion increasing from 18 to 56 per cent as we moved from the lower to the upper end of the one-standard-deviation range around mean local unemployment. The magnitudes were slightly lower with women. Likewise, low-educated persons and those living in low-wage regions were more likely to be living on a pension. Few of the retired women were single parents and many of them were grandmothers within the household.

Policies changed in 1998 in two important aspects. On the one hand, a gradual increase of the mandatory retirement age was announced, bringing it up from 60 to 62 years for men and from 55 to 62 years for women by 2010. Furthermore, a radical change of policy pushed the ratio of early to total retirement to 17 per cent in 1998 and 3–4 per cent in 1999–2001. The combined flows to early and disability pensions did not fall as dramatically as did entries to early retirement alone, and actually increased in 2000–01 (ONYF, 2001). We return to the effect of these policies in section 5.5.

5.3.9 Childcare benefit

Prior to 1996 and since January 2000, parents have been eligible for childcare benefit (GYED) until the child is aged two. The amount is 70 per cent of the average daily income, which constitutes the base of the sickness benefit calculation but can exceed a statutorily defined flat-rate amount. When the child is between two and three years of age, the parent at home is entitled to another type of childcare benefit (GYES) (eligibility can be extended to the tenth birthday of a seriously handicapped or impaired child). This monthly, flat-rate benefit is equal to the minimum old-age pension. To be entitled to childcare benefit, the person cannot receive any other regular income and cannot undertake work until the child is 18 months old. Beyond this age, the parent may work for up to four hours a day (there is no time limit when the work is performed at home). In 2006, GYES was extended to working parents too, effectively transforming this allowance into some sort of wage subsidy.

Childcare assistance (GYET) is payable to parents who are raising three or more children (the youngest has to be between three and eight years of age), and is the amount and subject to the same conditions regarding additional earnings and working hours as the GYES. The duration of any kind of childcare benefit is taken into account as a period of service in pension calculations.

Currently about 15 per cent of women under 45 years of age are receiving childcare benefit, with the proportion exceeding 30 per cent at 27–28 years. Men, though eligible for assistance, account for only 2 per cent of the recipients. As a rule, mothers receiving childcare benefit withdraw from the labour market, with only about 7 per cent of them being employed by ILO–OECD standards and 1 per cent searching actively for jobs, according to recent LFS data. LFS data from 1997–2003 gives the average period childcare as 4.2 years, varying between 2.3 years for college graduates and 5.6 years for mothers with primary school education.

Similarly to the case of early retirement, labour market conditions have a strong impact on flows to childcare. Estimates for 2000 in Köllő and Nacsa (2005) suggested that women living in high-unemployment regions were more likely to have children and, once they had children, were more likely to be on childcare benefit than were their counterparts in low-unemployment districts. The estimated difference between the 'best' and 'worst' regions amounted to about six percentage points. The level of education, another proxy of a person's labour market prospects, was closely correlated with the probability of having children but had no strong impact on the conditional likelihood of being on childcare benefit. However, the joint decision of having children and receiving childcare benefit was substantially higher for women with lower levels of education, particularly those with 0–7 years of education. Childcare as a labour market institution is addressed in section 5.5.

5.4 FLEXIBILITY: BEHAVIOURAL PATTERNS AND OUTCOMES

Consistent with what the international comparative literature suggests, Hungarian regulations do not seem highly restrictive. Wage setting is basically decentralized, more so than assumed in the country rankings extensively used in the international comparative research. Union density and coverage with collective wage agreements are low by international comparison. The minimum wage was increased substantially in 2001–02 but the minimum wage to average wage ratio remained 10 per cent below the median EU level and has been falling since 2002. The pecuniary costs of dismissals do not seem too heavy despite the existence of mandatory severance payments. Following a series of cuts, unemployment insurance covers only about 20 per cent of those actively searching for jobs. Only 18 per cent of those non-employed who want a job and 42 per cent of those who actively search receive any kind of social assistance.[5]

---

[5] The data relate to the end of 2001 and are based on the LFS.

Orthodox wisdom would predict high or rising employment on the basis of Hungary's institutional indicators and their direction of change. However, the overview in section 5.3 also draws attention to some specifics that call for caution. Despite changes in regulations, the combined flows to early retirement and disability pensions have remained high (after a transitory drop in 1998–99). Until recently, childcare schemes continued to provide a unique shelter for mothers with poor employment prospects. Socially useful and popular as they are, these institutions may curb labour supply as well as labour demand. (The costs of these schemes are low compared to expenditures on health, education, public administration, budget-financed investments and public debt payments, but they do contribute to high payroll taxes). Furthermore, the number of participants in ALMP fell substantially despite no remarkable change in the total number of people out of work – a kind of change generally considered detrimental to labour market performance. It should also be stressed that unconstrained wage setting, weak employment protection and parsimonious benefits do not guarantee high equilibrium employment. Wages may fall substantially without clearing the market if (some) firms have (some) monopsony power. Short-run considerations may dominate when dismissals have no costs. If the unemployed are not supported in their job search, they may not be able to afford a protracted period of searching for an adequate job.[6] These and similar considerations call for checking the outcomes empirically rather than blindly trusting baseline predictions.

5.4.1 Wage flexibility

The transition period brought about a degree of wage decompression unprecedented in the contemporary history of developed countries. The five-year change in the log wage differential between the 90th and 10th percentile of workers amounted to 0.16 in Hungary (1988–95), 0.19 in Poland (1988–95), 0.36 in the Czech Republic (1989–95) and 0.38 in Romania (1989–95). The magnitude of change was substantially larger than in the often-quoted cases of the United States in 1979–90 (0.07 with men and 0.14 with women) or the United Kingdom under Prime Minister Margaret Thatcher (0.12). Already in 1994, the log decile ratio of Hungary (1.33) exceeded that of the United Kingdom and was close to that of the United States (based on data from Katz et al., 1995, and Rutkowski, 1996a and 1996b). Educational and regional wage differentials have also been growing since the start of transition and have reached levels at or above the EU average.

The data hint at strong wage responses to changes in market conditions in the long run, but the study of wage flexibility generally focuses on how wages react to changes in the threat points of bargaining in the short run. (The threat points are usually approximated with ability-to-pay variables such as sales per worker or profit per

---

[6] Galasi (1996) demonstrated using Household Panel Survey data that while benefits increased reservation wages, they also raised the intensity of job search among the unemployed.

worker, on the one hand, and regional unemployment rates, on the other). Repeated cross-sectional estimates based on the WS (Nagy, 2001b, p. 70) suggest that the elasticity of net wages with respect to regional unemployment changed from close-to-zero level in 1989 to –0.1 in 1995–96, and fluctuated around –0.08 in 1997–2000. This is close to the elasticity of –0.1 regarded as a benchmark in the wage curve literature (Blanchflower and Oswald, 1994). The elasticity of wages with respect to sales per worker rose from 0.05 to 0.25 in the same period (Nagy, 2001b, ibid.). While these results capture behavioural changes over time, they are not controlled for regional fixed effects and fail to answer how wages respond to *changes* in ability-to-pay and outside options in the short run.

Models using panel data may bring us closer to answering this question. Köllő and Mickiewicz (2005) regressed wages on sales per worker and regional unemployment, relying on a panel of 300 large firms over 1996–99 and using a fixed-effects model with differenced variables and quantile regressions. All specifications estimate the elasticity of the wage with respect to sales per worker to be between 0.21 and 0.26, consistent with the cross-section estimates quoted earlier. They found that wages are usually not responsive to changes in unemployment but fall substantially when rising unemployment comes together with falling revenues.[7] Commander and Faggio (2003) used the Amadeus data set and estimated the productivity elasticity of the wage to be substantially higher (0.68) in first-differenced equations.

Collective wage agreements seem to have a measurable impact on wages. Neumann (2002) analysed the effect of collective agreements on wage levels and wage dispersion by estimating individual earnings functions for 1998. He concluded that collective agreements reduced the occurrence of low wages albeit without significantly affecting the level of the wage. He arrived at this conclusion by controlling the wage equation for the firm's average product; that is, assuming that collective agreements and sales per worker were exogenous and independent of each other. Kertesi and Köllő (2003a) estimated the union wage gap using the same data and assuming that market concentration results in high levels of sales per worker (monopoly rents) and high levels of unionization simultaneously. This assumption is conducive to a reduced-form wage equation, with concentration, unionization and their interaction on the right-hand side. Estimating the impact of these variables on industry-level earnings rents (coefficients of industry dummies in individual earnings regressions controlled for other wage determinants), they found the interactive effect to be rather strong. The elasticity of the industry wage rent with respect to industry-level collective bargaining was found to be zero at low levels of market concentration and 0.2 in the case of highly concentrated markets.[8] The

---

[7] If, for instance, sales revenues fall by one-fifth and local unemployment increases by one-fifth, wages are expected to fall by one-twelfth. The same change in unemployment has no measurable impact when the firm's revenues are on the rise.

[8] Coverage was measured as the combined number of workers in firms concluding collective wage agreements relative to total employment within the NACE-2 industries.

elasticity of the industry rent with respect to market concentration ranged between zero (no collective agreements) and 0.26 (full coverage). The results were driven by a relatively small group of industries with high levels of market concentration, unionization and wages. The group included petroleum extraction and refining, the energy sector, mail and telecommunication, rail, air and public transport, and the tobacco and chemical industries. The comparison of the Hungarian industrial wage structure with those of several European market economies reinforced that these industries indeed paid (and continue to pay) high wages relative to their Western counterparts. However, the fundamental results were similar to Neumann's in suggesting a weak effect of collective bargaining in the bulk of the competitive sector, where unionization and/or market concentration is at low levels.

5.4.2   Demand elasticities

Kőrösi (2000 and 2002) addresses the elasticity of demand for homogeneous labour with respect to wages using short panels of enterprises and a variety of econometric specifications. The models using lagged output and wages did not provide stable long-run elasticities; the short-run elasticities rose in absolute value during early years of the transition and fell afterwards (this related to the output elasticities, too). The demand elasticities estimated for more recent periods by Kőrösi (2002), Halpern et al. (2004) and Kertesi and Köllő (2003b) are all significantly negative and fall between –0.2 and –0.5 depending on the type of firm and type of labour, suggestive of a relatively low responsiveness of demand to changes in labour costs (table 5.5). However, the estimates do fall within the range observed in developed market economies (see an overview in Hamermesh, 1996). They are also rather similar to recent estimates for Poland (–0.2) and Romania (–0.3) presented in Commander and Faggio (2003).[9]

The minimum wage hikes of 2001 and 2002 provided a quasi-experimental test of these demand flexibility estimates. Halpern et al. (2004) calibrated a macro-model relying on, inter alia, the demand elasticity estimates quoted in table 5.5, and predicted a 0.47–1.1 per cent fall in aggregate employment as a response to the first hike. Analysing the observed changes, Kertesi and Köllő (2003b) concluded that aggregate employment fell by 0.5–1.1 per cent depending on assumptions made on the effects on some unobserved sectors (budget sector, micro-firms).

5.4.3   Adjustment costs

The labour demand models quoted in the previous section do not address the issue of adjustment, and implicitly assume quadratic adjustment costs, that is, expenses growing at increasing rate with the magnitude of employment change irrespective of

---

[9] Commander and Faggio (2003) estimate an elasticity of –0.7 for Bulgaria, a value similar to that found in Hungary at early stages of the transition.

Table 5.5   Estimates of the labour cost elasticity of labour demand for Hungary

Model	Period	Type of firm, type of labour	Estimates	Source
Differenced single equation C-D		*Homogeneous labour*		
Estimated with OLS	1992	Large exporting firms	−0.80	Kőrösi (2000)
	1993–95		−0.56	
	1996–99		−0.23	
Estimated with OLS	1992–95	Medium and large firms[1]	−0.61	Kőrösi (2002)
	1996–97		−0.32	
Estimated with IV[2]	2000–01	Firms 5–20 employees	−0.39	Kertesi and
		Firms 51–300 employees	−0.43	Köllő (2003b)
		Firms over 300 employees	−0.04	
Translog cost function		*Large firms*		
Estimated in repeated cross-sections with SURE[3]	1996–99	Unskilled labour[4]	−0.47	Halpern et al. (2004)
		Young skilled labour[5]	−0.14	
		Old skilled labour[6]	−0.19	

Notes: [1] From the model with the variables in first differences, p. 12. Mean of the annual estimates. [2] Exposure to the minimum wage increase used as an instrument. [3] Mean of the annual estimates. [4] Lower than secondary education. [5] Secondary or higher education, lower than median experience. [6] Secondary or higher education, higher than median experience.

its direction. This is a strong assumption that can be violated in several ways in practice. Kőrösi and Surányi (2002) estimated models of adjustment costs and found these costs to be significantly lower than those estimated for Western Europe. Their preferred specification suggested average costs of 3.6 months' wages as compared to estimates reaching 12–14 months' wages in developed market economies (surveyed in Hamermesh, 1996).

The practice of temporary lay-offs is one of the specifics making the United States labour market more flexible than that of the EU. It seems that Hungary's practices fall closer to those of the United States, in that temporary lay-offs occur on a large scale. Though the available data are insufficient for assessing the share of temporary lay-off unemployment in total unemployment, in general the 1994 and 2001 NLC–EJS surveys of exit to jobs consistently suggest remarkable magnitudes. The 1994 survey does not directly observe whether the workers entered a new job or re-entered their old jobs, but the proportions could be estimated using information on the pre-unemployment and post-unemployment employers. Similar estimates together with direct observations are

Table 5.6   Exit to new jobs versus re-entry to old jobs among UI recipients finding
employment in April, Hungary, 1994 and 2001 (percentages)

	April 1994 Estimated	April 2001 Estimated	Observed
Entry to new job	61.0	32.3	44.5
Re-entry to old job	19.3	39.9	37.2
Unknown	19.7	27.8	18.3
Total	100.0	100.0	100.0
New/(old + new)	0.24	0.55	0.46

Source: Data from NLC–EJS; own computations.

available in the 2001 survey. The data summarized in table 5.6 suggest that the share of re-entry rose from an estimated one-quarter in 1994 to one-half in 2001. Since both surveys were conducted in April, at the start of the agricultural and construction season, the figures are evidently upward-biased. Nonetheless they hint at a substantial and growing share of temporary lay-off unemployment.

The temporary lay-off periods observed in the NLC–EJS were of a seasonal character from the firms' but not from the workers' point of view. Rehired workers' unemployment spells typically lasted for six months, and re-entry was mostly directed at agriculture, construction, and hotels and restaurants. However, the median rehired worker had two long job spells (lasting for 3.7 years on average) in the ten years preceding the interview, which were interrupted by three shorter spells of unemployment. It seems that firms actually disperse the burden of seasonal adjustment among their employees rather than regularly sending the same people on yearly unemployment holidays.[10]

5.4.4   Labour turnover

In table 5.7 we present a descriptive regression estimating the probability that a worker observed in the WS was hired in the year preceding the survey year. We use the 1998 wave of the survey that was supplemented with information on unionization and product market characteristics. The model is capable of providing rough information on turnover, as we are able to control the equation for changes in the firm's level of employment. The coefficients of other explanatory variables thus capture variations in the share of newly hired workers across firms with similar rates of net job destruction or job creation.

---

[10] It is perhaps worth mentioning that the Hungarian UI system is not experience-rated and therefore provides hidden subsidies to seasonal industries, as argued by Feldstein (1976) and others.

Table 5.7   The characteristics of newly hired workers, Hungary, 1998 (probabilistic regression)

Variable	Coefficient	Mean	Standard deviation
Change in the firm's level of employment			
1997–98 (log)	.0562***	−.014	.282
Experience	−.0151***	21.7	10.6
Experience squared	.0002***	583.0	464.4
Male	.0039	.601	..
Years in school	.0004	11.1	2.4
Non-manual job	−.0205***	.301	..
Managerial job	−.0404***	.018	..
Shift work	.0117***	.289	..
Regional unemployment (log)	−.0116***	−2.722	.491
Budapest	.0038	.247	..
5–20 employees	−.0385***	.065	..
21–50 employees	−.0080	.105	..
51–300 employees	−.0100**	.301	..
301–1000 employees	−.0064*	.210	..
Capital–labour ratio (firm, log)	−.0035***	.454	1.559
Owner: domestic private	.0310***	.502	..
Owner: foreign	.0417***	.273	..
No majority owner	.0205***	.030	..
Firm covered by collective agreement (dummy)	−.0807***	.461	..
Market concentration[1] (log)	.0097***	−1.315	.787
Collective agreement x market concentration (log)	−.0275***	−.455	.702
Mining	−.0172	.005	..
Manufacturing	.0175***	.407	..
Energy	−.0035	.052	..
Construction	.0135*	.051	..
Wholesale and retail trade	.0304***	.116	..
Hotels and restaurants	.0352***	.021	..
Transport	.0342***	.123	..
Banking and insurance	.0560***	.036	..
Services	.0563***	.070	..
Other	.0204	.0232	..
Constant	.2526***	..	..

Notes: [1] Market concentration is measured as the share in sales of the three largest firms in NACE-3 industries (178 distinct values). .. = not applicable.

The dependent variable is 1 if the worker was hired 6–18 months before the survey, and 0 otherwise. The reference categories are manual job, more than 1000 employees, majority state ownership, agriculture. Adjusted $R^2 = 0.0633$. Robust standard errors. Significant at the *** 0.001, ** 0.05, * 0.1 level. The unmarked coefficients are not significant at the 0.1 level.

Source: Wage Survey sample of 88,614 workers in firms observed in both 1997 and 1998.

Table 5.8   Employees with 0–6 months' tenure as a percentage of total
employment, Hungary, 1997–2001

	1997	1998	1999	2000	2001
Hungary	8.2	8.5	7.1	6.9	6.3
Czech Republic	7.0	7.0	6.3	..	..

Notes: Tenure is measured in completed months. .. = not available.

Sources: Cazes and Nesporova, 2003, table 4.6, for the Czech Republic; LFS for Hungary.

The results suggest that the newcomers are younger, more likely to be manual work-ers, and hired for shift work. Consistent with expectations, the equation hints at slightly lower turnover in high-unemployment regions, firms with a high capital to labour ratio and state enterprises. The turnover rates appear to be higher in the tertiary sector, par-ticularly services. The differences by education and gender are statistically insignificant.

More importantly, turnover appears to be significantly lower in companies covered by collective agreements, with the effect of unionization on turnover being strongest in highly concentrated industries. Likewise, market concentration only restricts turnover at unionized firms. Firm size per se seems to reduce rather than increase the share of newcomers. Note that the combination of high market power and high union density is also conducive to high wages in Hungary, as was discussed earlier, pointing to departures from a pure competitive model.

Though monopoly power and falling demand elasticities hint at imperfections in the Hungarian labour market, these do not seem to be particularly severe. A com-parison of tenure data from Hungary and the Czech Republic (acknowledged to have a high-mobility labour market compared to the rest of the Central and Eastern European countries) suggests no significant difference between the two countries. While the proportion of newly hired workers was falling in Hungary in 1997–2001, it was marginally higher than in the Czech Republic in those years when a comparison was possible (table 5.8).

5.5   WELFARE SCHEMES

The combination of laissez-faire regulations and extremely low employment levels evidently direct the analysts' attention to supply-side and incentive issues. In this section we try to summarize the available research results on unemployment benefits, retirement and childcare schemes.

5.5.1   Unemployment benefits

Studies of how tightening UI benefits affected outflows to jobs have repeatedly found no significant effect. These results have been reinforced by several impact studies of the reform of the benefit system in 2000. Galasi and Nagy (2001a) followed two cohorts of UI recipients – workers starting their UI spells right before and right after the reform – and used non-parametric models to analyse changes in their exit-to-job hazards. Similarly to an earlier study on the effects of the 1993 reform (Micklewright and Nagy, 1994), they found no increase in the probability of job finding as a result of lower benefits. In a second study (2001b), Galasi and Nagy followed two cohorts of UI exhausters – one group eligible for UA and the other for SB. Workers were interviewed six months after UI exhaustion about their labour market careers and benefit status. The results were a minor, statistically insignificant increase in workers' probability of finding a job and a major, two-digit fall in benefit receipt. The main consequence of the benefit reform, they argued, was the drop in benefit receipt – a simple cut of the social safety net without a marked impact on incentives.

Fazekas' municipality-level analysis (2001) provides part of the explanation for the decline in benefit receipt. He estimated that mortgaging the real estate property of recipients reduces the ratio of SB recipients to UI exhausters (SB/UIX) by 4.2 percentage points holding other variables constant. The effect of the public works requirement on benefit receipt was analysed by regressing SB/UIX on the ex ante ratio of public workers to SB recipients (PW/SB lagged). A one-standard-deviation difference in the municipality-level PW/SB ratio reduced SB/UIX by 3 percentage points. Other things being equal, village dwellers were less likely to receive SB, which was interpreted as an indication of more effective monitoring in smaller communities.

Finally, Köllő (2001) analysed the exit-to-job rates of UI recipients in April 2001, 15 months after the benefit reform. He found that the benefit–wage ratio had no effect on exit but that remaining eligible did have an impact. However, the disincentive effect of benefits was significant with, and only with, skilled workers who have secondary or higher education.

The research results are consistent in suggesting that variations in the benefit replacement ratio have a weak impact on job search behaviour and exit from unemployment in Hungary. Gábos and Szívós (2001) demonstrate using Household Budget Survey data that only about 9 per cent of the income of unemployed households (families with at least one unemployed member) is accounted for by unemployment compensation. Consequently, a small change in the benefit exerts a weak influence on the value of being unemployed, and is unlikely to have a marked impact on the labour market. The exhaustion of benefit eligibility, on the other hand, affects the worker's non-wage income more fundamentally and has been found to affect job search behaviour, mirroring findings in other countries (see for instance Katz and Meyer, 1990, for evidence for the United States).

5.5.2 Retirement policies

Starting to increase the retirement age, effectively abolishing unemployment-alleviating early retirement schemes and tightening disability pension checks in 1998 were risky steps. Closing this important escape route from the labour market

Figure 5.2 Change of employment of pensioners and non-pensioners, by age and sex, Hungary, 1992–97 and 1997–2003 (percentages)

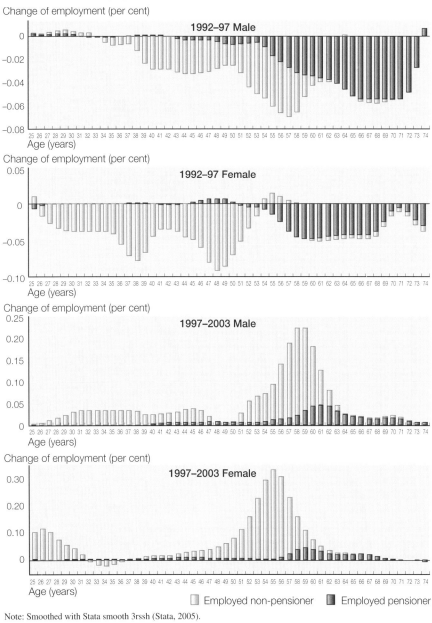

Note: Smoothed with Stata smooth 3rssh (Stata, 2005).

Source: LFS, October–December 1992, 1997, 2003.

could have led to growing unemployment in the generations affected. However, the measures also blocked another established form of employment adjustment, that of forcing the elderly to retire, and so extended the working career of many older workers. The measures also reduced (but did not eliminate) the scope for using the early retirement pension as a subsidy to informal and/or part-time employment. It seems that the balance of these and potential other effects was finally positive: employment grew substantially, up to 25–30 percentage points among people in their fifties and early sixties. This is shown by the bar charts of figure 5.2, looking at changes of employment by single year of age in 1992–97 and 1997–2003 (the post-reform period).[11] While the net effect of the reform package has not been clarified as yet, it certainly made it easier for these large positive changes to happen.

A closer inspection of the data reveals that in 1997–2003 employment ratios grew in the retired as well as the non-retired population: what happened was more than just a shift of some people from a low-activity state (pensioner status) to a high-activity one. We apply a simple descriptive decomposition to show the structure of employment change. From equations (1a) and (1b) giving cohort t's employment ratio as a weighted average of pensioner (P) and non-pensioner employment ratios (E^P and E^{NP}), in periods 0 and 1, we derive decomposition (1c). The first and the second components capture the effects of changes in non-pensioner and pensioner activity rates respectively, while c_3 quantifies the impact of a change in pensioners' share.

(1a) $\quad F_{1t} = P_{1t} E_{1t}^{P} + (1 - P_{1t}) E_{1t}^{NP}$

(1b) $\quad E_{0t} = P_{0t} E_{0t}^{P} + (1 - P_{0t}) E_{0t}^{NP}$

(1c) $\quad \Delta E_{t} = \Delta E^{NP}(1 - \overline{P_t}) + \Delta E^{P}\overline{P_t} + \Delta P_t (\overline{E_t}^{P} - \overline{E_t}^{NP}) = c_1 + c_2 + c_3$

Figure 5.3 shows the contribution of the three components to growing activity for cohorts aged 40–70 years. The data suggest growing employment among non-pensioners in the typical base-period of the early retirement age range (50–55 years for women and 55–60 years for men), and fast-growing activity among pensioners, especially men, between the old and new retirement ages (55–58 years for women and 60–62 years for men) and older. This is explained by the possibility of retiring between the two age limits (without deduction) when a worker has reached the required years-in-work limit. Many of these retirees continue to be employed legally, and typically part time, by their former employers while they also collect old-age pensions. While the reforms most probably contributed to increasing employment of the elderly, it seems that they did so partly by a shift from subsidizing early retirement to subsidizing the employment of old-age pensioners.

---

[11] The series were smoothed with Stata's 'smooth 3rssh'(Stata, 2005).

Figure 5.3 Components of change in the employment ratio by age, sex and
pension status, Hungary, cumulated percentages 1997–2003

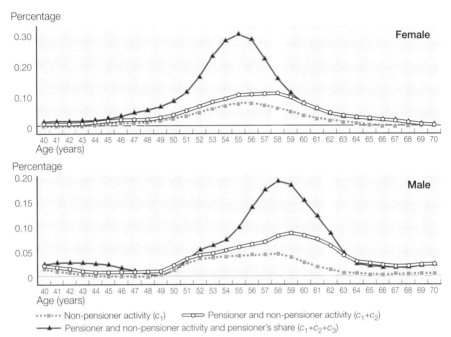

Note: Smoothed with Stata smooth 3rssh (Stata, 2005).

Source: LFS, October–December 1992, 1997, 2003.

5.5.3 Childcare

Unlike retirement schemes, childcare programmes have remained widely available
and generous until recently. Following a period of austerity in 1995–98, eligibility for
the GYES was extended to all mothers, irrespective of work history, and the GYED
was reintroduced in 1999. The effect of these reforms and other variables on the
duration of childcare spells is studied in table 5.9.[12]

The marginal effects from a discrete time duration logit (Jenkins, 1995) presented
in table 5.9 measure inactive childcare recipients' probability of exit to jobs
conditional on the age of their youngest child. The estimates point to high education-
specific differentials, especially in high-unemployment municipalities. Exit rates
were higher in case of multi-family households, though the effect was not significant

---

[12] We thank Mónika Bálint (Institute of Economics) for constructing the database and taking part in the estimations.

Table 5.9 The probability of exit to job from a childcare spell in 1995–2003 in Hungary (effects measured in a discrete time duration model)

	Municipality-level unemployment rate	
	>11%	≤11%
Male	0.675	1.203**
Age	0.341***	0.365***
Age squared	−0.005***	−0.006***
0–8 years in school	−2.749***	−1.378***
Vocational attainment	−1.101***	−1.158***
Secondary attainment	−0.811***	−0.817***
Age of youngest child	3.129***	5.091***
Age of youngest child squared	−0.387***	−0.674***
Number of children aged 0–6	−0.640***	−0.639***
Type of support: GYED	1.781***	1.849***
Type of support: GYES	2.094***	1.805***
Two or more families in the household	0.400*	0.480
Local nursery	0.396***	0.149
1996	0.054	0.179
1997	−0.222	−0.089
1998	−0.162	−0.040
1999	−0.802***	−0.421
2000	−0.706***	−0.797***
2001	−0.397*	−0.577**
2002	−0.480**	−0.444*
2003	−0.836*	0.732
Number of observations	23.816	23.466
Wald Chi-squared	530.32***	561.15***
Pseudo-R^2	0.127	0.131
Mean exit rate (%)	1.57	1.91

Notes: Significant at the * 0.1, ** 0.05, *** 0.01 levels. The reference groups are female, college attainment, type of support: GYET, one family, no nursery, 1995. The estimation method is a discrete time duration model in the logit form following Jenkins, 1995. Marginal effects are in per cent. The dependent variable is 1 if the respondent was employed by ILO–OECD criteria in quarter t+1. Exits to unemployment and inactivity are treated as censored outcomes, using a pooled sample of 36 quarterly LFS waves from 1995 to 2003. Estimates are measured as the ratio of registered unemployed to personal income tax payers and presented separately for high and low municipality-level unemployment rates. The mean quarterly exit rates are 1.57 per cent in the former and 1.91 per cent in the latter sub-sample.

Source: Data from LFS, 1995–2003.

at conventional levels. The presence of a local childcare institution (nursery) increased the probability of exit by one-quarter in villages or towns with high local unemployment, hinting at the lack of local job opportunities and the need to commute to the workplace. (Nurseries were widespread under communism. During the transition more than half of the nurseries were closed. In the period under investigation as much as 75 per cent of the mothers of the high-unemployment sub-sample lived in municipalities with no nursery.)

It seems that the extension of the childcare system in 1999 led to massive inflows of women with low employment probabilities, as suggested by a dramatic fall of the exit rate in both sub-samples. This effect was amplified by the re-introduction of GYED, which provides high compensation in the early stage of a childcare period, and often ends in a shift to the GYES. While in low-unemployment areas the exit rate returned to its previous level by 2002, and grew further in 2003, it remained persistently low in the high-unemployment areas.

5.5.4 Dilemmas

While Hungary's permissive early retirement schemes and generous childcare programmes are often blamed for supporting protracted withdrawal from the labour market, in some respect they also *increase* flexibility by paving the way to part-time employment and other flexible forms of participation. While part-time employment is non-frequent in Hungary among prime-age workers (4 per cent working usually less than 30 hours a week in 2003), remarkable shares are observed with workers above the retirement age (32 per cent). Furthermore, it seems that part-time employment is particularly widespread among workers who receive either a pension or childcare benefit. Part-timers accounted for 3.2 per cent of the workers who received no transfer whereas the respective shares were 39 per cent with working old-age pensioners, 50 per cent with employees receiving disability pension, and 63 per cent with working mothers on childcare. Altogether, nearly 40 per cent of the part-time workers received either a pension or childcare benefit in 2003.

Most analysts blame employers' fixed costs, such as screening and training costs, and the flat-rate health contribution (*eho*) for keeping the share of part-time employment low by European standards. We do not find these explanations particularly convincing. According to the available estimates, Hungarian adjustment costs are small compared to Western Europe, and the introduction of the *eho* in 1999 can hardly explain why part-time employment was so low throughout the transition period. The data suggest that workers' fixed costs may have more to do with the problem. Given that the non-labour income net of pecuniary fixed costs is higher for people receiving a pension or childcare benefit, this group may be more willing to accept part-time jobs at the prevailing hourly wage rate.

This conclusion is consistent with what we observe in table 5.10. The hourly wages of part-time workers receiving a pension or childcare benefit are only marginally higher than those paid to full-time employees: they work 51.3 per cent less and earn 47.3 per cent less than full-timers. By contrast, workers not receiving transfers seem to accept

Table 5.10 Working hours and earnings of part-time workers, Hungary, April–June 2001

Pension or childcare	Weekly hours		Regression-adjusted wage as % of wage paid to observationally equivalent full-timers[1]	
	Hours	(full-timer=100)	Monthly	Hourly
Yes	19.1	48.7	52.7	110.1
No	20.9	51.1	68.3	134.9

Notes: [1] Regressions using data from the LFS–S, April–June 2001. Controlled for gender, age, education, 10 industry dummies, 10 occupation dummies, 5 firm size dummies, unionized firm dummy, Budapest dummy and the local unemployment rate.

part-time jobs conditional on relatively high hourly wages: they work 48.9 per cent less and earn only 31.7 per cent less, which is tantamount to a margin of 34.9 per cent above the hourly wage rate paid to observationally similar full-timers.

5.6   CONCLUSIONS

A worker or employer entering the contemporary Hungarian labour market faces relatively few binding regulations. Jobs are not strongly protected. The key elasticities and mobility indices do not hint at major institutional failures. Unemployment is low: one of the lowest in Europe. Whether one can regard the labour market flexible on these grounds largely depends on whether one does or does not include the problem of lasting inactivity in the discussion. We have argued it should be included. Accordingly, the trade-off addressed in this chapter is between social conflict and flexibility rather than job protection and flexibility. From the start of transition, Hungary has followed a policy of letting the hard-to-employ groups leave the labour market, supported by a pension, childcare benefit or social benefit. It is a policy that reduces flexibility in the first place (since few of the people in question search for jobs) while also allowing greater flexibility – this increase is conditional, however, on pensions, childcare benefits and social benefits being used to subsidize part-time employment and locally organized welfare economies. Finding a balance between protection of the 'unemployable', subsidization of part-time employment and creation of incentives to return to the labour market seems to be the hard nut to crack for Hungarian policy-makers.

ANNEX 5.1 DESCRIPTIONS OF DATA SETS

Wage Survey (WS)

The WS is an annual survey conducted by the National Labour Centre (NLC) each May since 1992. In the waves used in this chapter the sampling procedure was as follows. The firm census provided by the Central Statistical Office (CSO) serves as the sampling frame. It is a legal obligation for each firm employing more than 20 workers to fill in a firm-level questionnaire and provide individual data on a 10 per cent random sample of the employees. Budget institutions irrespective of size have to fill in the institution-level questionnaire and provide individual data on all employees. Firms employing fewer than 20 workers according to the census are sampled in a procedure stratified by four-digit industries. The firms contacted are obliged to fill in the firm-level questionnaire and provide individual demographic and wage data on all employees. The observations are weighted to ensure representativeness. About 180,000 individuals employed in 20,000 firms and budget institutions were observed in 1999–2001.

Labour Force Survey (LFS)

The LFS is a representative quarterly household survey conducted by the Central Statistical Office (CSO) since 1992. Data are collected about each member of the surveyed households and an 'activity questionnaire' is filled in by those aged 15–74. The survey has a rotating panel structure with, each quarter, one-sixth of the sample dropped after spending six quarters in the survey, and replaced with a randomly chosen new cohort. The number of observations varied between 82,000 and 85,000 in 1999–2001. Individuals can be identified across waves. The cases are weighted by the CSO to ensure representativeness. All calculations in this chapter used these weights.

LFS supplementary survey, April–June 2001

The LFS does not collect wage data. In this particular wave respondents working as employees or cooperative members (22,415 out of 30,485 workers employed by ILO–OECD standards) were asked to state their last month's gross or net earnings. The gross value of net earnings was calculated by the CSO using tax tables. We used the gross figures as reported by the CSO and weighted the cases followed in a spell panel with their base period weights of April–June 2001.

National Labour Centre–Exit to Jobs Survey (NLC–EJS), April 2001

Between 22 March and 7 April 2001, the NLC interviewed all workers leaving the UI register to take up employment. The workers were interviewed when they contacted the office to collect the documents necessary to start the job. They were asked about their minimum and maximum expected gross monthly earnings in the first months after being hired. The file used in Chapter 5 contains the data of 105,957 recipients in the stock on 22 March 2001 and interviews with 9,131 workers finding a job. Of them, 8,811 workers provided wage data. The wage and benefit concepts used in the chapter are (i) gross monthly earnings in the four calendar quarters prior to the last UI spell, adjusted for wage inflation between the time of job loss and March 2001; (ii) the mean of the minimum and maximum expected earnings; and (iii) the monthly values of the pre-tax daily UI benefit assuming 30.5 days per month.

LITHUANIA

6

Boguslavas Gruzevskis* and Inga Blaziene**

6.1   INTRODUCTION

With the collapse of the Soviet Union, Lithuania experienced huge political, economic and social transformations. These transformations had a direct effect on the labour market of Lithuania, significantly changing employment relations and triggering the creation of new labour legislation and labour market institutions. In this respect, Lithuania's situation is very similar to that of the other transition countries. Overall changes in the economic situation and liberalization of employment protection legislation have reduced both employment security and social security for workers, but employers are still dissatisfied with the current situation and feel disadvantaged vis-à-vis their competitors. One feature particular to Lithuania that might be stressed in this context is its particularly low labour force organization: according to different sources, Lithuania stands at the bottom of European rankings by level of union density as well as by coverage of collective agreements.

The main source of statistical data used in this chapter is the labour force survey (LFS). Although the LFS was started in Lithuania in 1994, comparable data are only available from 1998 and some indices used in this report have only been collected since 2000. Whereas too short data series might reduce the reliability of some identified trends, the main focus in this chapter is on spatial rather than time-related comparisons.

As labour market inflows and outflows and job-tenure data analysed here show, the Lithuanian labour market can be characterized in general as neither too fluid nor too dynamic; indeed it is fairly stagnant. On the other hand some flexibility indices in the country (such as temporary employment) are rising.

---

* Institute of Labour and Social Research, Vilnius University. ** Institute of Labour and Social Research, Vilnius Gediminas Technical University.

Changes in employment protection legislation in Lithuania could be described as liberalizing. After the adoption of the new Labour Code in 2002 (which came into force on 1 January 2003) a significant part of labour relations regulation was transferred to the local or enterprise level (and became the responsibility of the social partners). However, because of the abovementioned low level of labour force organization, a substantial number of the provisions of the Labour Code are inoperative in practice and the employers are the main actors determining labour relations. Nonetheless, employers are still unhappy with the existing employment protection legislation, considering it too strict.

On the social security side it should be said that existing passive and active labour market measures as well as social security policy measures (as they relate to labour market and social security policies) have been insufficient to compensate the loss of employment protection. Unemployment and social assistance benefits as well as active labour market policies secure only very low standards of living and are not nearly enough to stimulate the human development of the unemployed. Moreover, our research indicates that there is a 'negative' complementarity[1] (Auer and Cazes, 2003) between employment protection and passive labour market policies and that there is no well-conceived linkage between employment protection and active labour market policies in Lithuania.

The transformation of the Lithuanian economy as well as changes in the labour market had an increasing negative impact on the combination of employment protection and labour market policies, and did not provide the relevant level of flexibility to firms and security to workers.

There have been cardinal changes in the sphere of flexibility and employment security since Lithuania's accession to the European Union on 1 May 2004. Accession brought with it a new and significant mobility of qualified labour, coupled with rapid economic growth, which created a skilled labour shortage. This stimulated employers to pay more attention to employee incentives and to support government initiatives to increase employment security. There were also a number of legislative amendments and new legislation adopted over 2004–06 which considerably increased social security.

The Law on Works Councils came into force on 1 January 2005. Works councils were established in around 10 per cent of enterprises inspected by the State Labour Inspectorate in 2005. Unfortunately, no systemized information about their activities has been made available so far, but their activities are expected to contribute to minimizing the scope of informal employment and violations of remuneration for work (delayed payments in particular), to increase transparency of remuneration and to have a positive impact on payment for overtime.

---

[1] The term 'complementarity' here means the lower the employment protection, the lower the security guarantees; i.e., the more an employee is underprotected in the labour market (is working under temporary contract or so-called 'oral agreement', receives wages cash in hand, etc.), the smaller the chances this employee will be able to receive unemployment benefit (or higher benefit) (see Auer and Cazes, 2003, p. 5).

In the light of these recent trends, the new economic and political environment of today's Lithuania should radically change the present situation and stimulate social dialogue – one of the prerequisites for the development of flexicurity.

Social and employment policy-makers as well as labour market institutions and actors should adapt their measures and attitudes towards the changing situation in order to promote new developments. The Government should create social dialogue which is favourable to and stimulates the business environment; active LMP should shift its social orientation towards an emphasis on employability. The social partners should fundamentally change their attitudes to each other as well, moving from an attitude of confrontation to one of partnership. Employers should pay serious consideration to the expansion of worker loyalty through different means (financial, competence improvement, career possibilities), while employees should be prepared to face changing circumstances and be ready to supply the qualities they are expected to provide.

The stable growth of the economy, coupled with the rise of average and minimum wages, are nonetheless crucial preconditions for developing flexicurity. The poverty–unemployment trap problem that persists in Lithuania does not motivate low-qualified employees with children to start work and can induce informal employment or undeclared work. It should be noted that these problems have been addressed recently by increasing the minimum wage and the minimum taxable income, and personal income tax is going to be reduced in the near future. The Value Added Tax Law and Personal Income Tax Law are scheduled to include significant exemptions for the self-employed. The development of small and medium-sized enterprises (SMEs), the network of business incubators, as well as guarantee funds and business information centres, are promoted by different means. All these measures should not only increase employment diversity, but also increase employment flexibility and the availability of different options in the labour market.

6.2   MAIN CHARACTERISTICS AND ISSUES OF THE LITHUANIAN LABOUR MARKET

6.2.1 Demographic trends

Lithuania is experiencing rapid demographic changes. Due to a diminishing birth rate and comparatively large-scale emigration, the Lithuanian population is steadily decreasing. At the beginning of 2004, the population stood at 3.45 million; by 2005 this had dropped to 3.42 million and at the beginning of 2006 was at only 3.4 million. In the period 2000–06 the Lithuanian population decreased by almost 110,000. Lithuanian Statistics forecasts a further decline, estimating that by 2010 the population is likely to have fallen to 3.32 million and to 3.24 million by 2020. The actual reduction might be even more significant, in light of the rapid labour force migration.

At the beginning of 2006, the majority of the population in Lithuania (66.2 per cent) comprised urban residents; the working-age population made up approximately

63 per cent of urban residents and approximately 57 per cent of rural residents. At present urban residents aged 60 years and over account for 19 per cent of the population, while rural residents in this age group represent 24 per cent, as the decreasing birth rate and longer average longevity are creating an ageing society. In 2005 pensioners made up 21 per cent of the total population. According to forecasts made by Lithuanian Statistics, by 2030 as many as 27 per cent of Lithuanian residents will be over 60 years old.

6.2.2 Recent employment trends

The recent growth of the Lithuanian economy is beneficial to employment. The key labour market indicators show significant improvements: labour force demand is growing and employment is increasing, while the unemployment rate as well as its territorial differentiation is shrinking.

More and more permanent jobs are being created in the economy. Data from the Lithuanian Labour Exchange (LLE) show that territorial labour exchanges are registering annually approximately 132,000–137,000 vacancies. In 2003, there were 1.4 million employees in Lithuania, half of them women, representing a growth of 6.4 per cent since 2001; by 2005, the employed population had grown to 1.47 million. It should be noted that during 2001–05, gross domestic product (GDP) grew three to four times faster than employment.

The employment rate has kept growing as the number of employed increases, reaching 63.3 per cent in 2005 (see figure 6.1). However, national policy-makers forecast that Lithuania will not reach the EU employment target of 70 per cent by 2010.

The employment rate varies by population group. Male and female employment rates are at around the same level, at 65.2 and 58.9 per cent in 2005. The youth (aged

Figure 6.1 Actual and forecast number of employed persons (15–64 years) and employment rate (percentages), Lithuania, 2000–10

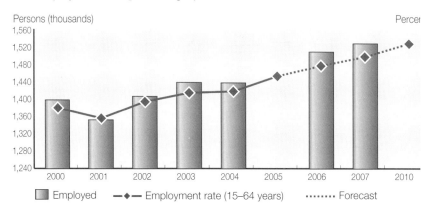

Source: Ministry of Social Security and Labour, 2004.

15–24 years) employment rate has been falling year by year and in 2005 was at 20.4 per cent. This tendency might be explained in part by the permanently increasing numbers of students: according to Lithuanian Statistics the number of pupils and students per 10,000 population during the 1990–2003 period increased by 27 per cent; the number of graduates from universities in Lithuania even doubled over 1993–2003. The employment rate for the 25–54 years age group continues to grow – increasing from 75 per cent in 2001 to 78.8 per cent in 2003. The employment rate of older people (aged 55–64 years) is growing as well, standing at 46.8 per cent in 2005.

In 2003, 54 per cent of those employed worked in the service sector; 28.1 per cent in industry and construction; 17.9 per cent in agriculture, hunting, forestry and fisheries. The developments in 2004 and 2005 have had a positive impact on the employment structure, with a decline in the share of employment in agriculture, hunting, forestry and fisheries to 14 per cent in 2005. Separate sectors of the economy differ in terms of male and female employment. In 2003 the number of women employed in the public sector exceeded that of men by a factor of 1.8, whereas the private sector employed 1.3 times more men than women. The sector of education remains predominantly female, with women workers accounting for 81 per cent of all individuals employed in this field. Employed men predominate in public administration and defence, compulsory social insurance and transport, warehousing and communications.

6.2.3 Incidence and persistence of unemployment

In the transition from a planned to a market economy, Lithuania experienced a considerable reduction in output (GDP), followed by a rapid decrease in the population in employment and an increase in unemployment levels.

In 2001, Lithuania recorded the highest numbers of unemployed during the entire period of independence (2.2 million) (figure 6.1). The highest unemployment rate in the country was recorded that year as well (figure 6.2). Although the

Figure 6.2 Registered unemployed, Lithuania, 1992–2005 (thousands)

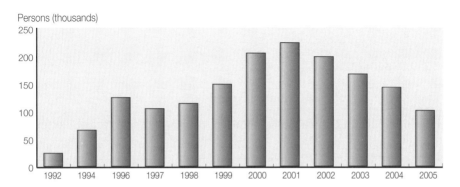

Source: LLE.

Figure 6.3 Average annual unemployment rate, Lithuania, 1995–2005

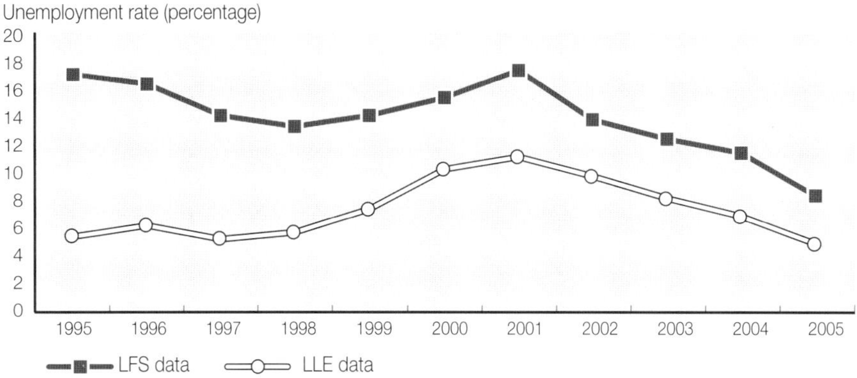

Unemployment rate (percentage)

Source: LFS and LLE.

unemployment rate has been steadily decreasing since 2002, in 2003 the unemployment rate in Lithuania still amounted to 10.3 per cent according to LLE data and to
12.4 per cent according to LFS data, meaning that approximately every tenth
economically active person in Lithuania was classed as unemployed. Although the
recent economic growth and free movement of labour has significantly reduced the
unemployment rate in 2004–05, unemployment continues to be one of the most
painful social and economic problems in Lithuania, with approximately 100,000
unemployed in 2005.

The unemployment rate of men in Lithuania is traditionally higher than that of
women, but there is a trend towards a levelling up of the rates during recent years;
according to LLE data, in 2002 the female unemployment rate (9.5 per cent) even
exceeded that of males (9.2 per cent) for the first time. (In 2005 the female unemployment rate had fallen to 5.1 per cent, and that of men to 3.2 per cent.) These trends
support the theory that female unemployment increases faster than male during
periods of an overall decrease in employment levels, and conversely male unemployment decreases faster during an overall employment increase. A possible explanation
could be the fact that the economic recovery has been more favourable for those
employed in activities where traditionally a male workforce is dominant, such as
construction, civil engineering, industry and transportation. An additional explanation might be that often the motive for registering at the labour exchange is to receive
social benefits. Women (especially those with lower qualifications) raising children
are the most likely group to be caught in the poverty trap and are more willing to
receive the available benefits and stay at home instead of working at a relatively low
wage. Another explanation might be related to higher degrees of informal
employment, which affect more men than women.

Lithuania has witnessed a marked difference in the unemployment rate by age
(see figure 6.4). Youth unemployment has been significantly exceeding the average

Figure 6.4 Unemployment rate by age group, Lithuania, 2003 (percentages)

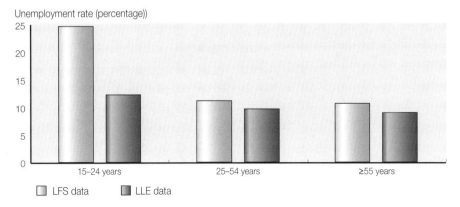

Source: LFS and authors' calculations based on LLE data.

unemployment rate according to LLE as well as to LFS data (see figures 6.3 and 6.4). The most problematic element of this phenomenon is that about 50 per cent of the youth registered at the local employment offices have no vocational education at all.

From 2002, when Lithuania introduced pre-retirement age unemployment benefits (valid for those within two years of eligibility of the old-age pension),[2] the number of unemployed individuals in this age group increased by 15–20 per cent. It should be added that the reintegration into the labour market of unemployed workers of this age has been a problem since 1995.

According to the data of the population census of 2001, Lithuania is quite a homogeneous country in terms of its ethnic composition: native Lithuanians comprise 83.4 per cent of the total population, Poles 6.7 per cent and Russians 6.3 per cent. The number of inhabitants of other nationalities (Belarusians, Ukrainians, Germans, Tartars and others) in 2001 accounted for less than 4 per cent of the population.

Lithuanians represent 83.4 per cent of the total workforce, while Russians and Poles account for 6.9 per cent and 7.8 per cent respectively, and other nationalities make up 2.5 per cent of the total workforce. Lithuania has integral and consistent legislation protecting the rights of national minorities.

Young people from ethnic national minorities are provided with adequate opportunities to learn Lithuanian and at the same time are guaranteed the opportunity to learn their mother tongue and preserve their national identity. However, a certain proportion of adults whose knowledge of the official language is quite limited, and whose secondary education and professional skills are not well developed, are less prepared to compete on the labour market.

---

[2] The retirement age for men in Lithuania is 62 years and 6 months, while that for women has been raised from 59 years to 60 years (2006).

Figure 6.5 Distribution of the length of unemployment, Lithuania, 2005
(percentages)

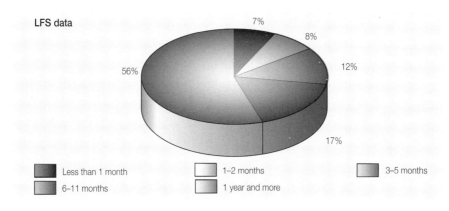

Source: LFS and LLE.

According to the data of the population employment survey conducted in 2002 by Lithuanian Statistics, the unemployment rate among national minorities was higher than the average rate in the country. The overall unemployment rate in Lithuania in 2002 was 13.8 per cent: among native Lithuanians it was 12.8 per cent, Russians 20.3 per cent, Poles 17.8 per cent and other national minorities 17.4 per cent. Those differences might be determined partially by the fact that immigrant populations are more often concentrated in socially and economically less-developed areas where the overall economic activity of the population is lower.

According to LLE data, in 2003 approximately one-quarter of those unemployed were in unemployment for one year or longer; according to LFS data it was almost a half, and by 2005 the share of long-term unemployed in the overall structure of unemployed had increased to 56 per cent (see figure 6.5). The fact that figures are much higher according to LFS data means that a lot of unemployed, who for one or another reason are not competitive and therefore do not expect to find a job, are simply not registering at the territorial labour exchanges. It should be noted that this increase in the share of long-term unemployed as well as in the average length of unemployment in Lithuania (from 7.1 months in 2002 to 9 months in 2005) took place against a background of economic growth and a decrease in the average unemployment rate.

When comparing those members of the labour force with vocational qualifications and those without, we see that more than half of the unemployed population in Lithuania has no vocational qualifications whatsoever, while among employed persons this percentage is only around 30 per cent (see figure 6.6).

Low levels of vocational qualifications and vocational skills among the unemployed are not to be attributed to an imperfect labour market policy, but rather

Figure 6.6   Share of vocational qualifications among unemployed and employed
persons, Lithuania, 2005 (percentages)

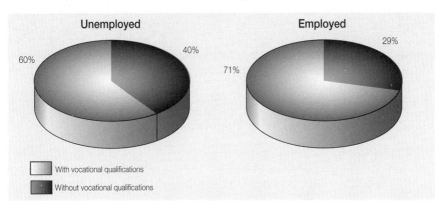

Unemployed   Employed

60%   40%   71%   29%

With vocational qualifications
Without vocational qualifications

Source: LFS.

to the education and vocational training policy, particularly given that even among
young people registered with the employment service 50 per cent have no vocational
qualifications. It should be mentioned that in 2004–05, alongside the significant
decrease in overall unemployment, the share of unemployed with problems of
integration (for example, individuals with disabilities, those returning to the labour
market after a long period of inactivity and individuals with drug and alcohol
problems) increased.

6.2.4   General conclusions and forecasts

Over 2002–03 the Lithuanian labour market experienced a critical turning point:
unemployment started to decrease and the demand for labour increased.
Nevertheless, low labour mobility and adaptability as well as the inadequate balance
still characterize the Lithuanian labour market. The comparatively low occupational
and territorial mobility of the workforce, and the low or inadequate skills of the
unemployed, mean that difficulties in providing employers with a qualified labour
force still persist. Individuals not ready for the labour market or with professional
qualifications no longer in demand represent a large share of the unemployed; there
is also a high proportion of unemployed without working skills.

Employment of workers living in rural areas, most of whom are employed in the
low-productivity agricultural sector, remains another matter of urgency. The
decommissioning of the Ignalina Nuclear Power Plant is likely to cause additional
economic and social problems in Lithuania (the first unit was closed in 2004, the
second is planned for 2009). Addressing these problems will require huge costs and
support from other EU Member States.

The labour market forecast is built on the assumption that the stronger economy of the country, factors stimulating its growth and the sound use of support from EU structural and cohesion funds will have positive effects on the development of business, employment, job creation and employment relations. The development of modern technologies, and in particular information technologies, will facilitate the creation of good-quality, well-paid jobs requiring high qualifications, using the available workforce potential and increasing investment in those sectors of the economy that need qualified workers.

6.3   FLEXIBILITY AND SECURITY: THE INSTITUTIONAL BACKGROUND

6.3.1   Employment protection legislation

In order to assess the employment security situation in Lithuania, we shall look at the impact of the country's employment protection legislation (EPL). Three phases of development in EPL should be singled out: the first phase – until 1991; the second phase – from 1991 until 2003; and the third phase – from 2003.

The first phase is characterized by the legal norms of the Soviet Union, which stipulated employment security. The norms encompassed strict regulations on labour relations between the management staff of enterprises and organizations and the employees, restricting the possibilities to dismiss an employee without sufficient motivation unless there was any fault on the employee's part. Moreover, the Labour Legislation Code of Soviet Lithuania provided a range of guarantees to secure employment for those employees who were dismissed.

The second phase began in 1991 after the restoration of independence. In addition to the reform of other laws, Lithuania had also to amend its labour law. To adapt labour legislation to the changing reality and to allow labour relations to develop in the appropriate direction – i.e. legitimating market economy conditions – the following new labour laws were enacted from 1991: Law on Employment Contracts, Law on Wages, Law on Leave, Law on Collective Agreements and Contracts, Law on the Regulation of Collective Labour Disputes, Law on the Settlement of Labour Disputes, Law on Occupational Safety and Health, as well as accompanying legal acts. However, for political and other reasons labour laws were often subsequently amended, resulting in inconsistencies and gaps.

It should be mentioned that Soviet labour law provisions considerably determined the content of the second-phase employment protection legislation; only the category of enterprise or organization management staff was revised to apply to the 'employer'. The employers' previous administrative obligation to secure employment for their employees became the obligation to make high lay-off payments (in the period of 1992–93 this was the equivalent of up to 36 average monthly wages).

The inadequate fit between the labour norms and the actual capacities of enterprises gave rise to a labour market phenomenon which had never been known in Lithuania until that time: 'hidden unemployment', whereby employees would stop working for two or more months but were not officially dismissed. The maximum dismissal benefit was later reduced to six average monthly wages and the obligation to employ dismissed employees was transferred from the management staff of the enterprise (or employer) to the Lithuanian Labour Exchange.

The third phase features the adoption of a new Labour Code in 2002 that came into force on 1 January 2003. The latter may be regarded as a unified codified source of Lithuanian labour legislation.

In October 2004, after more than two years of debate between the social partners, the Lithuanian parliament finally adopted a law introducing works councils. According to the law these new employee representative bodies may be established in enterprises with 20 or more employees where there is no trade union present.

The Government made other new resolutions which elaborate on and give detail to the appropriate Labour Code provisions, namely a procedure for estimation of working period; peculiarities of specific employment contracts; procedure and conditions for annual, additional and extended annual leaves; shortening of working time as well as payment; the procedure for placement of foreign workers temporarily working in Lithuania, in Lithuanian enterprises; the procedure for the qualification requirements and examination; and a list of offices subject to the tender procedure.

A significant characteristic of the new Labour Code and other legal acts regulating labour relations in the third phase is the further liberalization of the termination of an employment contract without any fault on the part of an employee.

Summarizing, we may say that within the period of 1991–2005 a new employment security system was established in Lithuania, moving from strict state regulation to direct relations between employers and employees, as well as giving meaningful support to employment using labour market policy measures. In our opinion, however, this new system is insufficient to ensure employment security (protection). While the current system ensures opportunities, there are no conditions needed to realize these opportunities; or, in other words, the opportunities created do not correspond to the real conditions.

We see the main reasons for this shortfall as follows: low labour force organization (weak role of the trade unions and works councils; insufficient social dialogue at the micro-level);[3] high unofficial employment; insufficient information given to employees; inefficient labour market policy measures; and a tax system unfavourable to employment.

On the other hand it should be noted that, according to employers, the existing labour legislation in Lithuania is still too strict. Since the new Labour Code came into effect in 2003, the Secretariat of the Tripartite Council of the Republic of Lithuania has received around 300 proposals (the majority of which were from

---

[3] By different estimations the level of unionized workers in Lithuania is around 10 per cent or less, and the coverage by collective agreements is between 5 per cent and 15 per cent. The overall disunity of trade unions and insufficient qualifications of trade union representatives aggravate the situation.

employers' organizations) regarding the amendments or supplements to 150 or so articles of the Labour Code. The main theme of these proposals is the liberalization of labour relations.

6.3.2 An analysis of labour turnover and job tenure data

Overall labour turnover in Lithuania is comparatively low: the labour turnover index calculated as a sum of aggregate accession[4] and separation[5] rates (based on LFS data) in 2003 was 26 per cent. For the most part, this index was substantially higher in other Eastern and Central European countries – with the exception of the Czech Republic – varying between approximately 30 per cent and 60 per cent in 1998–99 (see Cazes and Nesporova, 2003, p. 56).

Analysing the inflow and outflow data presented in table 6.1, it should be stressed that outflow data actually reflect the recovery of the Lithuanian economy. During the period 2000–03 the outflows from employment to unemployment as well as from employment to inactivity were declining.

Data provided by the LFS show that men are more mobile than women. In 2003, men have a labour turnover index of 30.5 per cent, compared with an index of only 21 per cent for women in the same year. There were higher flows of men changing from one job to another, moving from unemployment to employment, as well as moving from employment to unemployment. Women were more mobile than men during the period of observation for one index only – moving from inactivity to employment – which was presumably related to the upswing of the Lithuanian economy.

Labour turnover markedly decreases with age. If the labour turnover index calculated for the 15–24 years age group in 2003 was 63.7 per cent, the same index calculated for the 25–44 years age group amounted to 25.9 per cent and for the age group over 45 years only 17.1 per cent. This overall trend is induced by related differences in all types of inflows as well as outflows (with the exception of the flows from employment to inactivity, where the level for the age group over 45 years is inherently higher).

The extremely high level of employment flexibility in the age group 15–24 years is related primarily to the relatively high level of flow from inactivity to employment in this group. Another reason is that the employees of this age are more willing (voluntarily or involuntarily) to change their jobs.

Average job tenure is the main indicator of labour market stability. It is calculated as the length of time that currently employed individuals have spent with their present employer. In Lithuania during 1998–2003, average job tenure fluctuated around the level of 7.5 years.

---

[4] The accession rate is calculated as a sum of aggregate flows from unemployment to employment, from inactivity to employment and from one employment to another, divided by average employment in a given year.

[5] The separation rate is calculated as a sum of aggregate flows from employment to unemployment, from employment to inactivity and from one employment to another, divided by average employment in a given year.

Table 6.1 Labour market inflows (accession rate) and outflows (separation rate) as percentage of average employment, Lithuania, 2000–03

Flows	2000	2001	2002	2003
From unemployment to employment	..	3.8	4.5	3.7
From inactivity to employment	..	2.1	2.8	2.6
From employment to employment	..	7.5	8.7	7.7
Total accession rate	..	13.4	16.0	14.0
From employment to unemployment	6.3	4.7	3.9	3.1
From employment to inactivity	3.5	2.2	1.7	1.2
From employment to employment	..	7.5	8.7	7.7
Total separation rate	..	14.4	14.3	12.0

Notes: .. = not available.

Source: LFS.

The gender patterns of average job tenure in Lithuania are similar to those observed in other transition countries (Cazes and Nesporova, 2003, p. 67). Average job tenure in Lithuania is longer for women than for men, a feature which might be related to the abovementioned higher mobility of men in the labour market.

Normally, job tenure increases with age. However, job tenure in Lithuania is on average lower than in other transition and industrialized countries in all age groups. It should be noted that if the average tenure in the age groups 15–24 years and 25–44 years is more or less close to those observed in transition and industrialized countries, the average job tenure in the age group over 45 years in Lithuania is particularly low. The average job tenure of 11.2 years or lower in this last age group was not found in any of the analysed countries (with the exception of Estonia, 1999) (see Auer and Cazes, 2003, pp. 72–5, and Cazes and Nesporova, 2003, p. 72) and has been in decline (during the period 2001–03 it decreased from 11.8 to 11.2 years).

This feature of the Lithuanian labour market might be explained first of all by the fall of average job tenure in the pre-pension age as well as by comparatively weaker employment protection and lower adaptability of older workers. Relatively weak trade unions are often unable to protect older workers, who more often than the younger ones, are dismissed during the restructuring processes as they are (or are considered by employers as such) less adaptable, having lower qualifications or less demanded professions.

6.3.3 Development of flexible forms of employment

While the numbers of employed persons fluctuated during the period 1998–2003, the shares of wage employment, self-employment, and family workers remained constant. Hired employees represent 80 per cent of total employment, while around

17 per cent are self-employed and 3 per cent are family workers. Wage employment is the most typical form of employment for both sexes, but more men than women are self-employed, while women dominate in family work. These patterns remained unchanged for both sexes during the period 1998–2003.

During 1998–2003, around 90 per cent of employees had full-time jobs and only about 10 per cent had part-time jobs. The share of part-time employment declined during 1998–2005, with a particularly sharp fall in 2003–05. Women more often than men have part-time jobs and this tendency is increasing: the difference between the share of women and men with part-time jobs in 1998 was 2.2 percentage points, rising to 4.3 percentage points in 2003.

Approximately half of employees with part-time jobs hold them voluntarily and the other half have them because they could not find full-time jobs. During 1998–2003 involuntary part-time employment in Lithuania increased significantly (in 1998, 32.7 per cent of all part-timers chose such kind of employment involuntarily, whereas in 2003 this share was 53 per cent).

Comparing full-time and part-time employment by age and sex, we can see that in all age groups women hold part-time jobs more often than men. The share of young people with part-time jobs has been steadily declining, but the patterns are inherently different for young men and young women. There has been an increase in the share of workers of retirement age holding part-time jobs, again mostly women, which reached almost 40 per cent of this age group in 2003.

In general, the share of part-time employment in Lithuania is low. This is related to the low level of remuneration, which means that employees are not really interested in shortening their working time. From the data presented one can presume that only workers of retirement age are interested in part-time employment as this represents an income in addition to an old-age pension.

As the share of employees with additional jobs is related to the economic level of the country, the overall increase in living standards since 1996 in Lithuania (with the exception of the 1998 economic crisis) has been followed by a steady decrease in multiple-job holding, from 8.3 per cent in 1999 to 5.7 per cent in 2005. Since the LFS does not provide information on multiple-job holding for the years 1991–95, it can only be assumed that the figures were much higher during this period.

Temporary employment in Lithuania grew from 5.5 per cent to 7.2 per cent during the period 1998–2003, but the trend began to reverse in 2004–05 and by 2005 stood at 5.8 per cent. Women are hired under permanent contracts more often than men. In 2005, 96.7 per cent of women and 92.9 per cent of men were employed under permanent labour contracts.

There is no comprehensive information on informal employment in Lithuania. Estimates derived from different surveys allow us to make a very rough assessment of the situation. Primary evaluations of the extent of informal employment might be gained from the relatively high figures on the difference between insured employees and the working-age population in Lithuania, which works out at a ratio of approximately 1.2 million to 2 million (a difference not exclusively attributable to informal employment).

Lithuanian Statistics in 2002–03 performed a special survey in order to evaluate the extent of informal employment. According to this survey, informal employment in Lithuania amounts to 10–15 per cent of total employment. These estimates refer to primary and secondary or multiple activities, but do not include data on the self-employed or individuals employed in agriculture.

According to estimates from the Institute of Labour and Social Research based on surveys performed in 1995–97, approximately 60 per cent of all private sector employees did not declare their full income over the period. According to the information provided by the State Labour Inspectorate, the sectors in which this was most common were construction, agriculture, wholesale, retail trade and car repairs.

Analysis of national social insurance statistics allows us to conclude that the 2004–05 economic growth and shortage of qualified labour had a positive impact on the decrease in informal employment. In 2005 the number of individuals covered by state social insurance increased more than twofold with respect to 2004.

6.3.4 Active and passive labour market policies

The overall level of expenditure on labour market policies in Lithuania in general is very low. The level of expenditure on passive and active labour market policies, expressed as a share of GDP, is one of the lowest among industrialized as well as transition countries, reaching only 0.28 per cent of GDP in 2003. In absolute terms, expenditure on labour market policies in Lithuania increased by more than LTL 12 million (EUR 3.5 million)[6] in 2005, but the total spending still represented only 0.23 per cent of GDP.

Despite low levels of overall expenditure on labour market policies, we should stress that there is a trend towards 'activation' of labour market policies in Lithuania. Participation in active labour market policies as well as the level of expenditure on those policies has risen consistently since 1991 (with the exception of the period of economic crisis in 1999–2000 when the expenditure on passive LMP was intensified to respond to the increase in unemployment). The expenditure on active labour market policies expressed as share of GDP grew from 0.09 per cent in 2000 to 0.16 per cent in 2003, whereas the share spent on passive policies during this period decreased from 0.18 to 0.12 per cent of GDP. In 2005, after the introduction of the Law on Unemployment Social Insurance, expenditure on passive policies increased, but still remained lower than spending on active policies (LTL 71.3 or EUR 20.6 and LTL 92.6 million or EUR 26.8 respectively).

We will analyse below whether these trends should be valued positively and what impact they have on employment security, and whether the drop in spending on passive labour market policies has been compensated by the increase in active policies.

---

[6] Exchange rate as of 1 May 2004.

Active labour market policies

The ratio indicating job placement as a share of registered unemployment provides a very rough estimate of how many unemployed individuals registered with the employment service find jobs. During the years 1995–2003, this figure fluctuated around 40 per cent and was highly correlated with the economic fluctuations (see figure 6.7), a trend which continued into 2004–05.

Despite the fact that job placement is strongly related to growth and decline in the economy, it should be noted that the public employment service is becoming more and more active in promoting the trade-off between labour force supply and demand. The employment service has developed its Internet services and is actively collaborating with employers. Since 1997 it has regularly performed surveys of employers in order to find out the number of employees to be dismissed and placed, as well as drafting one-to-two-year regional forecasts of the needs for particular professions. This kind of information is forwarded to the Ministry of Education and Science and to educational institutions, enabling them to promote vocational training which is adequately adapted to the needs of the economy.

Participation in active labour market programmes as well as expenditure on them has been rising consistently since 1991. In 2003, individuals participating in active programmes made up almost 61 per cent of the annual registered unemployed. In 2005 this indicator increased to 79 per cent: 129,900 out of 163,900 registered unemployed were provided with active labour market programmes.

Judging by the official statistics, Lithuania has been consistently implementing the provisions of the European Union Employment Strategy and the National Employment Programme, which provide for the promotion of participation of

Figure 6.7 Job placements as a percentage of registered unemployed and annual real GDP growth, Lithuania, 1995–2003 (percentages)

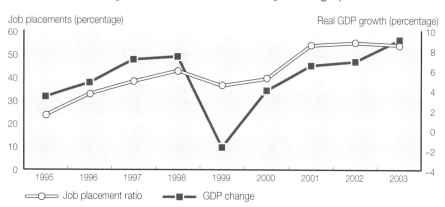

Source: LLE.

unemployed in active labour market programmes. While the assessment of these changes is on the whole positive, we should mention some drawbacks of active labour market policies.

The main active labour market programmes in Lithuania are job clubs, vocational training, public works, supported works, subsidized jobs and new business loans. A major part of expenditure on active labour market programmes is spent on vocational training and public works (in 2003, 67 per cent of total expenditure was spent on these measures, in 2005, more than 70 per cent; the latter was mostly influenced by the increase of expenditure on public works). About 50 per cent of individuals participating in active labour market programmes took part in vocational training and public works.

Vocational training organized by the employment service involves those unemployed individuals to whom the labour exchange cannot offer work because of their professional qualifications or health, as well as those unemployed without any educational attainment. Lithuanian labour market policy provides for the promotion of vocational training programme participation, particularly among the long-term unemployed, so participants are paid a training benefit which is 30 per cent higher than their unemployment benefit.

According to the data of the labour market vocational training survey performed by the Institute of Labour and Social Research over the period 1998–2000, 60–70 per cent of respondents stated that the participants lacked recent practical experience (this was particularly emphasized by the young and long-term unemployed).

Since 1998, the Lithuanian Labour Market Training Authority has been carrying out regular assessments of the efficiency of labour market training programmes, in collaboration with the Institute of Labour and Social Research. The job placement of vocational training programme participants 6, 12 and 18 months after the end of training is measured and approximately 40–68 per cent of participants find jobs after 12 months. During 1998–2001 the level of job placement remained unchanged but has begun to grow since 2002 (especially in construction and metalwork). Labour market training authorities continually analyse the results of the surveys and improve the training programmes accordingly to improve their fit with the needs of the market.

The public employment service organizes public works together with municipalities or other institutions. Persons employed in public works are paid by the hour, at a rate no lower than the hourly minimum wage. Unemployed participants are not paid unemployment benefit unless the wage is lower than this benefit, in which case the employment office pays the difference. Public works are also organized for those unemployed not eligible for unemployment benefits and/or with no qualifications or work experience, making these programmes of particular importance in rural areas and in other areas with high unemployment rates.

Programmes of public works in Lithuania usually involve the long-term unemployed and, unfortunately, serve more to reduce social exclusion than to assist the unemployed to return to the labour market. Public works are also insufficiently coordinated with other active labour market measures, and they do not address the needs of unemployed individuals with higher qualifications.

165

During the early stages of unemployment among individuals who do not have appropriate information about employment possibilities or proper education, or who are simply not motivated, so-called job clubs are organized. The special needs of each participant are considered: they are motivated and encouraged to choose an occupation currently in demand, and oriented towards appropriate skills training, including training in the preparation of a curriculum vitae and in communication technology.

In 2003, 53,800 jobseekers or every fifth individual registered with the employment service participated in job clubs; in 2004 this figure dropped to 51,100 in 2005. Every second participant in these measures was long-term unemployed and every fourth was a young person aged under 25. Sixty-eight per cent of job club participants acquired job-seeking and communication skills; half of them received counselling which changed their negative attitude towards employment opportunities.

Despite the fact that the number of unemployed participating in this labour market policy programme has been rapidly growing since 1994 (during 2000–05 this programme involved the highest number of participants in active labour market programmes), the quantitative indices used to evaluate the programme fail adequately to reveal its efficiency and the quality of its services. The indices used should be weighted, for example the number of hours per participant in the programme, and/or qualitative indices used, for example the percentage of participants in the programme who went on to find a job or who enrolled in vocational training programmes. Short surveys of participants, measuring the content of the programme against the needs of the unemployed, would be beneficial. The number of formally established job clubs could also be reduced.

Summarizing the application of active labour market policy measures in Lithuania, one should say that the high participation figures do not always disclose the efficiency of the measures in place. While vocational training is more or less effective in involving unemployed individuals in the labour market, other measures, particularly public works and job clubs (during 2000–05 these programmes involved more than 70 per cent of all participants in active labour market programmes), raise some doubts. With 70 per cent of registrations with the employment service being re-registrations, the success of the programmes is questionable.

During 2004–05, resources from the Employment Fund and EU structural funds were used to develop active labour market policy measures better attuned to the needs of employers. Efforts were made to organize fund-supported temporary job replacements for unemployed individuals. The individuals covered temporary vacancies left by employees taking leave, with no requirement on the employer to continue the contract beyond this period. In addition, 18 new labour market training programmes were developed. In order to evaluate the effectiveness of the new programmes, a research project was set up at the beginning of 2006 to demonstrate changes in the labour market status of participants.

Over the period under analysis, regular efforts were made to increase the attractiveness of active labour market policy measures for employers: the related bureaucracy was minimized and funding was increased. However, some employers were found to be profiting from the financial support they received and delaying payments to programme participants working under contract for them.

Passive labour market policies

The main passive labour market policy measure is unemployment benefit. Unemployment benefit in Lithuania is paid for a period of six months. Until 2005, when the Law on Unemployment Social Insurance came into force, the amount thereof varied from LTL 135 to 250 (EUR 39 to EUR 72), depending on the duration of former employment and payment of social insurance contributions, and was reduced by 20 per cent every two months.

On the whole, the procedure for paying unemployment benefit in force in Lithuania before 2005 strictly regulated eligibility. Only unemployed individuals with at least 24 months' state social insurance contributions within the previous three years were entitled to unemployment benefit. For this reason, unemployment benefit, which at the same time was very low, was paid to an extremely small number of beneficiaries. The average unemployment benefit in 2004 amounted to about EUR 50 per month or approximately 40 per cent of the minimum wage and 21 per cent of the average wage; moreover, this ratio regularly declined (see figure 6.8). In terms of coverage, the share of registered unemployed receiving unemployment benefit gradually decreased after 1995 from around 30 per cent to around 12 per cent in 2003 (see figure 6.9).

The main reason for the reduction in the number of beneficiaries of unemployment benefit was an insufficient period of social insurance contributions. The share of unemployed receiving unemployment benefits did not increase even in the period 1999–2001, when unemployment accelerated. We do not have fully reliable data to explain this phenomenon, but the main reasons for such a situation might be two. First, the initial casualties during the recession were temporary and/or informal workers, who were not eligible for unemployment benefit. Second, because of the decrease in

Figure 6.8 Average unemployment benefits (UB) as a percentage of the average net wage (AW) and the minimum wage (MW), Lithuania, 1995–2005

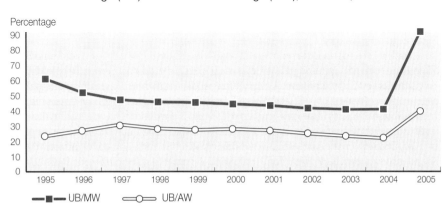

Source: Authors' calculations based on LLE and Lithuanian Statistics.

Figure 6.9 Share of unemployed receiving unemployment benefits, Lithuania,
1992–2005 (percentages)

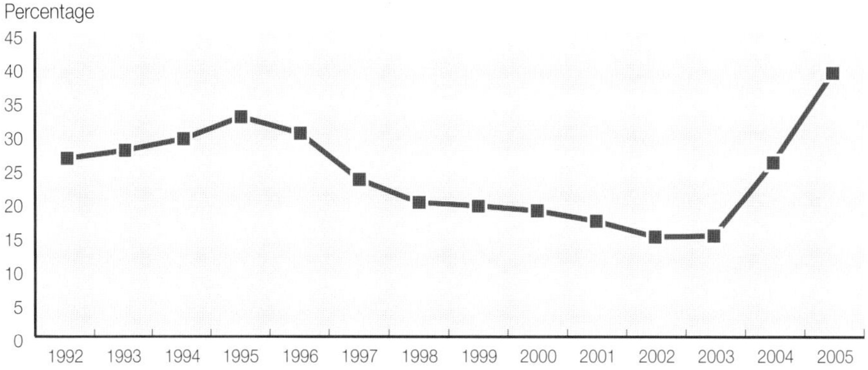

Source: Author's calculations based on LLE data.

overall living standards during the economic downturn, some of the registered unemployed were interested only in the receipt of social benefits and had not worked recently or long enough to have a sufficient period of social insurance contributions.

Until 2004 Lithuania witnessed a constant increase in the number of unemployed finding jobs under fixed-term contracts (in 2003 almost one-third of all movements from unemployment to employment were under temporary contracts), as well as an increasing overall extent of temporary employment in the country. This was particularly the case in construction and agricultural economic activities as well as in light industry and agricultural production processing. However, since 2004 these trends have changed: under the new conditions of labour shortage, employers are increasingly employing workers under permanent contracts.

The overall situation regarding passive labour market policies up until 2004 was not helped by employers withholding social insurance contributions in periods of financial difficulty, nor by the high level of informal workers generally.

It can be argued that the restrictive nature of the passive labour market policies offered up to 2004 encouraged individuals losing their jobs to seek new work more quickly. However, given the economic situation in Lithuania at the time, the regional differences in unemployment and the dynamics of job vacancies (particularly in regions with a predominantly rural infrastructure), as well as the underlying reasons for the low level of support for the unemployed, these polices should be qualified as negative ones.

The situation changed radically after the introduction of the Law on Unemployment Social Insurance, which came into force on 1 January 2005. Invoking the provisions of this law, new methods were applied to the calculation of unemployment benefit, which nearly doubled as a result and amounted to almost LTL 330 (EUR 96) in 2005 (up from an average of LTL 174 or EUR 50 per month in 2003). According to the new law, the period of social insurance contributions required for eligibility to the benefit was reduced, increasing the share of individuals receiving unemployment benefit in the total number of registered unemployed.

The European Employment Strategy provides for the reduction of the role of passive labour market policy measures in favour of active ones. However, these changes should not reduce the level of social security or living standards of the unemployed, as was the case in Lithuania prior to the recent reforms.

6.4 INTERACTIONS BETWEEN EMPLOYMENT PROTECTION AND LABOUR MARKET POLICIES

6.4.1 Identification of the trade-offs

Overall employment security in Lithuania during the period under analysis significantly decreased. This came about through changes in legal provisions regulating employment protection and as a consequence of the trends in the general development of the economy. Liberalization of employment protection legislation, low levels of labour force organization and new economic conditions, reflected in short average job tenure and a rise in temporary and informal employment, had the combined effect of reducing employment security in the workplace.

Attempts were made to compensate the decrease in overall employment security through labour market policies introducing employment insurance schemes as well as active labour market policies assisting those who had lost their jobs to reintegrate into the labour market. The diversity of labour market vocational training courses was increased and their quality improved. Vocational consultation and guidance was improved as well, and the activities of job clubs were extended. Since 2001, local employment offices have regularly introduced initiatives, and employment services on the Internet have also been extended. However, as the analysis of passive and active labour market policies has revealed, labour market policies have compensated for the loss of employment security only to a modest degree.

Up until 2005, the weight of passive labour market policies steadily decreased, resulting in shrinking average unemployment benefit and reduced numbers of unemployed receiving unemployment benefits. On the whole, this decrease was related to changes in the labour market.

The wide extent of unofficial employment, the increase in the number of persons employed under temporary as well as civil contracts, and a large proportion of unemployed individuals re-registering with the employment office, resulted in a situation where fewer and fewer applicants were eligible for unemployment benefit as they had worked for insufficiently long periods of time. This resulted in a drop in the average amount of unemployment benefit as well as in the share of beneficiaries, and on the whole social guarantees shrank for workers losing their jobs.

Therefore we can conclude that there was a negative complementarity between employment protection and passive labour market policy in Lithuania up to 2004 – the lower the employment protection, the lower the security guarantees. The Law on

Figure 6.10 Shares of long-term unemployed, re-registered unemployed and newly registered unemployed in total unemployment, Lithuania, 2005

Unemployment Social Insurance that came into force in 2005 increased approximately threefold the amount of unemployment benefit and simplified eligibility conditions. However, it is too early to observe its impact on the interaction between employment protection and passive labour market policy.

Along with shrinking employment protection, Lithuania has been witnessing insufficient growth in the efficiency of its active labour market policies. The efficiency of labour market policies may be estimated using the set of the following three indices and their dynamics: share of long-term unemployed in the total number of unemployed; average length of unemployment; share of re-registered unemployed in the total number of registered unemployed.

On average, the long-term unemployed made up about 30 per cent of the total registered unemployed and about 50 per cent of the unemployed recorded by the LFS. The share of long-term unemployed in the total number of registered unemployed in Lithuania steadily increased up until 2002. This trend reversed in 2003 as a result of the fall in the total unemployment rate (according to LLE data the number of long-term unemployed decreased in this period by around 29 per cent and according to LFS data by around 17 per cent, while the total number of unemployed in 2002–03 decreased by 16 per cent and 9 per cent according to the two sources). During the period 2003–05 the total number of long-term unemployed decreased from 40,800 to 23,600. However, the share of long-term unemployed among all registered unemployed did not decrease and in 2005 comprised 27 per cent (up from 25.7 per cent in 2003).

Of the 'new' unemployed, a special survey performed by the Lithuanian public employment service in 2002–03 revealed that about 70 per cent of individuals signing up with the employment service were persons re-registering and only 30 per cent were new registrations. The structure of registered unemployed may be very roughly illustrated by figure 6.10, showing the relative proportions of long-term unemployed, newly registered unemployed and re-registered unemployed.

The data on the overall structure of unemployment allow us to conclude that active labour market policies in Lithuania, which have been steadily growing, are not efficient since the majority of unemployed persons registered with the public employment service never manage to gain a permanent hold on the labour market.

We may conclude that there is no trade-off between employment protection and active labour market policy in Lithuania. Active labour market policies, on the whole, are not attuned closely enough to the needs of individuals with higher qualifications or education. Nor do they secure permanent re-entry to the labour market for those with lower skills and education. Thus, one can say that in the main active labour market policies do not compensate adequately for the decrease in employment protection.

Conclusion

Summarizing the information presented in the chapter so far, it is true to say that both active as well as passive labour market policies are more attractive to the low-skilled (who may end up in jobs paying less than EUR 200 per month), and are far from securing decent working or living conditions for these persons.

For individuals with higher levels of qualifications and education who might be expected to find well-paid jobs, active as well as passive labour market policies hold little attraction and – on the whole – bear little relation to full compensation for the decreased level of employment protection.

It can be concluded that there are two separate groups of labour market participants in Lithuania. We may call them a 'successful' block and an 'unsuccessful' block (a close linkage with the primary and secondary labour markets is likely, but more detailed analysis would be needed to determine this exactly).

The first, successful, block consists of persons with higher education and a marketable profession, who are able and motivated, expect a high wage, and manage to adapt to new economic conditions and find their place in the new labour market. These individuals seldom lose their job, and if they lose or change it, they look for a new job themselves and do not apply to the employment office, because, as we have already seen, they are not interested in either the passive or active labour market programmes on offer.

The existence of this block is evidenced in the first instance by the overall labour turnover, which is relatively low in Lithuania, and by data on the distribution of employment by job tenure characterized by a relatively high and steady growing share of employees with job tenure from five to ten years. It is further evidenced by the distribution of the unemployed by education and the relatively small share of individuals registering as unemployed for the first time.

The second, unsuccessful, block consists of individuals with a low level of education or 'unmarketable' skills, with little possibility of finding a job and consquently low motivation, who have not managed to adapt to new economic conditions and rely regularly on the public social assistance system.

Some of this group would be made up of individuals who have some informal work and, in principle, are not interested in finding a job in the formal economy (or at least do not expect to find a 'good' job) and are satisfied with casual or undeclared earnings supplemented by some level of state assistance in the form of benefits or allowances.

It is clear that the services and policies provided by the employment service play only a secondary role in terms of employment promotion and security in Lithuania. In this respect, attention needs to be focused on employment protection schemes. This requires the development of social dialogue at the micro (enterprise) level, as provided for in the Labour Code, since it plays a crucial role.

6.4.2   Reforms affecting the linkages

Employment protection legislation

The reforms in employment protection legislation are in fact related to the improvement of the Labour Code provisions. The process of liberalization of employment protection legislation began at the outset of transition, but the newly enacted Labour Code provides for a range of flexible means to regulate labour relations.

While employers are on the whole dissatisfied with the reforms thus far, workers' representatives believe the provisions of the Labour Code to be adequately liberal and to permit flexible labour relations. They consider it necessary to tighten control over enforcement of the Labour Code provisions and to enhance the social guarantees linked to employment.

The amendments to employment protection legislation currently under consideration are influenced by two contradictory tendencies. Employers are seeking to reduce restrictions on the application of flexible forms of employment as well as dismissals, citing the character of the production process and market fluctuations. Trade unions, by contrast, are trying to enhance control over the enforcement of the Labour Code provisions and to sustain secure guarantees in the field of employment.

Enforcement of employment protection legislation

Approximately 40 articles in the Labour Code include the phrase 'provided for in collective agreements'. Given that (according to information provided by the secretariat of the Lithuanian Tripartite Council) collective agreements cover only approximately 10 per cent of employees, many of these provisions have not been put into operation.

On the whole, improvements are related to the promotion of social dialogue, although there have been attempts to propose alternative mechanisms for the implementation of Labour Code provisions. For example, both employers' organizations and the Ministry of Economy have proposed that employers be allowed to temporarily approve procedures relating to provisions of the Labour Code until such a time as a relevant collective agreement has been concluded in the enterprise.

It is difficult to evaluate the enforcement of employment protection legislation through lawsuits or labour courts, as there are no institutionalized labour courts in Lithuania and the information provided by the National Courts Administration on labour lawsuits is very scarce. A study is needed to evaluate the situation fundamentally.

According to data provided by the National Courts Administration, the number of labour lawsuits initiated in 2003 was 2,532 and comprised 2 per cent of the total civil suits initiated, while in 2005 these figures were 1,980 and 1.3 per cent. The main reasons for initiating labour lawsuits concern remuneration (60 per cent) and dismissals (17 per cent). Unfortunately the information available is too scarce for any firm conclusions to be drawn.

Additional protection through collective bargaining

Only a small proportion of workers belong to trade unions and only about one-tenth are covered by collective agreements. Enterprises where employees are represented and where collective agreements are concluded usually provide for additional protection in cases of employment termination, such as prolonging the notice period or granting the employee days off to look for a new job. However, in the vast majority of firms in Lithuania the interests of employees are not represented and so collective bargaining at the enterprise level does not play an important role.

The situation might be improved through sectoral collective agreements (currently only one sectoral collective agreement is in place). The social partners are discussing this issue more and more, but there are significant obstacles. Sectoral organizations of employers are not willing to undertake this step or to take on additional responsibilities, while sectoral trade union organizations have neither the administrative nor the financial capacities to change the situation. Despite these shortcomings, in February 2003 the Lithuanian Trade Union Confederation initiated an appeal to the main employers' organizations regarding the conclusion of sectoral agreements. On the whole, employers supported the initiative, but only one sectoral organization of employers started concrete discussions.

A national collective agreement is often said to be the way out of the existing situation, allowing many contentious issues to be discussed and agreed upon. Such an agreement has not been concluded in Lithuania yet, though in 2005 a national bipartite agreement was signed, relating to the single issue of the implementation of job evaluation.

Labour market institutions and policies

The Law on Support to the Unemployed, in force in the period 1990–2004, has now been divided into two separate laws: the Law on Unemployment Social Insurance, which came into force on 1 January 2005, and the Law on Promotion of Employment.

The Law on Promotion of Employment was adopted by Parliament in June 2006 and came into force on 1 August of the same year. It provides for the ultimate development of cooperation between social partners by improving labour market

173

institutions and policies, reducing administrative regulation and creating economic incentives for employers to participate in labour market policy measures.

In consideration of the provisions of the EU Employment Strategy, the law also attempts to enhance the employability of those out of work and increase opportunities for their adoption on the labour market. Funding of training for the unemployed is to be extended, increasing this from the current 12 months to 24 months. With the view of promoting participation of young people in training programmes, various incentive mechanisms are to be introduced. Unemployed individuals will be compensated for accommodation costs for a certain period of time (up to three months), for example, if they have to relocated for training. The law also forsees closer coordination of unemployment allowances paid by the Employment Fund and social support policies administered at the local level.

The draft law also provides for increased pay-offs to those employers organizing enterprise-level training and accepting students for work experience. Employers' representatives would also be enrolled on the boards of vocational education schools, colleges and universities, participate in drafting study programmes and sit on thesis panels.

Income protection

The minimum wage was frozen at its 1998 level of LTL 430 (EUR 125) per month for fully five years, after which point it rapidly increased. In September 2003 it was raised to LTL 450 (EUR 130), from 1 May 2004 to LTL 500 (EUR 145), and from 1 July 2005 up to LTL 550 (EUR 159) per month.

Despite this rapid rise, increasing almost 30 per cent in two years, the minimum wage in Lithuania still remains one of the lowest among the EU countries. The minimum wage set in July 2005 amounted to 40 per cent of the average wage in the third quarter of that year.

As we have seen, the situation regarding unemployment benefit has undergone radical change since the introduction of the Law on Unemployment Social Insurance in 2005, with its new method of calculating eligibility and levels of benefits. Unemployment benefit now consists of two parts: fixed and variable. The Government sets the rate of the fixed part. The variable part amounts to 40 per cent of the beneficiary's average monthly wage over the previous three years, although the aggregate unemployment benefit should not exceed 70 per cent of insured income.[7] After three months, to encourage unemployed individuals to take up employment or actively participate in labour market policies, the variable part of the unemployment benefit is reduced by half.

The provisions of the new law ensure a more reliable control of eligibility, sustain the motivation of unemployed individuals searching actively for a job and maintain better coordination of active labour market policies with the social assistance system.

---

[7] Insured income is the average earned income on which social insurance contributions (pension, health insurance, maternity benefits, etc.) are paid; the annual calculation of the level is approved by the Government. In 2005 the level of insured income was LTL 1,084 or around EUR 314.

Moreover the new unemployment benefit system has been integrated with the exisiting social insurance system.

6.4.3 Labour force migration

To date there have been no systematic labour force migration surveys in Lithuania, so the specific number of Lithuanian nationals employed abroad is not known. According to different data in 2001–05, between 250,000 and 300,000 Lithuanian nationals were employed abroad. According to Lithuanian Statistics, only 56,100 citizens emigrated during this same period, with a consequent migration balance of approximately 29,200 individuals (see table 6.2). This would imply that Lithuanian nationals have been approaching foreign countries as hosts of potential employment opportunities rather than as places of residence.

Trends are beginning to be observed among the young, in particular university graduates, in terms of destination countries. Germany, Ireland, Spain, the United Kingdom and the United States are the most common choices for emigration and labour migration; among the Scandinavian countries, Denmark, Norway and Sweden are favoured more and Finland is less attractive. Belarus and Russia have in recent years been chosen by an older Russian-speaking population (usually at retirement age), though since 2003 Russia has become increasingly popular among a wider section of the labour force, including highly qualified white-collar workers.

Labour migration to Ireland and the United Kingdom greatly increased in 2003–05. From the labour force of the new EU countries, workers from Lithuania were the most active (after Poland): In the 12 months following accession, Ireland received around 18,000 applications and the United Kingdom around 26,000 applications from Lithuanian citizens.

The effect of significant labour migration of this kind is generally seen to be negative. There is a shortage of skilled labour, which is expected to limit production development and the opportunities to apply new technologies more efficiently. However, we believe that in the Lithuanian case a degree of skilled labour shortage can be interpreted as a positive factor. It encourages employers to use the workforce more

Table 6.2   Migration to and from Lithuania, 2001–05

Year	Immigration	Emigration	Net migration
2001	4 694	7 253	−2 559
2002	5 110	7 086	−1 976
2003	4 728	11 032	−6 304
2004	5 553	15 165	−9 612
2005	6 789	15 571	−8 782

Source: Lithuanian Statistics.

efficiently and increase labour productivity, which in turn directly contributes to the increased competitiveness of the Lithuanian economy. Indeed, the positive consequences have been notable: there has been employment growth and unemployment reduction, as well as an increase in domestic consumption fuelled by the income earned in foreign countries being spent on the national market. EU enlargement has played a key role in the recent economic upturn in Lithuania. It has created opportunities for Lithuanian nationals to participate more actively in the EU labour market, not only ensuring better employment and employment-related earnings for the Lithuanian population, but also helping Member States to fill the gaps in their national labour markets and contributing to the overall strengthening of economic capacities in the EU.

In 2005 a survey commissioned by the Ministry of Social Security and Labour showed that only 1.3 per cent of Lithuanians plan to leave the country permanently, whereas around 15 per cent of the population indicated that they plan to leave for a period of time. According to this survey and the data of Lithuanian Statistics, we may conclude that the migration process is beginning to stabilize: every year between 15,000 and 25,000 citizens leave the country and between 7,000 and 12,000 return. These trends might be expected to persist until 2010–12, though the Lithuanian Government is actively looking for measures to limit emigration (especially the emigration of skilled labour).

6.5   POLICY CONCLUSIONS

For the period analysed we have found that the labour market in Lithuania has neither a high level of flexibility nor high levels of employment or income security.

In the future, the situation should essentially change. The economy is developing rapidly. The upturn in economic growth which began in 2002, accompanied by free movement of labour, has and will continue to have a direct effect on the whole labour market and on labour relations.

The changing economic environment will inevitably influence active labour market policies. The increasing mobility of labour will stimulate employers to invest more in employee loyalty. The rapid increase in the average wage which began in 2004 (in 2004 the average wage in the Lithuanian economy increased by 8 per cent, in 2005 by 11 per cent) should reduce the problem of the poverty/unemployment trap as well as involve the inactive population in the labour market. With the newly enacted Law on Unemployment Social Insurance, employment and income security during periods of job loss will increase significantly.

On the other hand, at least some of the many proposals put forward by employers relating to the liberalization of employment protection legislation are likely to be considered and will result in increasing employment flexibility.

Increased employment flexibility coupled with increased employment and income security is believed to be a stimulus for the development of social dialogue, beginning at the enterprise level. The institutions pursuing employment and labour market policy in the country should be ready for these changes, as rapid growth of the economy is of benefit to all the social partners – employers, workers and the State. Meanwhile current labour market policy is insufficient, in our opinion, to meet the new requirements of the actors on the Lithuanian labour market and to respond to the changes in the country's social and economic situation.

The main problem appears to be that labour market policy is understood in a narrow sense as assistance to those who have lost their jobs; therefore labour market policies are not well enough coordinated with other measures, such as taxes, social support and vocational training. A variety of labour market training programmes, the organization of training and the improvement of vocational skills do not adequately respond to the needs of the labour market. The public employment service offers almost no training programmes for those unemployed with higher education. Active labour market policies insufficiently target regular job placement for the unemployed. Consequently, policies are more cosmetic than actively intervening where needed, which should be no surprise if we consider their financial resources.

In principle, these labour market imperfections may be explained by the peculiarities of transition, when the labour market was continuously developing under conditions of surplus labour, as was the case between 1991 and 2002.

Accommodating to the changing environment, the Government should:

- promote social dialogue at the enterprise and sectoral level, and initiate national collective agreements, using administrative and economic incentives;

- work towards resolving the issue of declaration of trade union membership;

- establish and implement a procedure for registering collective agreements;

- support vocational training for the socially excluded;

- increase funding of active labour market policies.

In its turn, the Lithuanian Labour Exchange and Labour Market Training Authority should:

- extend the variety, form and length (as necessary) of labour market training programmes;

- enhance the attractiveness of labour market policies for employers and encourage their participation;

- pursue permanent monitoring and evaluation of the effectiveness of labour market policies in terms of re-employment of participants;

- enhance the effect of active labour market policies on self-employment;

- improve and develop measures promoting motivation of the unemployed;

- develop cooperation with non-governmental organizations (NGOs) and private employment agencies.

The main goal of the social partners in this field is bring about fundamental changes in attitudes towards their role in social dialogue and the opportunities on the labour market. Confrontation between employers' and workers' organizations, which dominates in Lithuania, must become cooperation.

To this end, the disparate trade union organizations and their various positions on the main social economic issues need to be consolidated and coordinated. In addition, it is necessary to make a start on the signing of national and sectoral collective agreements. Targeted training systems, dissemination of good practices, and joint civic actions (such as organizing ecological initiatives, festivals or sport competitions) would also help to promote closer cooperation between the social partners.

At the enterprise level, measures should be implemented to:

- promote enterprise loyalty among employees through, for example, financial incentives, improvement of competencies and career advancement

- enforce social solidarity provisions, such as job placement of the disabled and more favourable conditions for studying employees

- encourage more active participation in implementing active labour market policies

- reduce violations of laws regulating informal employment and labour relations.

These measures should improve confidence between the social partners and reduce strain on labour relations. Lithuania should promote positive cooperation between the social partners as well as the concept that workers and employers are on the same team and that only their joint efforts can achieve the best result.

In order to enhance conditions of flexicurity, the social partners should be called upon to play a greater role in employment protection and security, aided by better adapted active labour market policies.

In terms of the development of social dialogue, it should be stressed that in Lithuania, where social partner institutions and their negotiation abilities are observed to be weak, the Government should pursue a more targeted policy that actively promotes cooperation between the social partners and develops an appropriate legal environment.

It is equally important to ensure that the scale of liberalization of employment protection legislation in Lithuania is closely coordinated with both the actual economic conditions and the social goals of the state. Is two months' notice plus severance pay of two or three months' wages too great a burden to place on employers? Would it be appropriate to reduce these obligations on employers? Lithuanian employers can be characterized as having a 'consumer' attitude towards the labour force, insufficiently assuming responsibility for the social security of their employees. The right balance between the responsibility of employers and that of the State should be found through teamwork.

To summarize, the rate of employment flexibility and social security did improve in 2004–05 in Lithuania and the basic reason for this was increased employability and income guarantees. Increased payments in cases of job loss, greater variety and more generous funding of active labour market policy measures reduced the complementarity between employment protection and passive labour market policy in Lithuania. In addition, active measures became more attractive to unemployed university graduates, and permanent employment opportunities improved for unemployed individuals with lower skills.

However, it should be noted that while the total number of unemployed dropped, the share of unemployed individuals not ready to join the labour market (those with no vocational training, for example, or returning to the labour market after a prolonged absence) increased in the total number of unemployed. Accordingly, integration of such unemployed individuals requires more financial resources and time. Therefore, although recent labour market policy measures have begun to ensure better employability, statistical indicators may insufficiently reflect this because of the varied structure of unemployed individuals.

Unfortunately, there have not been cardinal changes in the development of social dialogue and cooperation of social partners at national and sectoral levels; social dialogue is very vague at the sectoral level, employers still avoid assuming more responsibility and problems are usually tackled at enterprise level only. Some positive changes in this area are worth noting, however. In 2005, national unions of employers and employees signed the first bilateral agreement (on the application of a job evaluation methodology) and one collective agreement (in agriculture) was registered with the Ministry of Social Security and Labour.

6.6   FUTURE PERSPECTIVES

Lithuania is planning to further develop employability and income guarantees. As the time of writing, the Seimas of the Republic of Lithuania is considering the Law on Employment Support, which should broaden the range of active labour market policy measures and increase their funding. Training allowances for the unemployed may increase up to two minimum monthly wages, while the creation of a new job for a person with disabilities may be worth 22 average wages. The period of subsidized vocational training is also due to increase, and there are plans to compensate territorial mobility costs for the unemployed and to develop e-services.

The growing number of works councils and their role in social dialogue may stimulate the signing of collective agreements. In its turn, this may increase flexibility of employment relations (as set out in the Labour Code) and constructive cooperation between the social partners at enterprise level. In addition, investment by employers to foster employee loyalty, including through social guarantees, should grow. The social responsibility of enterprises is being more and more widely discussed in Lithuania and employer participation in various social and labour market programmes is increasing. The cooperative development of such active labour market programmes should nonetheless be in parallel with close monitoring of their implementation and efficacy.

It should be stressed that the recent economic growth as well as free movement of labour create particularly favourable conditions for a new stage of flexicurity from the perspective of human and social development. In a modern society, only united and purposeful efforts are able to guarantee socially valuable results and the stable development of society.

POLAND

7

Gabriela Grotkowska,* Mieczyslaw W.Socha* and Urszula Sztanderska*

7.1   INTRODUCTION

On its accession to the European Union (EU) on 1 May 2004, Poland joined with the distinction of having the worst employment of labour resources of any Member State. In the fourth quarter of 2004 the number of unemployed in Poland exceeded 3 million, with an unemployment rate of 18 per cent and 54.9 per cent of the population over the age of 15 unemployed or out of the labour market (figure 7.1).

Figure 7.1   Employment, unemployment and out of the labour force, Poland, 1992–2004 (thousands)

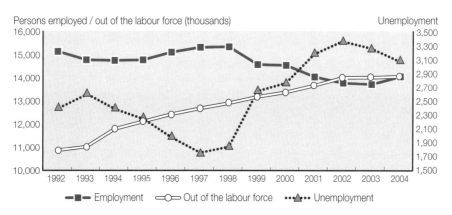

Source: LFS.

* Department of Economics, Warsaw University.

181

Both of these indicators, unemployment and non-employment rates, are among the highest of the OECD countries. Between August 1998 and the fourth quarter of 2004 the Polish economy suffered a net loss of at least 1,550,000 jobs, and the unemployment rate doubled (GUS, 2005a), despite the fact that the economy recorded a positive real GDP growth rate each year (GUS, 2005b).

Such a dramatic worsening of the labour market situation raises very important questions for observers of the Polish labour market. To what extent can the fall in employment and the rise in unemployment be related to a deterioration in the economy, and to what extent should it be linked to restructuring and adaptation to EU standards? Does the Polish economy suffer more than other countries from institutional barriers that hinder the creation of new jobs and reallocation of workers (see Boeri and Terrell, 2002; Riboud, Sanchez-Paramo and Silva-Jaregui, 2002; Svejnar, 2002)? If so, in which sectors? What role has social policy played in the process of stimulation of economic activity and labour force mobility? To what extent has social policy favoured social security and counteracted the growth of the army of people loosely linked to employment and the labour market?

In this chapter, we focus on much more narrow problems as far as both scope and time horizons are concerned. We try to answer the question of how, during a period of structural changes and a worsening economic situation, public labour market policy tried to reconcile two sets of incompatible goals: ongoing liberalization of the labour market and provision of the necessary level of social protection to employees. Why in Poland have we not yet managed to reconcile flexible labour markets, employment and income security with a high employment level?

We show that in spite of the many positive changes in labour market institutions which have been aimed at increasing the flexibility of the labour market it is difficult to discern signs of improvement in employment, labour force mobility or unemployment. On the contrary, after 1998 the dynamics of the labour market have weakened and there has been a significant growth of vulnerable groups less and less tied to work and the labour market. However, it is difficult to blame this situation on existing labour market rigidities alone.

How, then, can we explain the failure to achieve efficient coexistence between labour market flexibility and high levels of income and employment security? Lack of a comprehensive vision of the desired degree of flexicurity and the fragmented character of the changes implemented are the first possible explanations. Another is a lack of cooperation between the social partners in resolving the inconsistency between labour market flexibility and social security. Another possible reason is that improved labour market flexibility may not be sufficient to trigger employment growth during a period of slow economic growth and low demand for labour – particularly in the post-communist economy, where overstaffing still exists.

Although formal flexibility is growing, the high level of unemployment means that this may not be true of behavioural flexibility. The rising importance of employees' skills, particularly in relation to the inflow of young members of the labour force, is one of the most important aspects of increasing labour market flexibility. Generally speaking, young employees bring a higher level of general education and a greater capacity to move around in the social and professional environment, while older workers have become more rigid in their behaviour and want to defend their jobs or have become inactive. The result is greater stress on different forms of premature withdrawal from the labour market. The Government, in turn, has supported regulations that were supposed to limit the budget costs of such behaviour, gradually restricting access to different forms of movement to inactivity. Such policies have made some workers even more determined to protect their jobs.

Moreover, in the period of the arrival of the baby boom generation on the labour market, developing industries have found it easier to acquire younger workers, who are relatively cheaper and better prepared, at least as regards general human capital. Restructuring of employment has taken place at least partly by employing new entrants for new jobs. New jobs are scarce and the chances for redeployment of older workers very limited, severely diminishing their mobility. These conditions – reduced access to long-term income support for the unemployed; entry to the labour market of the better-educated baby boom generation; very high unemployment – as well as certain legal regulations making it easier to dissolve labour contracts and various incentives for restructuring, may not favour growth of employment and unemployment reduction.[1] Finally, the failures discussed may result from other market inefficiencies and institutional problems in the transition economy, such as in the capital market, corporate governance and the business environment (see Svejnar, 2002).

Although the Government tried to increase the flexibility of the Polish labour market through the liberalization of legal regulations, the action undertaken was somewhat fragmentary and there seems to have been an absence of any coherent vision of the reconciliation between increased labour market flexibility and maintaining proper levels of employment and income protection. What is more, public expenditures on active labour market policies (ALMPs) fell. As a result, an enormous number of low-skilled individuals, with low levels of attachment to the labour market, were not offered adequate programmes aimed at improving their employability or changing their skill levels, nor were new jobs created for them. For a significant part of the population remaining inactive, social assistance became the main source of income. This did not encourage them to actively seek work or acquire the skills demanded by employers. The role and involvement of the social partners in the formulation and implementation of employment policy was also insufficient, particularly at sectoral and local level.

In spite of the failings to be seen in institutions and in the Government's labour market policy, we cannot categorically state that the institutional rigidity of the Polish labour market lies behind its labour market problems. On the contrary, changes introduced recently have clearly improved its flexibility. Lack of improvement as far as employment growth and unemployment decline are concerned is probably a result of the recent nature of the latest reforms and of barriers existing on other markets that

---

[1] This question has been noted and documented by Cazes and Nesporova (2003, Chapter 4, in particular) for the broader group of post-communist countries.

hampered the job creation process. Relatively high labour costs and fiscal redistribution (for a country with relatively low GDP per capita) may be another important constraint.

Reversing negative trends in the labour market depends to a large extent on the modernization of the economy as a whole, including the public sector, and on an economic recovery capable of increasing the demand for labour. Without it, further deregulation of the labour market may prove to be ineffective, since the reduction of employment protection does not result in increased employability of the unemployed. Greater formal flexibility, accompanied by high unemployment, has made people's actual behaviour more rigid.

The remainder of this chapter is organized as follows. Section 7.2 gives a description of the labour market performance. In section 7.3 flexibility and security are analysed. The interdependence between labour market policies and employment protection is the subject of section 7.4. The chapter ends with conclusions and policy recommendations.

7.2   LABOUR MARKET CHARACTERISTICS AND ISSUES

During the period 1998–2004, real GDP rose by 22 per cent,[2] but according to the Polish labour force survey (LFS) the number of people employed dropped by 8 per cent. On the other hand, the registered unemployment rate rose from 10.4 per cent to 19 per cent.

The characteristic feature of the changes in the Polish labour market over the period 1998–2004 is the declining level of utilization of labour resources, expressed in a fall in participation and employment rates and in growth of unemployment rates in each labour force group (see table 7.1). According to the LFS, between November 1998 and the fourth quarter of 2004 the population aged 15 years or more grew by 3.8 per cent, indicating the arrival of the baby boomers of the 1980s on the labour market. In the same period, the employment rate dropped from 51 per cent to about 45 per cent, actual employment dropped by 8.3 per cent and the number of inactive persons rose by 9 per cent. As a result, in 2004 there were only a thousand more people with a job of some kind (aged 15 and more) than there were individuals remaining out of the labour market.

Changes in the level of employment were combined with changes in employment structure. First of all, the number of employed workers with low levels of education dropped considerably. Only employment among persons with tertiary and general secondary education has grown.

Participation and employment rates are higher and unemployment rates are lower among men than women. A very interesting feature is that from 1998 until the second quarter of 2004, women with higher education experienced a lower decline in activity

---

[2] The rate of GDP growth declined from 6–7 per cent in the mid 1990s to 1 per cent during 2001–02. However, it grew again to almost 6 per cent in 2004.

Table 7.1   Participation rates, employment rates, unemployment rates, by sex, age
            and education as a percentage of the population, Poland, 1998 and 2004

	1998			2004		
	Males	Females	Total	Males	Females	Total
Participation rates						
Total	64.9	50.0	57.1	62.7	47.9	54.9
Aged 15–24 years	42.2	33.2	38.5	39.3	31.3	35.4
Aged 25–44 years	92.7	85.3	85.9	93.1	80.5	86.9
Aged 44+ years	49.9	46.7	41.3	48.9	33.0	40.1
Tertiary	83.9	81.2	82.4	81.4	78.2	79.7
Post-secondary	79.0	80.3	79.9	77.1	71.0	72.6
Vocational secondary	78.4	69.9	74.0	72.8	62.0	67.4
General secondary	47.4	48.1	47.8	50.7	43.2	45.6
Basic vocational	80.2	64.0	74.0	74.9	58.8	68.6
Primary and lower	36.2	23.1	28.8	31.6	18.0	23.8
Employment rates						
Total	58.9	43.9	51.0	52.2	38.5	45.1
Aged 15–24 years	35.0	26.0	29.6	25.8	18.4	22.2
Aged 25–44 years	79.0	69.6	77.5	79.7	65.5	72.6
Aged 44+ years	34.5	31.9	38.5	42.2	28.5	34.6
Tertiary	81.8	78.3	79.9	76.7	72.2	74.2
Post-secondary	72.8	73.5	73.2	65.2	59.3	60.8
Vocational secondary	73.1	62.5	67.6	63.0	50.0	56.4
General secondary	42.2	41.1	41.4	41.6	33.8	36.3
Basic vocational	71.7	53.5	64.7	59.7	43.1	53.2
Primary and lower	31.4	19.5	24.6	23.9	13.4	17.9
Unemployment rates						
Total	9.3	12.2	10.6	16.7	19.5	18.0
Aged 15–24 years	21.3	25.5	23.2	34.2	41.0	37.2
Aged 25–44 years	8.0	11.9	9.8	14.5	18.7	16.4
Aged 44+ years	6.6	7.3	6.9	13.7	13.3	13.6
Tertiary	2.5	3.5	3.0	5.8	7.8	6.9
Post-secondary	7.8	8.3	8.4	15.4	16.5	16.2
Vocational secondary	6.8	10.6	8.7	13.5	19.4	16.2
General secondary	10.8	14.4	13.5	17.9	24.8	20.4
Basic vocational	10.6	16.4	12.5	20.3	26.7	22.4
Primary and lower	13.4	15.6	14.4	24.1	25.6	24.8

Source: Authors' calculations based on the published results of the LFS (fourth quarter).

Table 7.2   Population, labour force and employment by sex and status of
employment, Poland, 1998 and 2004 (thousands)

	1998			2004		
	Total	Males	Females	Total	Males	Females
Population aged 15+	30 061	14 306	15 755	31 196	14 870	16 326
Labour force	17 162	9 283	7 878	17 139	9 323	7 816
Not in the labour force	12 899	5 023	7 877	14 057	5 547	8 510
Unemployment	1 827	863	964	3 081	1 555	1 526
Employment	15 335	8 421	6 914	14 058	7 768	6 290
Private sector	9 476	5 554	3 922	9 876	5 942	3 935
Public sector	5 859	2 867	2 992	4 182	1 826	2 355
Wage employees in private sector	5 413	3 144	2 270	6 113	3 709	2 404
Employers	622	440	181	556	390	166
Own-account workers	2 753	1 691	1 064	2 400	1 512	888
Unpaid family workers	687	280	408	807	330	477

Source: Authors' calculations based on the published results of the LFS (fourth quarter).

and employment rates and a lower increase in the unemployment rate than men with higher education. Female employment in general decreased at a slower pace during this period, particularly in the public sector. However, from the second half of 2004 labour market performance indicators have seemed to recover at a much faster pace for men than for women. This is a typical feature of the female labour market, as it is much less sensitive to changes in the business cycle.

The biggest drop in employment over the period 1998–2004 was among young people, reflecting a longer time spent in education as well as the particular sensitivity of demand for youth labour to the business cycle. The smaller decline in employment among older cohorts than in prime-age groups reflects the role of regulations protecting older workers from redundancy.

Two groups that suffered particularly severely on the labour market were those of public sector workers, where employment diminished by almost 29 per cent, and own-account workers, whose numbers dropped by about 12.8 per cent (table 7.2). On the other hand, the numbers of unpaid family workers and of wage employees in the private sector rose (by 17.5 and 12.9 per cent, respectively).

The structure of female employment by employment status has remained relatively stable. However, some interesting changes can be noted. First, the growth of employment in the private sector was significantly higher for men than for women (7 per cent and 0.3 per cent respectively); the difference is also significant if we compare wage employment in the private sector (it grew by 18 per cent for men and only by 5.9 per cent for women). Second, the share of women among employees in the public sector grew (by about five percentage points). Third, the drop in the

Table 7.3   Distribution of employment, by sex and level of education, Poland, 1998 and 2004 (percentages)

Level of education	1998		2004		% change in total employment 1998–2004	
	Males	Females	Males	Females	Males	Females
Tertiary	11.3	15.0	17.3	24.5	41.8	48.4
Post-secondary	1.4	5.9	1.8	6.2	16.1	–3.9
Vocational secondary	24.5	28.1	25.3	25.2	–4.8	–18.4
General secondary	2.9	9.8	5.2	11.3	62.9	4.3
Lower vocational	43.0	24.3	38.8	22.1	–16.8	–17.3
Elementary	16.9	16.9	11.6	10.7	–36.4	–42.2

Source: Authors' calculations based on the published results of the LFS (fourth quarter).

number of employers was significantly larger among men than among women (by 11.4 per cent and 8.3 per cent respectively), resulting in a slight growth in the female share of this form of employment. But it is also worth noticing that the employment of women as own-account workers diminished considerably (by 16.9 per cent), and faster than for men (by 10.6 per cent).

Transition is characterized by fundamental changes in the education structure of employees, and this continues to be the case in its later stages. As can be seen in table 7.3, employment of people with tertiary education during the period 1998–2004 grew by 41.8 per cent for men and 48.4 per cent for women, while the employment of persons with primary education dropped by 36.4 per cent and 42.2 per cent respectively, and of those with basic vocational education by around 17 per cent for both sexes. The fraction of the employed with tertiary education grew by more than 7.6 percentage points to 20.6 per cent, while the share of workers with primary education fell from 16.9 per cent in 1998 to 11.2 per cent in 2004.

According to data available from the LFS, only in two occupational groups – professionals and sales workers – did employment rise over this period, by 17.3 per cent and 0.4 per cent respectively. The biggest drop in employment has been observed among skilled workers (25.5 per cent), clerical staff (18.1 per cent) and elementary occupations (16.6 per cent).

As far as the structure of employment by firm size is concerned, a tendency can be seen for the share of small and big firms to decrease. In 1998, employment in firms employing between one and five people and those employing over 100 workers constituted 61.9 per cent of employment, while in 2004 the figure was only 58.6 per cent.

Table 7.4 shows the distribution of unemployment by sex, age and level of education over the period 1998–2004. The LFS shows enormous growth in the numbers of the

Table 7.4   Unemployed by sex, age and level of education, Poland, 1998 and
2004 (percentages)

	1998	2004	% change in total unemployment, 1998–2004
	Thousands		
Total number	1 827	3 081	68.6
Males	863	1 555	80.2
Females	964	1 526	58.3
	Share of total (%)		
Females	52.8	49.5	58.3
Aged 15–24 years	28.8	25.3	47.9
Aged 24–44 years	50.6	48.6	63.6
Aged 45+ years	20.6	26.1	109.1
Tertiary	3.4	6.9	243.5
Post-secondary	2.6	3.3	112.5
Vocational secondary	20.8	22.3	80.8
General secondary	7.9	9.3	97.2
Lower vocational	41.5	41.3	67.8
Primary and less	23.8	16.9	19.8
	Duration of unemployment (%)		
0–3 months	25.1	16.8	13.1
4–6 months	17.7	14.5	37.7
7–12 months	21.8	19.8	53.5
13–24 months	23.0	25.9	89.5
25+ months	12.4	22.9	212.8
	Unemployed by reasons for entering unemployment (%)		
Job losers	54.1	15.7	−60.3
Job leavers	6.6	3.2	−33.3
Re-entrants	19.9	54.0	271.6
New entrants	19.4	27.0	90.1

Source: Authors' calculations based on the published results of the LFS (fourth quarter).

unemployed by 68.6 per cent (confirmed by the registers of the employment service, which show an increase of 63.8 per cent). All labour force groups contributed to the overall increase in the number of unemployed, but the largest increases were for men (by 80.2 per cent), the older age groups (by 109.1 per cent) and those with the highest level of education (by more than 243.5 per cent for people with tertiary education). The different dynamics of unemployment growth for individual groups caused changes in its structure, resulting in decreases in the shares of women (by 3.3 percentage points), youths and individuals with primary education (by 3.5 percentage points), while the share of older unemployed rose by 5.5 percentage points and that of workers with higher education by 3 percentage points. However, workers with basic or vocational education still make up almost 60 per cent of the unemployed while prime-age individuals make up almost half the total unemployed in Poland.

Growing difficulties in finding a job have been reflected in decreased frictional unemployment and increased structural unemployment. The share of the unemployed searching for less than three months for a job has decreased from 25.1 per cent to 16.8 per cent, while the share of the unemployed looking for a job for longer than a year but less than two years increased from 23 per cent to 25.9 per cent. Finally the share of persons looking for a job for over two years increased from 12.4 per cent to 22.9 per cent. This last group more than doubled in numbers. Such an unemployment structure favours the persistence of unemployment, or even hysteresis.

If we take the unemployment rate as a measure of unemployment severity, the situation of the younger age groups is the worst, since their unemployment rate at the end of 2004 exceeded 37 per cent. People with a low level of education are also in a very difficult situation (an unemployment rate higher than 23 per cent). The female unemployment rate in each year has been higher than the male unemployment rate, but the difference has steadily decreased and in 2004 was only 2.8 percentage points. This was the result partly of the relatively higher level of women's education and the enormous outflow of women, particularly those with a low level of education, from employment and unemployment to economic inactivity. On the other hand, relatively more men are described as long-term unemployed than women (49.2 per cent and 48.5 per cent respectively). The proportion of women searching not longer than three months for a job was lower than in the case of men for each year analysed. The average length of job search has grown in both groups and was at the end of 2004 about 16.7 months for women and 16.5 months for men.

During the period analysed the growth rate of the inactive population has been greater (8.9 per cent) than that of the population over 15 years old (3.8 per cent). As a result, the non-employment rate rose from 49 per cent in 1998 to 54.9 per cent in the fourth quarter of 2004. Despite quite similar growth rates of the population of men and women, the number of economically inactive men grew faster (by 10.4 per cent) than the number of inactive women (by 8.0 per cent). The numbers of the inactive aged 45–64 years and youths have grown most (by 50.2 per cent and 5.4 per cent respectively), while the number of inactive prime-age persons diminished by 11.5 per cent.

Up to 78 per cent of inactivity can be attributed to education, retirement or physical disability. Since 1998, the share of people inactive due to retirement has grown, while the share of inactivity due to disability and diseases or family reasons has fallen. However, the highest growth has been observed in the group of people discouraged by unsuccessful job search. The share of discouraged workers in the unemployed population rose from 11.3 per cent in 1998 to 14.6 per cent in 2003. The total passivity of people aged 45 years or more who do not participate in any form of improvement of their skills or qualifications is another worrying feature.

The combination of the recession with the restructuring of the economy and the entrance of the new young cohorts into the labour market might have been expected to result in growing labour market inflows and outflows (see Grotkowska, Socha and Sztanderska, 2005). In fact, since 1998 a diminishing fraction of the population has been moving between employment, unemployment and inactivity. While in 1992 during each quarter on average 8.1 per cent of the population aged 15–64 changed position on the labour market, moving from one status to another, in the year 2002 such flows accounted for only 4.1 per cent. The probability of remaining in unemployment has grown the most (by 11.6 per cent on average between 1992–97 and 1998–2002) and the probability of remaining in employment the least (by 1.2 per cent between the two periods).

Unfortunately, owing to a change in the definitions of permanent and temporary workers, we cannot comment on the changes taking place in these groups over the whole of the period analysed. However, for the period 2001–04 comparable LFS data indicate a sharp increase (by 76.6 per cent) in fixed-term employment; this is particularly the case among women, where the use of these contracts has increased by 86.1 per cent. Even so, in the fourth quarter of 2004 temporary jobs were more common among men (26.5 per cent) than among women (22.5 per cent). The prevalence of fixed-term contracts among young people is particularly significant. While in 2004, 24.7 per cent of the working population on average were employed on fixed-term contracts, the share among those aged 24 years or less reached 64.7 per cent. This may indicate that most of the people entering the labour market for the first time are offered fixed-term contracts. At the same time, relative to other age groups fewer young people state that they have accepted these terms because they have been unable to find an indefinite contract (about 43.7 per cent versus about 54.7 per cent in prime-age categories).

In terms of the education profile of those on fixed-term contracts, generally speaking both the men and women employed on fixed-term contracts are less well educated than those on indefinite contracts. The shares of those with tertiary education are lower and the shares of vocational and primary education, particularly among men, higher than in the case of permanent employment.

The precise explanation for such an abrupt increase in fixed-term employment after 2000 is not clear. There are two main possible reasons: economic recession and legislative change. The unfavourable business cycle phase seems to have been the crucial factor. Fixed-term contracts offer employers an attractive way of achieving considerable reductions in dismissal costs and labour costs in general. The relevant change in legislation, on the other hand, was almost insignificant and only in place temporarily between 2003 and 2004, allowing the use of three consecutive fixed-term contracts per worker rather than two.

There have also been changes to the definitions of full-time and part-time workers over the period, but in 2004 more than 88 per cent of the working population work full time and this share has remained stable throughout the transformation period. Part-time employment was more popular among women than among men in 2004: although women constituted 45.1 per cent of total employment, they formed 56.8 per cent of part-time employment (2004). Another characteristic feature of this population is the overrepresentation of the youngest (15–24 years) and oldest employees (45 years and older). The former group constitutes 20.6 per cent of part-time employment (compared with 9.7 per cent in total employment), the latter 49.4 per cent (compared with 38.3 per cent). This form of employment is somewhat unpopular with prime-age workers. These are mainly employees with primary and general secondary education working on a part-time basis. The share of persons with primary education in part-time employment is 33.5 per cent (versus 13.2 per cent in total employment), while in the case of those with general secondary education their share is 8.4 per cent (versus 7.4 per cent). On the other hand, persons with tertiary education and vocational (secondary and basic) education are under-represented among part-time workers. In the case of persons with the highest level of education the ratio is almost 2 to 1: 18.2 per cent of total employment but only 9.1 per cent of part-time employment. The development of work on a part-time basis has been caused mainly by either employees choosing this kind of work (32.7 per cent of employment in 2004) or a lack of a full-time alternative (25.9 per cent).

Multiple-job holding shows no significant changes during the period 1998–2004. The number of people holding two jobs fell by 21.6 per cent, but their share in the total of full-time workers declined marginally from 9.4 per cent in 1998 to 8.8 per cent in 2004.

Unfortunately there is a lack of data concerning the scale of informal employment in Poland. However, the above information enables us to draw the conclusion that informal employment has tended to expand after 1998. This may be explained by the growth of employment in the informal economy by around 11.3 per cent (GUS, 1998, and GUS, 2004) and by the growth in the number of unpaid family workers. On the other hand, the fact that the social security contributions paid by farmers are only one-sixth of the norm encourages many persons to register economic activity in agriculture while working in other industries. Indirect proof of this may lie in the phenomenon of multiple-job holding, which to a large extent concerns agriculture. It is likely that high indirect employment costs could have a similar impact on growth in informal employment, but for lack of more detailed information, we are not able to make a more thorough analysis of this.

7.3 FLEXIBILITY AND SECURITY: THE INSTITUTIONAL BACKGROUND

After an improvement in labour market performance in the period 1994–98, the situation dramatically worsened. The change of trends had a significant (although not immediate) impact on labour market legislation. Other factors that influenced institutional changes were accession to the EU and institutional convergence related to accession. Finally we may observe, although it is not well documented, a weakening of the political influence of trade unions.

Fundamental labour market reforms took place in the earlier years of the transition; since 1998, few changes have been introduced. Effective initiatives on the part of employers' organizations, mainly in the Tripartite Commission forum, have resulted in some new regulations facilitating dismissals of workers and concluding more flexible employment contracts. Since the beginning of 2003, the procedure for dismissing workers employed for indefinite durations has been changed mainly through the elimination of the obligation for consultation with a higher-level trade union organization in cases where the enterprise-level trade union had reservations concerning the dismissal. The right of dismissed workers to paid time off to search for a new job had been limited to those workers whose notice period was at least two weeks, whereas earlier (1996–2002) the employer had been obliged to pay for these days whenever terminating a labour contract. It is also now possible to hire a worker to temporarily replace another worker absent for justified reasons. For these contracts a very short (three-day) notice period is required. As mentioned above, for one year (up to the day of accession to the EU), the obligation to transform a third fixed-term contract into an indefinite contract was suspended. However, since 1 May 2004, prolongation of a second labour contract for a determined period results in its automatic transformation into an indefinite contract (with the exception of seasonal work or casual work of a cyclical character). Employers have received clear regulations determining compensation which their employees have to pay in the case of an unjustified early termination of a labour contract with failure to respect the notice period. In the case of indefinite contracts the compensation equals the remuneration for the notice period and in the case of fixed-term contracts it equals two months' remuneration (up until 31 November 2002 the amount of compensation was set by the labour court). However, employers are also threatened with a fine if they fail to meet their obligations and violate employees' rights (including issuing a civil contract instead of a labour contract, absence of written confirmation of the contract and its conditions, dissolution of the labour relationship in violation of regulations, and negligence regarding employees' records). They are also obliged to rehire employees dismissed without due notice or without compensation for this period.

As for group dismissal or redundancy regulations, four significant changes have recently been introduced. The first consists of a more general formulation of the reasons permitting a group dismissal. Currently these are all reasons not related to the workers, whereas until 2003 these were the only reasons specified by law that could motivate group dismissal. The second change is the obligation to provide trade unions with notice of an intended group dismissal within 20 days of the final decision (previously this period had been longer – 30 or even 45 days). The third change is the qualification for group dismissal procedure. Group dismissals have been redefined to include all dismissals involving at least 10 employees in an enterprise employing fewer than 100 workers, 10 per cent of the number of employees in an enterprise employing between 100 and 299 workers, and 30 employees in an enterprise employing 300 workers or more. This has resulted in more dismissals in large firms being regarded as group dismissals, while in small and medium-sized enterprises (SMEs) dismissals of several persons are not treated as group dismissals and do not come under special legislation. The fourth change in group dismissals is related to the broadening of the entitlement to compensation (severance payments) and consists in shortening the job tenure required for a right to a payment of one, two or three months' wages.

Generally speaking, changes in the legislation concerning group dismissals have reduced the number of cases where this procedure will apply to small firms and increased it with respect to large firms. They have also facilitated the implementation of the group dismissal procedure and entitled workers with relatively short job tenure to higher severance payments. The result can be seen as creating more flexible instruments of employment regulation. In the event of financial difficulties, employers may conclude an agreement with trade unions that suspend obligations resulting from the collective agreements and other labour rules and statutes (but not the Labour Code or other primary acts of law) for a period of up to three years.

Some regulations have been introduced that give employers more freedom as far as workers' duties are concerned, some elements of which may favour more stable employment. First, more liberal ways of setting work timetables have been introduced. The working week was also shortened from 42 to 40 hours. Second, small firms with 5–20 employees have been dispensed from an obligation to set formalized regulations concerning remuneration. Third, employment contracts have been formalized. Employers are now obliged to attach written information to the labour contract, within seven days of the acceptance of the job by the worker, specifying the characteristics of the job, the duties of the worker and the remuneration. This 'rigidity' gives employees the possibility of resigning in the event of changes in employment conditions, and facilitates for employers changes in work organization and dismissals of persons not wishing to adjust.

In the latest changes to the regulations, greater attention has been paid to part-time work. Employers are now obliged through the Labour Code to make an effort to transform a full-time contract into a part-time contract should the employee request it. Employers are obliged to inform workers (in the manner of their own choosing) about possibilities of full-time and part-time employment and to inform workers employed on a part-time basis about vacancies.

Although the legal foundations for industrial relations in Poland are to be found in the country's basic legislation and were regulated by law as long ago as 1991, they are considerably different from those observed in the developed market economies of Western Europe. The main differences are the multiplicity of relatively small employers' and employees' organizations, the lack of genuine cooperation within trade unions and within employers' organizations, the dominance of legal regulations and the undeveloped nature of social dialogue (for further information, see Grotkowska, Socha and Sztanderska, 2003).

Trade unions in Poland are grouped into three confederations: 'Solidarity' (NSZZ 'Solidarność', established in 1980), the All-Poland Alliance of Trade Unions (OPZZ, established in 1984) and the Trade Union Forum (FZZ, established in 2002).

However, some unions do not belong to any of these umbrella organizations. In Poland systematic data concerning trade union membership and structure are not collected.

Generally speaking, all trade unions have suffered from a decline in membership during the 1990s (Gardawski, 2003). It is estimated that between 2.2 and 2.4 million people were trade union members in 2002, accounting for 14.5 per cent of total employment and 20 per cent of full-time workers. Trade union membership is significantly rarer among those groups whose position on the labour market is relatively weak: young people (up to the age of 30), part-time workers, temporary workers and low-skilled persons. Only 7 per cent of those working in the private non-agricultural sector belong to a trade union. The share of trade union membership among employees is particularly significant only for mining (60 per cent) and transport (32 per cent). The highest rate of unionization (about 15 per cent) was recorded among persons with higher education (specialists, doctors, lawyers and teachers), followed by skilled workers. Only 10 per cent of unskilled workers have declared their affiliation to a trade union.

Most collective agreements are concluded at enterprise level. According to the National Labour Inspection data for the end of 2002, there were 8,683 collective agreements in force at that time, concluded mainly at enterprise level. Single-establishment collective agreements registered in 2002 concerned 117,653 persons. The highest number of multi-establishment collective agreements (75) was registered in 1998. In subsequent years, the number declined systematically, reaching 10 in 2001. No data are available on the time structure of the agreements and the populations they concern. The Ministry of Labour and Social Affairs estimates that multi-establishment agreements cover about 1 million employees (mainly in the public sector), employed by more than 4,300 employers. This is equivalent to more than 11 per cent of total employment.[3] Since there are no details on the contents of the agreement, we cannot judge the extent to which social partners agree on matters concerning the job security of employees covered by the agreements and the flexibility of their employment.

A low degree of synchronization of wage negotiations, on both the side of the trade unions and of the employers, is a characteristic feature of industrial relations in Poland. This does not help to formulate a uniform stance across the social partners.

The major change during the period analysed was the passing of a new law on the minimum wage, which came into force on 1 January 2003. According to the new legislation the minimum wage is negotiated in the Tripartite Commission for Social and Economic Affairs. Negotiated amounts are supposed to safeguard the real value of the minimum wage. In practice the minimum wage grows by the inflation rate, which means that in periods of real wage growth it falls in relation to the average wage. A differentiation of the minimum wage according to the employment period

---

[3] In 1997, collective agreements covered the employment contracts of 64 per cent of employees in state enterprises, 46 per cent of those employed in the budget sector and only 31 per cent of employees in the private sector (Kozek and Kulpińska, 1998). The budget sector includes public services financed from the public finance system (education, health service, administration etc.).

was also introduced, guaranteeing new entrants to the labour force not less than 80 per cent of the statutory minimum wage in the first year of employment and not less than 90 per cent in the second. However, in 2005, the law was amended to abolish the rule for the second year of employment, leaving special regulations only for the first year of employment. At the same time Parliament decided that the minimum wage would be increased each year by two-thirds of the projected rate of real GDP growth until it reaches 50 per cent of the average wage.

Modifications have also been made to the law relating to wage negotiation in public enterprises employing more than 50 persons. As of 22 July 2002, remuneration may be increased only by those employers who have demonstrated a profit in the previous accounting year.

In 1999 a fundamental reform of the social security system was introduced. One of the most important reasons for the reform was serious anxiety regarding the financial stability of the system, particularly in the long-run perspective of the gradual ageing of the population. Creating closer links between the amount of contributions paid into the system and future pension benefits was no less important. This process should give better incentives for greater economic activity and legalization of employment; a brief summary is set out below.

Financing of the social security system is based on an insurance scheme (contributions are the main source of financing) but direct government funding still regularly provides a subsidy (27 per cent of total expenditures of the Social Security Fund in 2002). There are four parts to the social security contribution: old-age insurance, disability insurance, sickness insurance, and work injury and occupational disease insurance. All in, the employer pays a social security contribution that may vary from 17.23 per cent to 20.12 per cent. The employee pays 18.71 per cent. Employers pay two additional contributions: for the Labour Fund (2.45 per cent) and for the Guaranteed Employee Benefits Fund, which covers wage arrears due to employees of bankrupt businesses (0.15 per cent).

All four kinds of insurance are compulsory for workers employed on labour contracts. For own-account workers (persons running non-agricultural business activities), sickness insurance is voluntary, while the other forms are compulsory and contribution rates are the same. An own-account worker pays both the employer and employee portions.

With regard to civil contracts (which became popular as a way of avoiding high indirect labour costs), in 2000 a rule was introduced which required all such contracts to include compulsory social insurance. Previously, social insurance was compulsory only for contracts concluded for more than 14 days, with accumulation of contract duration when the period between consecutive contracts was shorter than 60 days. However, social insurance does not include sickness insurance, and work accident insurance is not compulsory if the work takes place outside the employer's premises.

The basis for determining social security contributions is the income (real or declared) of the insured person; this is limited, in the case of old-age and disability insurance, to 30 times the average wage projected for a given year. For own-account workers, declared rather than actual income is the basis for the contribution calculation, though this cannot be lower than 60 per cent of the average monthly wage in the previous quarter. In 2005 an important amendment was introduced allowing individuals becoming economically active for the first time to pay social security contributions equal to only 30 per cent of the minimum wage. Preliminary statistics suggest that this measure has encouraged growing interest in setting up a business.

An employed person is also obliged to pay contributions for compulsory health-care insurance. These are calculated in relation to the pre-tax salary. In the case of own-account workers the calculation is based on pre-tax income. The contribution rate has risen and will continue to rise systematically – from 7.5 per cent in 1999 through to 8.75 per cent in 2006.

Besides the general system, there are special schemes for certain occupational groups. The social security system for farmers is particularly important, since its quarterly contributions for old-age and disability insurance, for work injury, sickness and maternity insurance are only a small fraction of the minimum contributions in the general social security system. This has resulted in the exodus of many own-account workers from the general social security system to the agricultural scheme. The scheme is open to all those with a farm of an area exceeding 1 reference hectare (a reference hectare takes into account the location and quality of land or special kinds of production).

The Polish personal income tax system is relatively progressive. There are three tax rates depending on the income earned by the taxpayer: 19 per cent, 30 per cent and 40 per cent. However, personal income tax thresholds were frozen in 2001 and have not followed inflation rates (which means a rise in the effective tax rate). The tax rate of 19 per cent is paid on yearly income up to PLN 37,024 (about €9,500[4]), and the rate of 30 per cent on income exceeding the previous threshold up to PLN 74,048 (about €19,500). Income exceeding PLN 74,048 is taxed at a rate of 40 per cent. The level of tax-free income remains relatively low (PLN 2,789.89 – about €750 – annually) resulting in a substantial tax wedge, particularly for low-skilled persons earning low wages. According to various studies, the effective personal income tax rate in Poland is between 17 per cent and 19 per cent. According to the Polish Ministry of Finance, in 2004 only 0.85 per cent of taxpayers paid the highest rate of 40 per cent, while 94.8 per cent paid the lowest rate of 19 per cent.

The amendments to the Labour Code introduced in July 2002 have resulted in a reduction in non-wage labour costs for employers. These changes, inter alia, abolished payment of wages for the first day of short-term illness, reduced overtime payments, abolished the obligation to establish formal rules governing work and pay in small firms (employing up to 20 persons), and limited the obligation to prepare a leave plan (unless a trade union demands one).

Difficulties in finding and keeping employment have resulted in strong demand for a permanent or at least periodical income, unrelated to work. Since the beginning of the transition period this has taken the form both of the creation of new sources of

---

[4] All conversions use the May 2006 exchange rate.

social income and of profiting from existing ones. Every possible form of income protection is intensely exploited. The introduction of any new form of social protection rapidly results in an increase in the number of people benefiting from it and hence in a rapid growth of expenditures related to this measure, particularly if the benefit has the character of an entitlement. This in turn is one of the reasons behind the budget deficit and high taxes.[5]

The income protection system has undergone a significant evolution in recent years. In the early 1990s, people who had difficulty finding a job would apply for an early-retirement pension or unemployment benefit. They repeatedly renewed their rights to these allocations, mainly through short-time employment. There was significant demand for disability pensions, mainly from individuals not entitled to early retirement, and pressure soon emerged for disability pension claims to be subject to assessment.

In 1997, special provisions for early retirement were abolished. Gradually, entitlement to early retirement for specific occupational groups (miners, teachers, railway workers, persons working in special conditions or women who had worked for at least 30 years) came to an end as well. To replace these allowances, pre-retirement allowances and pre-retirement benefits were introduced for the unemployed of pre-retirement age. In 2002, pre-retirement allowances were abolished in order to prevent a massive increase in the number of beneficiaries. As part of the reform of the social security system, the criteria for qualification for different disability categories were changed, substantially limiting the possibilities of obtaining disability pensions.

Gradually but systematically, during the period 1991–97 the allowance entitlements were reduced: one group after another was excluded from the population entitled to the allowance and the criteria for granting it were tightened (a means test was introduced such that the allowance could not be granted to an unemployed person with an income above a certain amount). As a result, in 2003 only 15.1 per cent of the unemployed registered with the employment service benefited from the unemployment allowance, compared to 20.3 per cent in 2000.

A significant portion of the population withdrew permanently from the labour market over the period in question, with a large number of relatively young people deciding to retire. The average retirement age in Poland is among the lowest in the EU: in 2002 it was 57.2 years (59.4 years for men and 56.1 years for women). In 2002, only 13.5 per cent of women retired aged 60 or more and 28.7 per cent of men retired aged 65 or more. In 1995 more than one-third of pensioners (over 1 million people) were below the retirement age. Restrictions on the access to early-retirement pensions, introduced in 1997, resulted in a decrease in this proportion to about one-quarter in 2002 (880,000).

While restricted eligibility for early-retirement pensions brought down numbers in the years 1997–2002, the share of people still benefiting from pre-retirement

---

[5] According to the methodology of the Ministry of Finance, public finance expenditures in 2001 reached 43.9 per cent of GDP (according to the OECD this share was 46.8 per cent) and grew to 44.4 per cent in 2002 (45.6 per cent according to the OECD).

allowances and benefits in this period grew substantially. At the end of 2001, 365,000 individuals were receiving pre-retirement allowances; in 2002, with the abolition of the granting of new allowances, the number of persons continuing to receive pre-retirement allowances decreased to 334,000, but at the same time the number of pre-retirement benefit beneficiaries rose from below 100,00 to 160,000.[6] As part of the so-called Hausner Plan[7] an estimate was made of the cumulative number of people who had withdrawn from the labour market through early retirement and were receiving pre-retirement allowances and benefits in 2002. The number had risen to 1.4 million. This illustrates the widespread tendency to exploit benefits that permit economic inactivity and is a proof of the inefficacy of active labour market policies as far as the pre-retirement age group is concerned.

Although receipt of a disability pension requires assessment of the existence of a disability (a factor independent of labour market performance), the level of disability confirmation is quite generous. Claiming disability pension has thus become another way of becoming economically inactive for those who have difficulty adjusting to the requirements of the labour market. The number of newly granted disability benefits (excluding those from the agricultural scheme) grew from 188,000 in 1989 to 243,000 in 1990 and 319,000 in 1991. Introduction of controls on disability certification, greater strictness concerning the definition of disabilities and a new rule stating that disability pensions are granted for a determined period of time resulted in a drop in newly granted benefits to an annual level of 150,000 during the period 1995–98, and a further reduction to 72,000 by 2002.

In the 1990s the system of social welfare was significantly changed as well. Since the self-governance reform (1999) all tasks concerning assistance have been entrusted to the local authorities, partly commissioned centrally, partly at the initiative and on the budget of the local authority.[8] For the period 1999–2001, on average about 900,000 families were granted some kind of help each year. About 700,000 families had periodical financial problems related, for instance, to unemployment. We have to take into account that unemployment was not the only reason for these difficulties and that other factors play an important part (for instance, in almost 500,000 cases there

---

[6] A right to pre-retirement benefits used to be granted to all individuals with adequate total job tenure (30 years for women and 35 years for men, or 25 and 30 years respectively if for at least 15 years the job was executed in special conditions or was of a particular character). Entitlement to pre-retirement allowance, on the other hand, is related to age: it is granted to all those who are no more than two years from the retirement age. In some cases (very long job tenure or job loss due to a group dismissal) the age may be lower.

[7] Minister Hausner prepared a diagnosis of the explosion in social expenditures that have caused growing problems with balancing the state budget and proposed a plan of its reduction. The Hausner Plan is the main social and budget reform prepared by the Government in recent years.

[8] The main task of *gminas* (municipalities) in Poland is to fulfil the common needs of local communities. However, since the reform of the public administration system implemented in 1999, local authorities execute the tasks of regional and central authorities and are funded accordingly. Since the second half of 2004, the system of family assistance has been similarly integrated. Up until 2004, part of the benefits were paid to families centrally and administered by separate services; for instance, while family benefits and childcare allowances were paid by the national Social Insurance Institution (ZUS), sets of school accessories were provided by schools. In the years 1998–2003 the payment of different benefits claimed for different reasons was abolished and the right to a benefit became means tested.

was a problem of a large family or a lack of one or both parents, and in more than 100,000 cases a problem of alcoholism). The current system of social assistance is aimed at helping families with particular problems, with unemployment not the only reason for their material and social difficulties. Sometimes the unemployment itself results from other family problems. It is therefore difficult to regard the current social assistance system as a scheme that replaces employment income for people who have difficulties in adjusting to the restructuring of the economy. Instead it can be said to provide some minimal income to families who have problems with social reintegration in general, not only as far as the labour market is concerned.

It should be noted that the attractiveness of different forms of replacement of employment income by social benefits has not increased in recent years and in fact has even fallen. At the start of transition, unemployment benefits, pre-retirement benefits, and retirement and disability pensions were linked to the average wage. The indexation method was then changed, replacing indexation on wage growth with indexation on price growth. With real wages progressively increasing, there was a gradual fall in the ratio of benefits to the average wage.

To sum up, it has to be stressed that the enormous rise during the period 1998–2003 in the number of people benefiting from different kinds of social payments was not a result of broader coverage of social entitlements or of their growing financial attractiveness. On the contrary, there was a gradual introduction of regulations that were supposed to reduce the attractiveness of such benefits or even to make access to them more difficult. However, this did not result in growing activity on the labour market. The practical obstacles to taking a job were stronger still.

In the period 1998–2002[9] a gradual decentralization of the national labour market administration took place. The reform made self-governance units and their authorities the main decision-makers, organizers and executors of active labour market policy. Employment councils at various levels – *voivodships* (higher-level administrative-territorial units) and *poviats* (lower-level administrative–territorial units) – became institutions formulating opinions on local labour market policy goals and tasks; these consist of representatives of employers' organizations, trade unions, farmers' organizations and local authorities. The state administration still determines the right to register individuals as unemployed and their unemployment benefit entitlement, and manages the payment of the benefit. It also determines entitlement to pre-retirement benefits and allowances, and administers their payment.

It seems that this step, aimed at shifting to the local level decisions concerning policy and its local implementation in significantly differentiated conditions, was a positive one. First reports of the employment councils indicate that they have undertaken some local-specific analysis and ordered action to be taken in the light of its results. There are, however, local self-governments and local councils that are

---

[9] A crucial change was introduced at the beginning of the year 1999 (implementing the law of 24 July 1998) with the fundamental division of the State into three administrative levels. However, actual decentralization of the State's different functions is still under way. The National Labour Office was closed down in 2000, for example, and local authorities were given sole authority over social benefits in 2004.

very passive in their action and clearly do not appreciate the positive long-term results of consistent labour market policy. They concentrate on short-term results related, for instance, to the material results of public works. We observe some loss of control of labour market policy in its entirety. Although the Government is able to coordinate local government action to a certain degree (mainly through the allocation of Labour Fund resources), it has not succeeded in obtaining an adequate level of coordination. Even the construction of an information system for the employment service was interrupted and required ministerial statutory entitlements on the setting of standards concerning computers and their software. Although the Government has initiated many programmes aimed at reducing unemployment, such as its widespread First Job programme, the results were not significant despite numerous participants.

The main reason for the low level of efficiency of labour market policies has been the reduction of expenditure on active policies. Whereas in 1998, 23.8 per cent of Labour Fund spending was allocated to active labour market policies, in 2002 the share was only 5.4 per cent. As a result, in 1998, when the number of the unemployed grew by 547,600, the number of basic programmes diminished by 30,000 (this drop ranged from about 4 per cent in public works and 5 per cent in training to 19.5 per cent in intervention works). Active labour market policies were concentrated on the implementation of the First Job programme, which was directed exclusively at school leavers who had finished their education in the previous 12 months. Almost 40 per cent of the Labour Fund resources for ALMP were allotted to this relatively small group. An average unemployed person who had not just left school had little chance of participating in an active labour market programme. This is particularly serious for low-skilled workers, who are faced with not only a low demand for labour, but with problems of access to education and professional training schemes that could improve their employability.[10] The structure of Labour Fund spending has improved in recent years, such that 14.4 per cent of its expenditure in 2004 was allotted to active programmes. This was reflected in growing spending on active measures per unemployed person: in 1998 it was PLN 707 (€173), then it fell to PLN 171 (€42) in 2002 and grew again to PLN 428 (€105) in 2004.

The 'mass exodus' from the labour market to all possible forms of social support is no surprise, as similarly structured and resourced labour market policies are simply insufficient to improve the employability of the unemployed. What is more, the engagement of other institutions in the labour market transformation process is very low – the level of resources assigned for training by employers is low and the education system is mainly concerned with the general education of young people rather than vocational training, and also suffers from financial shortages.

---

[10] It is usually the better educated who take part in training. Among employees, 4.3 per cent undergo training each quarter: the similar share among employees with tertiary education is 12.7 per cent; those with secondary education 4 per cent; and for those workers with education below secondary this level is about 1.2 per cent (Liwiński and Sztanderska, 2003).

7.4 LABOUR MARKET FLEXIBILITY, EMPLOYMENT AND SOCIAL PROTECTION

7.4.1 Identification of the trade-offs and complementarities

In the Polish economy there are two kinds of interdependence between labour market flexibility and employment and income security. The first kind is rather transitory and is related to the process of privatization of the economy.

Privatization has led to rationalization of employment (which usually means a reduction in the numbers employed) and hence provoked a growing need for social benefits (Bednarski, 2000). At the same time this process has been accompanied by a reduction in the coverage of social assistance offered by private enterprises. Relatively low wages (and incomes) result in keeping public expenditure, including spending on social welfare, high as a share of GDP. Growing income inequalities require a higher level of income redistribution to prevent social unrest, funded through high taxes and social security contributions. This results in high costs of employment per additional worker. While the reduction of the non-wage labour costs would lead to a drop in living standards for the poorest section of the population, high taxes result in some workers being pushed into the informal economy. A growing informal economy in turn increases insecurity on the labour market and stimulates demand for social transfers as a stable source of income. The high proportion of the population receiving disability pensions not always related to their actual state of health is one symptom of this process.

Another type of interdependence is more structural, and is associated with certain features of the market economy and with labour market and social policies, as well as with the level of economic development. A characteristic feature of the Polish economy is its high share of small business units, which have only a limited capacity to create new jobs.[11] As a result, some institutional solutions (internal to the labour market, but external to it as well) may have a disproportionate impact on the capacity for job creation in the SME sector. Uniform regulations concerning employment and dismissal conditions (particularly those regulating group dismissals); relatively burdensome procedures accompanying the registration of new firms; and complicated, non-transparent and frequently changing systems of accounts with the tax and social security administrations provide examples of such institutional factors.

---

[11] The drop in employment in Poland took place mainly as a result of the decrease in employment in large enterprises. This process was particularly intensive during the period 1998–2003 when there was still a legacy of excessive employment from the pre-transition era and the restructuring process intensified. The restructuring process was postponed mainly due to safeguard clauses in the privatization contracts, keeping state ownership in given sections and gradually disclosing the results of investments and technological progress. SMEs might have absorbed some of the effect of the dismissals in large enterprises, but during the recession period they too ceased to rely on hired employment. Their role has been concentrated rather in the development of self-employment. Therefore slower growth of the number of SMEs is clearly correlated with the slower growth of employment in SMEs.

In countries with relatively low levels of income per capita (in Poland it is more than 60 per cent below the European average), pressure to make up the backlog is bound to be enormous. Theoretically, it may be achieved through increased labour productivity or employment growth, or both. Labour market liberalization made this first possibility easier for employers. However, it happened at the cost of low employment and growing income inequalities. It is difficult to assess *a priori* whether maintaining stricter labour market regulations would have permitted higher employment through increased flexibility of internal labour markets and income growth. Polish experience indicates that with low demand for labour even further deregulation of the labour market would appear to be ineffective as far as the job creation process is concerned. At the same time, with limited resources devoted to labour market policies, it is difficult to determine the direction of the causality. For instance, is high labour taxation a cause of high unemployment or vice versa? In other words, are high taxes necessary for providing incomes for people without jobs?[12]

The share of people with a stable position on the labour market has increased. The adjustment process took a specific form and consisted mainly of workers withdrawing from the labour market and giving up searching for a job. The number of inactive people has therefore grown considerably. The workers most concerned were older workers and those with lower levels of education. These people used all the available means of securing incomes for themselves – particularly through entitlement to pre-retirement benefits. At an earlier stage in the process, disability pensions played a major role, but new regulations concerning these benefits caused a decrease in the number of newly granted pensions. As a result, the pressure on pre-retirement benefits and allowances intensified. Benefits were granted to the older unemployed with only a few years before old-age pension entitlement. Young, better-educated persons replaced economically inactive persons on the labour market. However, some of these could not find permanent employment and therefore turned to temporary employment, fixed-term employment or were employed only for the time taken to perform a given task. This is reflected in shortening of the average job tenure of people with tertiary education, of professionals and of persons aged 15–44 years (see Auer and Cazes, 2003, for data on OECD countries).

Generally speaking, stability of employment increased during the period 1998–2002, but this growth was not particularly significant. It is difficult to identify the labour market regulations that caused this phenomenon. Procedures for concluding employment contracts and dismissals were made somewhat more flexible. However, taxation did not decrease, the business cycle phase was definitely unfavourable and investment dropped. Such changes tended to strengthen the position of workers permanently linked to given employers (the insider effect) and made entry to employment difficult for workers from the outside. This phenomenon concerned, above all, young people from the demographic boom generation. As a consequence, persistence of unemployment or inactivity grew faster than stability of employment.

---

[12] However, research shows that employment is highly sensitive to labour costs. Some estimates indicate the elasticity of employment versus labour costs at 0.7 (Socha, 2005).

During the period of low GDP growth, the nature of Polish industrial relations favoured the strengthening of the position of insiders. The reconciliation of a flexible labour market with a high level of social security requires the cooperation of all social partners and a well-balanced programme for change. Instead, industrial relations have continued to be regulated mainly through central legal regulations and wage agreements concluded at the enterprise level. The lack of uniform employer and trade union representation at the national, sectoral and enterprise levels has tended to preserve a relatively high degree of state intervention in industrial relations processes.

The social partners' concentration on satisfying their own narrowly defined interests appears to be a significant weakness of social dialogue in Poland. Trade unions very rarely initiate actions aimed at promoting mobility of workers to new workplaces and almost exclusively concentrate on safeguarding existing employment. For their part, employers' associations lobby (quite successfully) for the reduction of barriers to dismissal and their role in employment promotion is also small.

The problem of assessment of the level of employment protection can be approached from two perspectives: de facto and de jure. As far as actual employment protection is concerned, this can be assessed on the basis of the characteristics of flows and dismissals. Data we have gathered suggest that the decline in economic growth was accompanied by a more-than-proportional decline in employment that affected mainly hired workers. The production crisis in the period 1998–2003 was far milder than the 1990–92 recession. In the recent period dismissals permitted significant productivity growth to be maintained, whereas at the beginning of the 1990s unemployment grew even though employment was protected.

This radically different adjustment pattern can be related to the significantly increased importance of the private sector in the economy. Labour turnover in the recent period has been distinctly higher in the private sector than in the public sector (about twice as high), although the share of the public sector in the economy has been falling. This suggests a higher degree of de facto employment protection in the public sector than in the private sector.

However, in both sectors a decline in separation rates has been observed (from 24.7 per cent to 19.0 per cent in the period 1999–2002, according to the registers), resulting in longer average job tenure. Among the reasons given for separation, employers' reasons rose from 22.5 per cent to 25.3 per cent. The overall separation rate decreased by 23 per cent in this period, but the rate of separations initiated by employers by only 13 per cent. We have to take into consideration as well the fact that a significant proportion of retirement decisions were forced on the workers by their employers. It is therefore impossible to discern any clear trend. An unfavourable stage of the business cycle tends to encourage a slowing down of flows into the labour market, but the decline in this period was mainly the result of a decrease in the number of separations initiated by employees, not by employers. It is hard to show at all clearly the impact of difficulties that employers may have been experiencing when dismissing employees.

Analysis of the unemployment rate suggests that the share of structural unemployment is still high and that there may be some fundamental reasons for unemployment growth besides demand factors. It seems that in Poland classic structural mismatch is a considerable problem, in terms of both skills and territorial profiles. Strong pressure pushing older workers and persons with lower qualifications out of the labour market indicates a definite shift in labour demand towards new and higher qualifications. Even formally, the same nominal education level of young persons and of older persons means different levels of qualification – not only because of the normal depreciation of human capital, but also because of the rapid changes that have taken place in the content of both education and jobs. Second, with real wages low and with a proportion of housing excluded from market regulation (housing in municipal and cooperative ownership), there remains a high degree of disproportion between living costs and wages. Territorial mobility is therefore rather limited, and this tends to perpetuate the regional disequilibria of the labour market. Third, wages are relatively rigid. Although the Gini coefficient of wage differentiation has risen, wages among workers with low qualifications are little differentiated. Fourth, we clearly observe an avoidance of high indirect labour costs, often using illegal methods, such as civil contracts instead of labour contracts, and non-registered employment. This suggests that labour costs in Poland are high. Although the unit labour cost is not particularly high, with demand constraints and large reserves thanks to technological progress, it appears that the economy does not reabsorb workers once they have left or have lost their job.

Sociocultural patterns of behaviour – some kind of negative adjustment or 'learnt helplessness' – may also play an important role. Previous easy access to social benefits and the importance of the natural-resource economy (for instance, farming or ownership of at least a smallholding) provide incentives to withdraw from the labour market. At the same time, the high level of inactivity demonstrates the relative inefficiency of all the activation policy measures undertaken in recent years, which have been limited in scope and impact. This is mainly a result of budget constraints, but structural mismatch probably goes deeper than the measures and resources of the active labour market policy can cope with.

7.4.2 Factors affecting the linkages between employment protection and labour market policies

The decline in employment protection in the private sector has been caused in large part by the recent increase in the number of fixed-term labour contracts, the ending of protection periods (of three to six years) in the privatized former state enterprises[13] and the statutory decrease in the employment protection level, although

---

[13] Usually privatization contracts were accompanied by a 'protection pack', negotiated with trade unions or workers' representatives, which specified additional conditions the new owner had to fulfil vis-à-vis workers. Research by the Institute of Labour and Social Policy shows that all packs included employment guarantees usually valid for three years (Bednarski, 2000).

as far as the legal aspects of the latter were concerned, these were of a fairly minor character and mainly concerned group dismissals.

The possibility of fixed-term employment has resulted in an increase in the population of temporary paid workers, which grew by a factor of 4.1 between 1998 and 2004, while the population of permanent paid workers fell by 26.2 per cent (the share of permanent paid workers fell from 94.2 per cent to 76 per cent). It seems that the significant increase in the numbers engaged on fixed-term contracts is the main sign of gradual growth in the flexibility of the Polish labour market. In real terms, employment protection appears to have fallen, particularly as far as newly employed workers are concerned. However, this has not resulted in any appreciable growth of mobility on the labour market.

Compliance with legal provisions regarding employment protection is reported to have been high. However, this opinion is based on fragmentary reports from the National Labour Inspectorate (PIP). According to the PIP, the number of infringements of the law on dismissals was relatively small and related mainly to failure to pay due compensation for dismissal with a shortened notice period, which was in turn largely a result of financial problems experienced by some employers. The PIP's reports do not indicate significant difficulties concerning dismissals (National Labour Inspectorate, 2003).

It is also known, although there is no statistical evidence, that there is a widespread phenomenon of disguised employment relationships, where employers offer workers civil rather than employment contracts: workers are encouraged to set up a firm (own-account employment) that accepts orders from former employers and in fact performs paid employees' tasks. This procedure is prohibited by law, but without the cooperation of the worker and the current employer it is almost impossible to prove that it takes place. The prevalence of the replacement of employment contracts by civil contracts is mainly due to its effectiveness in avoiding taxes.

A well-developed system of income protection for the unemployed and inactive has undoubtedly had a negative influence on the effectiveness of job search and strengthened the attractions of economic inactivity for those groups whose position is relatively unfavourable. According to estimates based on the latest national census (NSP), almost 14 million people in Poland benefit from different social allowances and benefits. This means that social system beneficiaries outnumber the population of formally employed (MgiPS, 2003). We observe a decline in the minimum/average wage ratio and the unemployment benefit/minimum wage ratio, though the former ratio may be regarded as high in the case of low-skilled persons, particularly on local labour markets where the wage level is low. There is no specific research on the behaviour of the unemployed, but general surveys indicate that many unemployed persons are passive, do not look for work or delay job search until the end of the period of benefit payment. Lack of control over the behaviour of individuals receiving unemployment benefit or disability pension, and shortcomings in the system to confirm active job search (required by the employment offices) result in a situation in which some unemployed work in the informal economy or are de facto economically inactive. The low share of persons now entitled to unemployment benefit indicates only that among the unemployed the share of persons out of work for less than a year is relatively small.[14]

The popularity of disability pensions comes as no surprise, since the average amount is 9 per cent higher than the minimum wage (2004). The possibility of combining social income with employment in the informal economy probably makes this relationship even more attractive from the point of view of its beneficiaries.

7.5   POLICY CONCLUSIONS

7.5.1 Labour market flexibility, employment and income security

Modernization of the Polish economy is still incomplete and the standard of living in Poland is still low by comparison with the European average. Moreover, the economy has had to face even stronger competition and restructuring pressure since accession. At the same time, the analysis presented above has indicated the economy's limited ability to create new jobs, the slow process of labour force reallocation and the continuing rigidity in some market institutions such as payroll taxation. While institutional reforms implemented by the Government have made the Polish labour market more flexible, there is still a need to increase the degree of flexibility of the Polish labour market in the context of existing challenges.

On the other hand, we can see that the patterns of labour market adjustment to changes in the economy since 1998 indicate a growing number of individuals loosely linked to the labour market (inactive and long-term unemployed), and growing differences between different labour force groups, particularly as regards their qualifications and the threat of social exclusion. This results not only in a significant share of people living below the poverty line, but a worsening social climate and growing support for populist political parties.

As already mentioned, among the reasons for the failure to reconcile growing labour market flexibility with employment security and social security are the fragmentary nature of changes, the low level of execution of implemented solutions and the centralized manner of their implementation. The law is the main instrument of regulation. In practice, there has not been much success in developing social dialogue at the lower levels of economy, while dialogue at the central level has been dominated by the political aims pursued by the social partners, not by social and economic goals. Given the lack of synchronization and the complexity of labour market reforms, even good partial solutions have not brought the expected results.

---

[14] The falling share of persons entitled to the unemployment benefit seems to be a result of two things. First, the share of long-term unemployed is growing; since the benefit is given for 6, 12 or 18 months (depending on the region and personal circumstances), this implies a falling share of individuals claiming benefit. Second, the structure of entrants to unemployment is changing: more individuals entering unemployment do not fulfil the requirements to claim benefit (in particular, having worked 365 days during the previous 18 months). This is related to the growing share of new entrants and re-entrants, and of employees on short-term contract, who have no right to benefits when unemployed.

However, the Government has obviously made mistakes as well. For instance, despite declaring its active stimulation of economic activity and employment, the Government launched policies that in fact promoted dis-activation. Generally speaking, labour market policy was aimed too much at outflows from employment and too little at creating new jobs and shifting people between old and new jobs. It strengthened the position of insiders, rather than weakening it, and therefore failed to increase functional flexibility. Limited solutions for external flexibility (for instance, rigid rules on group dismissals) at a time when the economic situation was worsening led to large-scale dismissals of workers instead of giving incentives to keep them in employment through increased flexibility on the internal labour market. The policy of income protection for the unemployed did not encourage an increase in the effective labour supply or improved efficacy of job search.

Then again, the failures of many programmes concentrated on a given labour force group lead us to reflect that during a recession, with limited public resources, the possibilities of improving the functioning of the labour market through increasing its flexibility are almost certainly more limited than in a period of economic boom.

7.5.2 Role of the social partners

Social dialogue in Poland is still at a fairly early stage of development (Grotkowska, Socha and Sztanderska, 2003). A tripartite dialogue between government, trade unions and employers clearly predominates over other forms of social dialogue, and it takes place mainly at national level (within the Tripartite Commission for Social and Economic Affairs).

Definite progress is being made in the process of building effective institutional and legal infrastructure for social dialogue in matters relating to employment and the labour market. This is indicated by such events as the development of dialogue at regional level within regional social dialogue commissions and at sectoral level within tripartite sectoral groupings. In this sense, in spite of differences with practice in the EU, possibilities for genuine inclusion of trade unions and employers' organizations in the process of labour market and social policy formulation and implementation have been created. The problem of the limited role played by the social partners therefore lies not so much in the legal basis for their active participation as in problems encountered among groups of partners. Difficulties in formulating one stance for all trade unions or all employers' organizations prevent any effective impact on policy formulation. At the same time, it seems that neither the trade unions nor the employers' organizations in Poland are as yet sufficiently mature to balance the need for social security and labour market flexibility in their respective stances. Trade unions concentrate on fighting (sometimes even violently) to maintain all social rights acquired by employees, while employers underline the crucial role of labour market flexibility in solving the economic problems of the Polish economy (unemployment). So far they have not made sufficient efforts to reconcile these two goals in their programmes.

An important direction seems to be improvement of the coordination within both trade unions and employers' organizations (particularly the latter). According to many cross-country studies, this factor is crucial for tackling the unemployment problem. In coping with structural and technological challenges, the Pact for Employment and Competitiveness should be considered as a method of achieving a higher level of employment and of social security.[15]

7.5.3 Policy recommendations

Within the EU, Poland is one of the Member States with the worst employment and unemployment rates. However, the first adjustment period and its consequent increased competition threatens to create greater restructuring pressure, as it is quite likely that there are still reserves of labour due to overstaffing in some sectors, for instance in mining, metallurgy, energy supply, railways and certain public services. This may worsen an already unfavourable situation.

We consider that important progress has been made in creating a legal environment with that fosters greater labour market flexibility. This positive assessment is based on changes in the labour law, the creation of legal conditions for cooperation between the social partners at all levels (including the Tripartite Commission and Employment Councils), the decrease in the ratios of social benefits to wages and a gradual reduction in access to benefits, limiting the access to really difficult cases in which external help is indispensable. Radical social and family policy reform (consolidation of allowances) is the best example of such a policy. Some policies are in the process of implementation within the framework of the plan for the rationalization of social spending. Among other positive changes, mention should also be made of the possibility of coordinating social and labour market policies and relating them to local situations.

Despite constant improvement, the system still has faults. There is a clear lack of coordination at national level, excessive territorial differentiation resulting not from the characteristics of the local labour markets but from the competence of local authorities. In many cases resources earmarked for labour market policies were reallocated to other local needs. All local authorities suffer from severe budget constraints that often make a rational decision on resource allocation impossible. The differences between local labour markets are widening and regional policy has so far been ineffective.

---

[15] Such a pact might be very helpful in building a better and more efficient labour market, since it seems that this is not a high priority for either of the social partners. Some trade unions have little interest in helping workers adjust to take on new jobs through updating or changing their skills and through support for more flexible forms of employment. Employers for their part are usually not interested in training their employees and rarely offer alternative employment to dismissed workers. It seems that these are the minimum requirements necessary to achieve better competitiveness and flexible flows from one job to another, and guaranteed modest wage growth in periods of falling unemployment in order to avoid inflation growth. However, the present system of negotiations appears to be stuck in the past: some trade unions only fight to keep existing employment levels and for better remuneration, while many employers try to cut employment to a minimum and pay little attention to the future employability of their workers.

We cannot assess unequivocally the changes in the education system. Numerous observers claim that popularization of education at the secondary and tertiary level is not being accompanied by an adequate level of quality.[16] There is a lack of direction in education regarding the evolution of the demand for labour; this tends to be due to a combination of lagged market signals, limited personal or family financial possibilities and the limited initial endowment of the education system itself, rather than a reflection of long-term labour market development. An exception is the gradual computerization of schools. Raising the level of education and – to a great extent – improving its general character provide some sort of protection against mistakes concerning its direction.

The analysis presented in this chapter confirms the existence of labour demand barriers in recent years. We do not think that labour legislation limiting the freedom of employers is the source. It seems that labour costs, particularly indirect ones, are still too high for the economy. On the one hand, it is not worthwhile for employers to employ additional workers; on the other, low wages discourage active job search and give an incentive for inactivity. Under strong influence exerted by the employers' organizations, changes in taxation aimed at the introduction of a flat-rate tax have been discussed and partly implemented. An alternative proposition would be to try instead to reduce taxes on the lowest incomes (for instance by raising the threshold of income exempted from taxation). The tax wedge results mainly from the high costs of social security contributions and, more generally, the high operating costs of state and public services. Pension reform, definitely necessary from a long-term perspective, imposes significant burdens on the state budget. The process cannot be reversed, but it could be more efficient to shift the financing of health insurance onto general taxes. In the long run, rationalization of the functioning of the whole public sector is unavoidable.

Two – apparently contradictory – tendencies have been a feature of the Polish labour market in the past five years: a decline in employment security and a slowing down of labour turnover. One might therefore conclude that a degree of employment protection legislation that allows for more flexible restructuring of employment has already been attained. Such reasoning could well be wrong.

The main threat to workers on the Polish labour market is high and persistent unemployment. With the unemployment rate as high as 20 per cent and the employment rate remaining below 50 per cent, and with increasingly severe difficulties in finding a new job, losing a job in almost any occupation puts the employee at risk of remaining permanently without work and income. This risk is highest in groups where unemployment is particularly high – mainly among the low-skilled labour force. In such a situation the resistance to dismissals is not because employment would be less protected at the new workplace but because there is no potential workplace to which to move. The shortage of jobs is relative and is a result of the deterioration of the business cycle and continuing substantial overstaffing in

---

[16] International comparative research by the OECD Programme for International Student Assessment (PISA) indicates a lack of functional skills among Polish pupils and students.

non-restructured sectors of the economy on the one hand, and low profitability of hired employment on the other. Low profitability is in turn the result of the high tax wedge and the low attractiveness of the supply of unskilled labour. In some branches (particularly those where new technologies requiring highly skilled workers are widely used) the fall in employment turnover should be related rather to the reluctance of employers to dismiss workers in whose skills they have previously invested. Restructuring pressure results in a tendency to reduce the numbers of low-skilled personnel and in increasing stability of employment for those workers with the highest qualifications. However, in most recent years this tendency has been reversed and a decline in job tenure has been observed even for people with tertiary education.

Our analysis indicates that it would be difficult to lower wages in the case of low-skilled labour, since their real level is already very low and a further drop (or even stagnation) would be likely to lead to a decrease in the participation rate for this group. A reduction in the tax burden and social security contributions mainly through increasing the income tax threshold for this section of the labour force would be one solution. However, the implementation of such a measure at a time of deficit in public finances would be possible only if the reforms aimed at reducing budget expenditures were successful.

Measures to improve the situation on the Polish labour market are dependent on the employability of those dismissed, meaning that they must have qualifications that are attractive to employers. Relevant active labour market programmes have been considerably restricted: restoring or even increasing the level of expenditure on such programmes is therefore necessary. Particular attention should be given to training in terms of its orientation and its implementation. A system allowing better insight into the qualifications of the unemployed in the context of the needs of the local labour markets is also needed. One of the most important obstacles to effective public policy aimed at adjusting qualifications to labour market requirements is the inefficiency of the public employment service. In the new administrative system this has been decentralized and the National Labour Office has been closed down. Satisfactory, national-level coordination of the work of the employment offices, popularization of effective counter-unemployment measures, increasing the level of professionalism of employment office staff (including hiring qualified personnel and reducing rotation) and curtailing the political influence on their functioning are absolutely vital. Currently, employment services are dependent to a high degree on political decisions by local authorities, including the choice of people to be employed in local offices.

It is worth noting that the general decline in labour market turnover seen alongside longer average job tenure and employment duration (and unemployment duration) is a result of two opposing tendencies. In the private sector, in the sections of the economy where markets are more competitive, obstacles to employment restructuring have been considerably reduced and the first results (shorter job tenures, higher share of fixed-term labour contracts) are already visible. At the same time, turnover fell significantly in those branches where the public sector predominates and where a monopolistic market structure prevails. This indicates that there is not much sense in searching for a recipe for restructuring through stricter employment protection, but rather through weakening the position of insiders, de-monopolization, faster privatization and implementing methods in the public sector that would expose it to competitive pressure. However, to obtain social acceptance for such solutions, the scale and efficiency of active labour market policy measures need to be improved, since only such an improvement can give a chance of restoring employability to workers threatened with dismissal. This policy should be region-oriented instead of being sector-oriented.

It seems that in sectors of the economy whose functioning is governed by the market and where the level of competition is significant, statutory regulation provides for proper equilibrium between employment security and labour market flexibility. However, this has not influenced the process of employment restructuring in the state sector and in branches where monopolistic or oligopolistic market structures prevail.

Acceptance of dismissals in state enterprises and large firms has been secured up to now mainly through implementation of various measures aimed at assisting the reduction of economic activity (early-retirement, disability pensions obtained in spite of still being able to work, pre-retirement benefits). This policy cannot be continued because of the financial burden that it creates and because of the negative impact on the economic activity of the whole economy.

Financial assistance for the unemployed cannot be further reduced, particularly the assistance granted for short spells. Consideration might be given to introducing unemployment benefits that are degressive over time. Access to benefits during the relatively short spells between different employment contracts would be universal and would be a better form of securing income for members of the labour force.

The above findings allow us to conclude that the labour market reforms that have taken place in recent years have been along the right lines. They have allowed employers to better adapt the demand for labour to the needs of the economy. The search for the equilibrium between employment security and labour market flexibility should now be concentrated on assisting labour force members to make a smooth adjustment to labour market challenges.

THE WAGE DIMENSION OF FLEXIBILITY AND SECURITY IN SELECTED CENTRAL AND SOUTH-EASTERN EUROPEAN COUNTRIES

8

*Mirco Tonin**

8.1   INTRODUCTION

Labour market security is determined by its capacity to provide decent and relatively stable living and working conditions to the population, while its flexibility is determined by its ability to adapt to new conditions. As described in chapter 1, discussions of flexibility are generally applied to four dimensions. External and internal flexibility refer to the possibility of adapting the quantity of labour through hiring and firing or variation in working time. Functional flexibility concerns the organization of work, while wage flexibility is the ability to adjust pay to respond to shocks and provide proper incentives.

The combination of flexibility and security in a particular labour market depends on the interaction of several of its institutions. In this comparative study we focus on the wage formation system of six of the Central and South-Eastern European (CSEE) countries: Bulgaria, Croatia, the Czech Republic, Hungary, Lithuania and Poland.

The chapter begins with an analysis of the wage determination system, where the changes that have occurred during transition are highlighted. The focus is on the formal and informal arrangements governing the formation of wages. The relevance of the informal economy and the non-respect of contractually agreed provisions in the countries under study should be kept in mind while reading all sections. Informal arrangements result in a higher degree of wage flexibility than that found when only formal arrangements are taken into consideration. Moreover, the comparison of official data on wages is made more cumbersome by the fact that the informal economy has different relevance in the various countries.

The degree of wage flexibility is assessed in section 8.3. First, we evaluate the responsiveness of the real wage to macroeconomic conditions and crises since 1989. Then the regional scale is considered, looking at the sensitivity of wages to local

* Institute for International Economic Studies, Stockholm. The author would like to thank the editors and Danijel Nestic for useful comments. All errors and omissions are solely the author's.

conditions. The variation of earnings along the sectoral dimension and along educational and professional lines is also examined. In the subsequent section, section 8.4, we investigate whether there is a wage floor in the countries under consideration. We look at how binding the minimum wage and unemployment benefits have been. Section 8.5 analyses the issue of labour taxation. The incidence of social security contributions and income taxation is evaluated. The last section concludes.

8.2   THE WAGE FORMATION SYSTEM

The way in which wages are determined has radically changed with the systemic transformation of the CEE economies. This section presents the development of the wage formation system from the high centralization typical of the socialist regime to the high decentralization prevailing today.

8.2.1 From high centralization …[1]

The strategy of forced growth that characterized the classical socialist system implied full employment and high investment rates. The full employment policy generated chronic labour shortages and labour hoarding by enterprises. The pursuit of high investment rates required a limitation of consumption, realized by bureaucratic control over real wages through a centralized wage tariff system and price control. While firms faced a soft constraint over their general budget (meaning they could expect to be systematically bailed out in case of persistent losses), the constraint over the wage fund was hard.

Wage dispersion was limited. Relative wages were responsive to relative excess labour demand along occupational and regional lines, while effort, productivity or company performance generally played a limited role. 'Material production' was favoured, in particular heavy industry, and the differentials in earnings of non-manual and manual workers were narrow. The reforms attempted in some countries, such as Hungary and Poland in the 1970s and 1980s, produced a weakening of bureaucratic control and resulted in runaway nominal wages.

The case of former Yugoslavia was different. Under the system of workers' self-management there were fewer incentives for labour hoarding and open unemployment was present. Moreover, less stringent bureaucratic control made wage restraint more difficult.

At the onset of transition, stabilization programmes characterized by tight monetary and fiscal policies were launched with the aim of maintaining macro-economic stability. These programmes usually included a restrictive income policy based on a punitive tax on excessive wage increases, with the purpose of controlling inflation by avoiding a price–wage spiral. The application of the system was usually soon restricted to public enterprises, while for the budgetary sector a wage tariff

---

[1] This section draws extensively on Kornai (1992).

system remained in force. In Hungary this tax-based income policy was introduced long before the political transition and lasted until 1992. In Bulgaria, the Czech Republic and Poland it was implemented in the aftermath of transition, lasting until 1995 in the Czech Republic and Poland, and continuing until 1997 in Bulgaria. The tax-based income policy had a serious drawback in that it reduced incentives for labour to reallocate toward successful firms by inducing enterprises, both profitable and unprofitable, to increase wages at the maximum allowed rate, sometimes through asset sales and cuts in investment (Cazes and Nesporova, 2003). Centralized tax-based income policy is no longer applied, largely replaced by a more decentralized wage formation system.

8.2.2 ... to high decentralization

Collective bargaining in the CEE countries has generally a more limited role than in the majority of the EU15 Member States. In the countries under consideration, with the exception of Croatia, the coverage of collective agreements is far from comprehensive. Moreover, the implementation of signed collective agreements is rather weak, with underdeveloped surveillance and enforcement mechanisms. Remuneration and more generally working conditions in a large part of the private sector and in particular in small and medium-sized enterprises (SMEs) are determined by bargaining on an individual basis or decided unilaterally by the employer. However, even the fact that salary is based on an individual contract is not to be taken for granted as employment without any type of contract or payments different from contractually agreed levels is widespread.

The level at which bargaining takes place matters in terms of economic outcome. According to economic theory, a high degree of centralization, with bargaining mainly at national level or decentralized bargaining at enterprise level, implies a lower level of unemployment and wages than that associated with intermediate, sectoral-level bargaining (Calmfors and Driffill, 1988).

In the countries under consideration, bilateral collective bargaining at the national level is rather underdeveloped, while national tripartite social dialogue has an important function. From the wage determination perspective this stage is relevant mainly in connection with minimum wage fixing and for public employees. In Hungary and Poland, recommendations for wage increases at sectoral and enterprise level are also drawn up in national-level negotiations, while in Croatia the tripartite Economic and Social Council has among its prerogatives the proposal of a harmonized wage policy (Djuric, 2003).

Social dialogue at the sectoral level, important in the EU15 Member States, is deemed to be the least developed level of bargaining in CEE countries (Ghellab and Vaughan-Whitehead, 2003). Sectoral-level agreements are generally few and their content weak, as the main stage of bargaining usually takes place at enterprise level (see Tonin, 2006). Croatia represents an exception in this respect, as bargaining at intermediate level is relevant (Rutkowski, 2003). Moreover, Croatia associates the highest estimated coverage rate to the highest unionization rate. At the opposite end of the spectrum is Lithuania, where collective bargaining at any level is extremely underdeveloped and the unionization of the workforce is particularly low. The few collective agreements in place are in the public sector, state-owned enterprises or privatized enterprises, while they are extremely rare in foreign-owned enterprises and SMEs (Babrauskiene, 2003).

The low coverage rates in the countries under consideration imply that salaries are determined through collective bargaining only for a minority of the workforce, and mainly at the enterprise level, resulting in a highly decentralized wage bargaining system. Croatia is the exception and it is interesting to note that among the countries under consideration it has the highest average wage in terms of purchasing power but not the highest productivity, as we shall see in the next section, suggesting that higher unionization and coverage combined with the prevalence of sectoral-level bargaining are indeed effective in pushing up wages.

The weakness of the social partners that should be involved in bargaining (trade unions and employers' organizations) is usually considered one of the main impediments to the development of collective agreements (Ghellab and Vaughan-Whitehead, 2003; Lado, 2002).

In an analysis of the wage formation system in CSEE economies it would be misleading to focus exclusively on formal arrangements. Two aspects are of particular interest for wages: employment under some type of informal arrangement and non-respect of formally agreed provisions. A widespread type of informal arrangement is, for instance, the payment of undeclared 'envelope wages' over the officially agreed amount.

To measure informal economic activity is difficult. However, some techniques have been developed to provide at least a raw estimate (Schneider and Enste, 2000). The relevance of the informal economy clearly emerges from the figures in table 8.1, in particular in Bulgaria, Croatia and Lithuania. The sectors where undeclared work is most common are agriculture, construction, social and personal services, and especially hotels and restaurants, businesses and retailing. Working, at least partly, in the informal economy is not exclusive to unskilled labour. Medical services and some types of business services also see a significant incidence of undeclared work.

The mirror phenomenon is the partial or non-payment of contractually agreed wages. In Bulgaria the problem of wage arrears is widespread, in particular in state-owned enterprises, while Croatia, Poland and Lithuania are also affected.

Payments above and below the contractually agreed wage greatly increase the effective degree of wage flexibility. It is however a 'perverse' type of flexibility, open to abuses, and one which in the case of envelope wages, for instance, reduces the effective taxation of wages for some categories of workers, leaving the fiscal burden to others. The reduction of the degree of informality and the negotiation of a combination of flexibility and security which applies to the whole workforce is one of the most important tasks facing these economies, for reasons of both equity among workers and fair competition among firms. Social partners with the capacity to play their role effectively, in particular at decentralized levels, could perform an important function in this respect.

Table 8.1   Bargaining, unionization and the informal economy, selected CSEE
             countries and EU15, late 1990s and early 2000s

	Collective bargaining coverage 1999–2001[a] (%)	Union density 1999–2001[b] (%)	Informal economy 2000[c] (% of GNI)	Undeclared work[d] 2002/3[1] (% of GDP)
Bulgaria	40[2]	30	36.9	22–30
Croatia	50–60	45	33.4	..
Czech Republic	25–30	30	19.1	9–10
Hungary	34[3]	20	25.1	18
Lithuania	10–15	15	30.3	15–19
Poland	40	15	27.6	14
EU15 (unweighted average)[4]	78*	44	18.8**	6–7***

Notes: Figures are estimates. [1] Czech Republic and Hungary: 1998. [2] At sectoral level for 2002–03. [3] Lado (2002) estimates coverage at 45%–50%. [4] Not including: * Greece, Ireland, Italy; ** Luxemburg; *** Ireland, Luxemburg, Spain. .. = not available.

Sources: [a] Carley (2002), except Markova (2003) for Bulgaria; Grgurev (2002) for Croatia. [b] Carley (2002), except Bandelj (2003) for Bulgaria and Croatia. [c] World Bank. [d] Renooy et al. (2004).

8.3   WAGE FLEXIBILITY

Wage flexibility has been defined as the ability to adjust pay to respond to shocks and to provide workers with proper incentives. In this section, we first relate real earnings to macroeconomic conditions during transition and study how wages responded to the transformational recession and subsequent crises. We then examine whether wages respond to variation in unemployment along regional lines and look at the variation of wages by sector, education and profession.

8.3.1   The development of real earnings during transition

All the countries under consideration experienced a deep recession at the outset of transition. As a consequence, both employment and real wages fell, except in the case of Hungary, where the drop in output was compensated by decreasing employment, and Lithuania, where the initial shock was absorbed mainly by collapsing wages.

As can be seen in figure 8.1, wages were hit hard by the surge in inflation that came with price liberalization in Bulgaria, the Czech Republic, Poland and Lithuania at the beginning of the 1990s. The conflict of 1991–95 heavily affected real wages in Croatia, falling to a third of the 1989 level in 1992–93 as a consequence of

Figure 8.1 Level of real wages, selected CSEE countries, 1989–2003

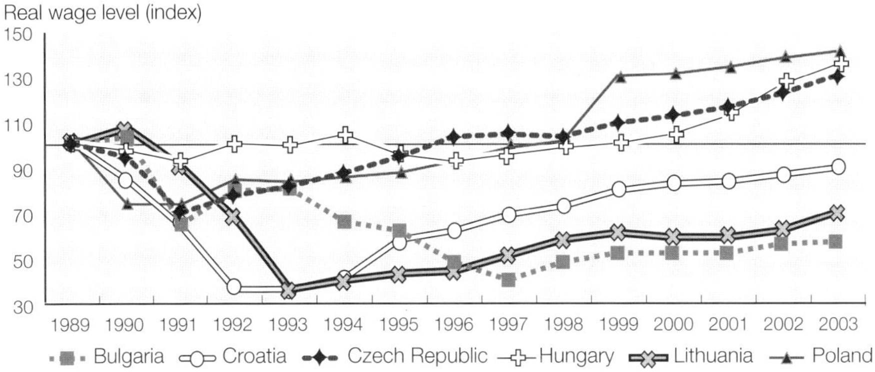

Real wage level (index)

Note: Deflated by CPI; index, 1989 = 100.

Source: CPI from UNECE; wage data from ILO; own calculations.

hyperinflation. Hungary is an exception. It had double-digit inflation for the whole of the 1990s but did not experience the dramatic increase in prices at the beginning of transition that affected other countries, as price distortions were less serious. Thus real wages remained quite stable.

Wages have generally continued to be responsive to the crises that ensued during the course of transition (Bulgaria 1994 and 1997; Czech Republic 1997; Hungary 1995–97). As for the situation in recent years, only the Czech Republic, Hungary and Poland had reached a wage level above the 1989 starting point by 2003. At the opposite end of the scale, Lithuania and more particularly Bulgaria are well below the 1989 level, experiencing stagnating earnings levels in the years around 2000 and only recently beginning to show signs of an upward trend. Croatia experienced a dramatic slump at the beginning of the 1990s but has been on a clear rising path thereafter. However, it has to be kept in mind that comparisons of the pre- and post-transition level of wages are cumbersome.[2]

The path of production after the initial shock of transition has been very different in the countries analysed. In the Czech Republic, Hungary and Poland the fall was contained, at least in comparative terms, and the recovery pushed production above the 1989 level in the following years. Bulgaria, Croatia and particularly Lithuania experienced instead a dramatic slump in terms of GDP and they are still below the pre-transition level. The path of employment has also been different. In Hungary

---

[2] The fact that monetary wages were just a part of work compensation during socialism and that prices were not the instrument used to regulate demand and supply makes the deflated nominal wage an imperfect estimate of the slump in the standard of living among wage earners. Moreover, the 1989 wage level does not represent an equilibrium reference point and comparisons may be sensitive to the specific price index used as deflator. See Tonin (2006) for more details.

Figure 8.2 Productivity measured as GDP per worker, selected CSEE countries, 1989–2003

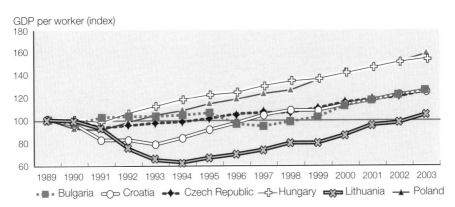

GDP per worker (index)

Note: Index, 1989 = 100.

Source: GDP and employment data from UNECE; own calculations.

employment fell to just 70 per cent of the pre-transition level in the mid 1990s and then slowly started to recover. Bulgaria and Croatia have similarly experienced a drop in employment, with signs of recovery visible only recently. The Czech Republic and Poland have kept a higher employment level throughout the period, but the trend in recent years is downward. The experience of Lithuania is one of a moderate decline, comparable to the Czech and Polish situation up until the end of the 1990s, followed by a dip around 2000 and a partial recovery in recent years. Figure 8.2 displays real GDP per worker as an index of productivity. In absence of distortions in the labour market, productivity and real wages should move in the same direction and it is possible to state that, with the notable exception of Hungary and Bulgaria in the first phase of transition, real earnings have broadly moved in line with productivity.

In Poland there is a strong similarity between the paths of real earnings and productivity. After a slight drop at the beginning of transition, output per employee recovered quickly, thanks to the rapid upturn in GDP, and since then has been on a steep upward trend. The Czech case looks similar, with a smaller GDP growth rate per employee. The path of wages in Lithuania also corresponds in shape to the developments of our productivity measure. At the beginning of transition Lithuania followed the behaviour of other countries of the former Soviet Union. In the face of collapsing GDP, wages dropped dramatically while employment remained much more stable, such that falling wages corresponded to falling GDP per worker (Boeri and Terrell, 2002). Real wages started to increase again once productivity began to rise in concomitance with a recovery in GDP and labour shedding. Croatia follows a similar path, with an initial period of decreasing wages and productivity followed by a phase where both were on an upward trend. In Hungary productivity has a similar

219

Table 8.2   Correlation coefficients of GDP per worker and real wages, selected
CSEE countries, 1989–2003

	Real wage deflated using CPI			Real wage deflated using GDP deflator		
	1989–96	1997–2003	1989–2003	1990–96	1997–2003	1990–2003
Bulgaria	–0.18	0.88	–0.22	0.53	0.95	0.32
Croatia	0.84	0.93	0.79	0.79	0.93	0.91
Czech Republic	0.94	0.98	0.96	0.99	0.99	0.99
Hungary	–0.05	0.96	0.70	0.43	0.99	0.85
Lithuania	0.98	0.84	0.78	0.97	0.88	0.92
Poland	0.58	0.93	0.95	0.85	0.96	0.97

Source: Author's calculations based on UNECE for GDP, CPI and GDP deflator; ILO for wages.

path to that of Poland, with the sharp fall in employment being in this case the main
force behind the rapid increase in GDP per worker after the initial drop. Real wage
growth, however, stagnated during the 1990s and has accelerated rapidly in recent
years. Bulgaria is the exception, as real wages have fallen dramatically and are
recovering at a very slow pace. The index of GDP per worker remained quite stable
for the first years of transition and is on the rise in recent years due to sustained
growth. Bulgaria experienced both a dramatic fall in the level of employment and a
protracted decline in real wages, while the trade-off between price adjustment
(decrease in real wages) and quantity adjustment (decrease in employment levels)
seems to have been effective for the other countries.

In table 8.2 we present the correlation between GDP per worker and the real
wage, calculated using both consumer price indices (CPI) and GDP deflators. The
numbers broadly confirm the analysis made by comparing figures 8.1 and 8.2. The
Czech Republic presents the strongest correspondence between the paths of GDP per
capita and real wages. Bulgaria and Hungary show a low correlation (negative when
the CPI is used) in the first period of transition, but in line with the other countries in
the subsequent sub-period. In general, in the period 1997–2003 real wages moved in
line with GDP per capita in all the countries under consideration, while discrepancies
emerged in the first period of structural adjustment.

Levels of earnings among countries can also be compared, provided that
differences in price level are taken into account.[3] Given a price level of 100 (gross
wage plus social security contributions paid by employer) for the Czech Republic,
employee compensations in Poland and Hungary are slightly lower, Lithuania is at

---

[3] According to Eurostat, the price level in the Czech Republic, Hungary, and Poland was around 52 per cent of the
EU15 level in 2002; in Lithuania it was 46 per cent and in Bulgaria just 33 per cent of the EU level, while in Croatia it
was 56 per cent.

around 60 per cent and Bulgaria at approximately 40 per cent, while Croatia enjoys a premium of around 10 per cent.

The first possible explanation of such a big disparity in workers' compensation is different labour productivity. As an approximation for the level of productivity it is possible to use GDP per person employed, expressed in terms of purchasing power standards. Again taking the Czech level as 100, Croatia is at around the same level, Hungary is slightly above at 109, Poland has 83 per cent of Czech productivity, Lithuania 74 per cent and Bulgaria has the lowest productivity per employed person at 54 per cent of the Czech level (data from Eurostat). These kinds of comparisons are just indicative, but taking the Czech Republic as a yardstick, Croatia and Poland have higher compensations than their productivity would suggest. The opposite is true of the other countries, with Bulgaria an outlier in this respect as its compensation level is much lower than its lower productivity would justify.

8.3.2   The variation of wages

The regional dimension

Labour markets in CSEE countries are characterized by wide regional variations. Unemployment rates in Polish voivodships in May 2004 ranged from just above 15 per cent in Mazowieckie, where Warsaw is located, to almost 30 per cent in Warminsko-Mazurskie, in the north-east of the country. In Lithuania, a much smaller country whose total population is comparable to that of a single Polish voivodship, the unemployment rate in 2003 ranged between 7.6 per cent in Vilnius county, where the capital is located, and 14.4 per cent in Telsiai county, in the north-west. The European Bank for Reconstruction and Development (EBRD, 2003) has underlined that during transition regional variation in unemployment has tended to grow and that policies to better integrate the domestic labour market are necessary.

Table 8.3 presents the coefficient of variation of regional unemployment based on territorial units of homogeneous size, illustrating the comparatively high dispersion of regional unemployment over the period 1999–2003 in the Czech Republic, and the relatively low dispersion in Lithuania. These regional differences are due to the combination of high levels of regional specialization of production inherited from socialism and large product-specific demand shocks characterizing transition (OECD, 1995). In the case of Croatia, war represents a further factor as parts of the country were affected with different intensity.

Regional disparities in labour demand are an important source of regional variation in unemployment[4] and wages could act as a re-equilibrating mechanism. The search for evidence concerning the relationship between unemployment and wages in CSEE countries has given mixed results (see Huber et al., 2002, p. 40, for a review). However, comparative studies have in the main found that wage flexibility

---

[4] The relative importance of regional disparities in labour supply or in labour demand in explaining regional dispersion in unemployment is discussed in the working paper version of the study (Tonin, 2006).

Table 8.3   Coefficient of variation of regional unemployment, selected CSEE
            countries, 1999–2003

	1999	2000	2001	2002	2003
Bulgaria	..	45.8	27.7	31.0	34.5
Czech Republic	38.6	44.3	44.4	48.2	44.6
Hungary	..	35.5	34.2	35.9	36.7
Lithuania	24.6	24.5	25.1	26.5	17.0
Poland	35.7	38.0	35.6	27.1	25.8

Notes: Based on NUTS categories. NUTS = Nomenclature on Territorial Units for Statistics. This is a five-level
hierarchical classification of territorial units drawn up by Eurostat. For data on Croatia at NUTS-II level, see Botrić et al.
(2004). .. = not available.

Source: Eurostat.

is comparatively high in Bulgaria and quite low in the Czech Republic. A simple
comparison between the regional dispersions of unemployment and wages for the
countries under consideration reveals the very limited variation in wages in the Czech
Republic and Croatia, despite a wide variation in unemployment, while in Lithuania
and Bulgaria the spread appears to be limited by the relatively small variation in
unemployment in the Lithuanian case and higher wage variability in Bulgaria.

An increase in wage flexibility along geographical lines could represent a useful
component in a policy package aimed at reducing regional imbalances, in particular
in countries such as the Czech Republic and Croatia where the responsiveness of
wages to local conditions appears to be subdued.

The sectoral dimension

Material production, and heavy industry in particular, was favoured in terms of earnings
during the socialist era. With transition the ranking of sectors according to average
earnings has quickly converged with that prevailing in EU15 countries. At present, in
all the countries under consideration people working in financial intermediation earn
much more than in the rest of the economy, while fishing, agriculture and hotels and
restaurants are the least well-paid sectors. The evolution of the dispersion of wages
across sectors in the last ten years as indicated by the coefficient of variation is presented
in figure 8.3. There is not a distinctive general trend, but the relative position of the
countries is quite well established. Croatia displays the lowest level of sectoral
dispersion, comparable in 2002 to the situation in France or the United Kingdom. The
Czech Republic is also characterized by low dispersion. Lithuania and Bulgaria instead
present much higher inter-sectoral variation.

Data on the distribution of wages across sectors should be treated with particular
caution. As seen in section 8.3, the incidence of informal activities and among these
the underreporting of wages greatly differs among the countries under study and

Figure 8.3 Sectoral wage dispersion measured by coefficient of variation, selected CSEE countries, 1993–2003

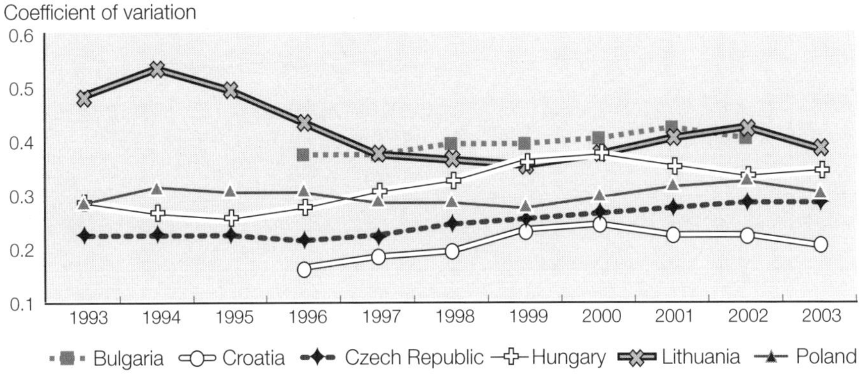

Note: Sectors as defined by NACE.

Source: ILO for sectoral wages; own calculations.

among different sectors of the economy. This may lead to the overestimation of the dispersion of earnings across sectors, particularly in the case of Bulgaria and Lithuania, and makes the low dispersion in the Croatian case even more striking.

It is also interesting to repeat at sectoral level the analysis of the correlation between productivity and earnings. Table 8.4 presents the correlation between sectoral value added and sectoral wages.

Bulgaria presents several sectors in which the correlation is negative or low. Of particular interest is the manufacturing sector, representing the most important single sector in almost all the countries under consideration, with a share between one-fifth and one-quarter of total value added. In the manufacturing sector, wages and productivity appear to go hand in hand in Croatia, the Czech Republic, Hungary and Poland, while in the case of Bulgaria an increasing productivity is paired with stagnating real earnings. It is also notable that the electricity, gas and water supply sector has a low correlation in the Czech Republic, Hungary and Poland, due to sustained wage growth well above productivity. This may point to rent sharing in sectors characterized by a certain degree of market power.

Dispersion by educational achievement and professional position

The previous regime's emphasis on education left the CSEE countries with a legacy of a generally well-educated workforce. However, the combination of an educational system stressing the acquisition of specific skills through vocational training with the sectoral and technological shocks that came with the transformation, made some of the skills acquired in the previous system quickly obsolete. Studies of several CSEE

Table 8.4   Correlation coefficients of sectoral real wage (deflated by CPI) and sectoral value added per worker, selected CSEE countries, 1996 to early 2000s

	Bulgaria 1996–2002	Croatia[1] 1996–2001	Czech Republic 1996–2002	Hungary 1996–2003	Lithuania[2] 1997–2003	Poland 2002
C: Mining and quarrying	0.86	0.34	0.69	0.97	−0.33	0.92
D: Manufacturing	−0.01	0.86	0.94	0.96	0.61	0.90
E: Electricity, gas and water supply	0.40	0.94	−0.43	0.21	0.94	0.22
F: Construction	0.15	−0.06	−0.37	0.52	0.54	0.92
G: Wholesale and retail trade; repairs	−0.02	0.90	0.94	−0.14	0.67	0.77
H: Hotels and restaurants	−0.40	0.88	−0.08	−0.40	0.27	0.61
I: Transport, storage and communications	0.71	0.76	0.89	0.91	0.55	0.94
J: Financial intermediation	0.32	0.58	0.83	0.89	0.47	0.94
K: Real estate, renting and business activities	−0.94	−0.57	0.80	−0.81	0.67	−0.87

Note: Sectors according to NACE categories. [1] Croatia: for categories F–I correlation is 1996–2003. [2] Lithuania: for categories C–D correlation is 1998–2003.

Sources: UNECE for CPI and sectoral value added; ILO for sectoral wages and sectoral employment.

Table 8.5   Gross average earnings by educational achievement as a percentage
of average earnings, selected CSEE countries, early 2000s

	Bulgaria[1] 2002	Croatia[2] 2001	Czech Republic 2001	Hungary[3] 2002	Lithuania[4] 2002	Poland 2002	Germany[5] 2001
Primary education	80	72	64	63	63	71	94
Secondary	84	92	106	103	73	94	118
Higher post- secondary	110	122	107	147	94	91	160
University	134	164	178	223	149	151	174
University/Primary	169	227	277	355	237	212	186

Notes: [1] Secondary is a weighted average of lower and upper secondary; university is a weighted average of degrees (specialist, bachelor, masters, doctorate), with the number of employees used as weights. [2] Net earnings. [3] Secondary is an average of vocational, general, and technical secondary schools. [4] Secondary is an average of basic and upper secondary. [5] Categories are: Volks-, Haupt- oder Realschulabschluss; Abitur; Fachhochschulabschluss; Hochschul- oder Universitätsabschluss.

Source: CSO.

countries (among them Bulgaria, the Czech Republic, Hungary and Poland) show that workers with vocational education had a higher probability of losing their job, a lower probability of finding new employment and suffered a negative wage premium compared to workers with general secondary education (Boeri, 2000).

Workers with adaptable skills have experienced an increase in their relative wage, however, as the wage distribution has become more responsive to market conditions and the adoption of new technologies and production methods has increased the demand for skills. There are nonetheless notable differences in the return from education among the countries under consideration.

In table 8.5 average earnings for different educational levels are presented. Compared to a country such as Germany, workers with primary education fare comparatively worse in terms of percentage of average wage earned, while the situation for the highly educated is more mixed. It is striking that the wage premium enjoyed by a university graduate over a worker who has completed only primary education is four times higher in Hungary than in Bulgaria. The Czech Republic also presents a wide variation of earnings among educational levels. While it is difficult to infer from the wage premiums enjoyed by more highly educated workers the level of success of a country in adapting to new technologies, these certainly represent an incentive for skill acquisition and thus can constitute a positive factor in the growth and catching-up processes.

Another way to assess the dispersion of wages is to look at the wage differentials across occupations (table 8.6). The country where the gap between the top level and the lowest level of pay is greatest is once again Hungary, immediately followed by Poland. Bulgaria, as in the case of educational differences, is at the opposite end of the

Table 8.6   Gross average earnings by major occupational groups as a percentage of average earnings, selected CSEE countries, early 2000s

	Bulgaria 2002	Czech Republic 2002	Hungary 2002	Lithuania 2000	Poland 2002	Germany[1] 2003
Senior officials and managers	199	205	218	187	230	196
Professionals	133	133	145	122	133	171
Technicians and associate professionals	117	107	105	95	102	123
Clerks	85	81	83	86	89	101
Service workers	59	68	64	70	60	64
Agricultural and fishery workers	67	64	59	56	67	..
Craft and related trade workers	94	84	77	89	84	84
Plant and machine operators	96	83	81	88	89	88
Elementary occupations	60	58	55	56	59	67
Senior officials and managers/ unskilled workers	3.3	3.5	4.0	3.3	3.9	2.9
Maximum/minimum	3.4	3.5	4.0	3.4	3.9	3.0

Notes: Data for Croatia are not available. [1] Gross annual earnings. .. = not available.

Source: CSO.

spectrum, with the lowest disparity between managers and people employed in elementary occupations. Lithuania also has a low level of variation along the occupational dimension. Again, people performing unskilled work fare comparatively worse than in Germany, while for senior officials and managers the situation is mixed.

8.4   IS THERE A WAGE FLOOR? THE MINIMUM WAGE AND UNEMPLOYMENT BENEFITS

Both minimum wage regulation and unemployment benefits can reduce wage flexibility by generating a wage floor and compressing wage distribution. On the other hand, they reduce income insecurity and protect workers with low bargaining power against the risk of receiving a wage insufficient to maintain a decent standard of living.

In the countries under consideration the minimum wage is set by the government after negotiations with the social partners through tripartite national bodies. The government usually has a pivotal influence, as it retains the right to make a unilateral decision should no agreement be reached. Minimum wages above the national standard can be negotiated by the social partners through bilateral bargaining.

Figure 8.4 Minimum wage as a percentage of the average gross wage, selected CSEE countries, 1990–2003

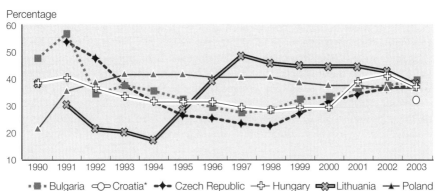

Note: Minimum social security threshold.

Source: Own calculations.

With the exception of Poland, in the aftermath of transition the minimum wage declined even more than the average wage. Reaching levels as low as 17 per cent of the average wage in Lithuania in 1994, it lost any protective function for vulnerable workers (Vaughan-Whitehead, 1995). In recent years, however, the minimum wage has showed a tendency to recover its value and has converged in the analysed countries to a level around 35–40 per cent of the average wage (see figure 8.4). These increases allow the minimum wage to act as an effective wage floor, in particular in sectors of the economy where earnings are lower and for categories of the workforce with low educational attainment or skills. At the outset of transition this role was played by unemployment benefits (Boeri and Terrell, 2002), but the shortening of duration and the reduction in replacement rates in recent years has greatly diminished their part and the degree of protection they afford in case of job loss (Tonin, 2006).

The effectiveness of the minimum wage as a wage floor can be assessed by looking at the percentage of the workforce earning this amount. In Lithuania in October 2003 almost 20 per cent of the workforce was working at or below the minimum wage. It was particularly prevalent in the hotels and restaurants sector, where the minimum wage was binding for 44 per cent of the workforce, and in trade and repairing, with a 29 per cent spike in the sectoral wage distribution at the minimum wage level. There is similarly a spike at the minimum wage level in Bulgarian wage distribution in 2002. In Poland in 2001, 6.5 per cent of the workforce worked at the minimum wage, with once again a particularly high incidence in hotels and restaurants (18 per cent) and trade and repairing sectors (14 per cent). In Hungary, after a substantial increase in 2001, 12 per cent of the total workforce was employed at the minimum wage. For the construction sector the incidence was higher (33 per cent), as in the hotels and restaurants (29 per cent) and trade and repairing

(24 per cent) sectors. By contrast, in the Czech case only 2.5 per cent of the workforce in the hotels and restaurants sector was employed at the minimum wage in 2002, and the percentage was much lower in the other categories.

If we take into account underreporting of wages, a spike in the distribution of earnings at the minimum wage level may not necessarily be an indication that the minimum wage is a binding constraint. The fact that the minimum wage seems to be more binding in those countries and sectors where the practice of paying envelope wages is considered to be more widespread suggests that this may indeed be the case.

Directly connected to this issue is the recent introduction in Bulgaria and Croatia of the minimum social security threshold, which prevents social security contributions being paid according to the minimum wage instead of at the supposedly higher actual wage (see Tonin, 2006, for more details). The risk associated with this arrangement is that if the minima do not represent in practice a minimum wage, then they make social security contributions regressive, forcing lower paid employees to pay more as a percentage of their salary than their higher paid colleagues.

The relevance of the informal economy may reduce the significance of the minimum wage in some countries. However, due to the fragmented nature of labour markets along regional lines or by age, the minimum wage continues to play an important role for parts of the workforce. With respect to this issue, a recent tendency to differentiate the minimum wage applicable to different categories of workers is noticeable in several countries: Poland and the Czech Republic have lower minima for the first years of employment or for young people, while Lithuania differentiates according to profession.

When fixing the minimum wage, both the needs of workers and their families and the capacity of enterprises to pay should be taken into account. On the one hand, fixing a minimum wage that is too low may fail to provide vulnerable workers with a decent income, thus creating a group of working poor. A too high minimum wage could on the other hand adversely affect the labour market position of these workers by reducing labour demand for their profiles or pushing them into the informal economy.[5] Indeed Kertesi and Köllő (2003c) find evidence that the 57 per cent minimum wage increase in Hungary in 2001 meant a loss of employment opportunities, in particular in small firms, and a higher probability of unemployment after its implementation for the workers for which the new minimum wage was binding.

Having a different, lower, minimum wage for young new entrants in the labour market takes into account both the weaker labour market position of these inexperienced workers and the fact that, usually not having a family to support, their minimal needs are lower. Considering that the unemployment rate for young people is usually double that of the general population in the countries under consideration, the policy of fixing lower minima for young workers may be useful. Moreover, by removing the risk of pricing out youths it would allow the general minimum wage

---

[5] The effect on employment of an increase in the minimum wage is however not a settled issue in economics. A minimum wage hike having the effect of increasing efforts or reducing search frictions may lead to a higher employment level; see Card and Krueger (1995).

to better reflect the needs of workers with families. A further issue is whether this differentiation should be extended to other areas. A natural candidate is the regional dimension. The cost of living is not uniform in the different regions and, moreover, there is a wide regional variation in labour market conditions. A differentiation of the minimum wage along the regional dimension, at least in the bigger countries, could therefore be a useful tool. Adjusting the minimum wage to the cost of living in different parts of the country, and thus having a more uniform minimum wage in terms of purchasing power, would also be more equitable than simple nominal equivalence.

8.5   THE TAX WEDGE

A strong influence on wage distribution is also exercised by the fiscal system. Of particular interest for labour market analysis is the tax wedge, namely the difference between the labour cost to the employer and the net take-home pay of the employee. The labour cost to the employer is composed of the gross wage plus the social security contributions paid by the employer and other payroll taxes, if any. To calculate the net take-home pay of the employee we need to subtract from the gross wage personal income tax and the part of social security contributions paid by the employee, and then add any cash benefit, such as dependent-related transfers. Hence the main components of the tax wedge are social security contributions and personal income tax.

It is striking that the tax burden on labour in the countries under consideration is very high, in some cases higher than in the average EU15 country and much higher than in the average OECD country. This is particularly true for Hungary, despite a decrease in 2003, while Bulgaria seems to provide the most favourable fiscal regime.

Other things being equal, a higher tax wedge reduces equilibrium employment: it affects labour demand by raising the total labour cost, and affects the labour supply by lowering the net take-home pay. Moreover, a higher tax wedge makes it more attractive to work in the informal economy or to underreport wages. Table 8.7 presents the main features of the tax systems in 2003.

Croatia has the highest total tax burden, as measured by the ratio of collected taxes to GDP, at a level similar to the average EU15 country. Hungary and Poland are just a step below, while Bulgaria and Lithuania belong to a different category altogether, with taxes representing a smaller portion of GDP. The way the total tax burden is distributed among different types of taxes also varies greatly, in particular the relative relevance of direct versus indirect taxation. The Czech Republic and Poland rely heavily on social security contributions, while in Lithuania personal income tax is particularly important. Hungary has a more even balance between the two taxes. In Croatia and Bulgaria it is indirect taxation, and in particular value-added tax, which represents a bigger share of tax revenues. Indirect taxation is generally considered to be less distorting than direct taxation. Therefore, the relevance of indirect taxes in Croatia mitigates the distortional effect of the high tax burden on labour, while in Bulgaria both the limited fiscal burden and the structure of the tax system are comparatively favourable to labour allocation.

Table 8.7   Main features of the tax system, selected CSEE countries and EU15, 2003

	Total tax (2002) as % of GDP	Personal income tax					Social security contributions as % of taxable income
		Number of tax brackets	Minimum rate as % of taxable income	Maximum rate as % of taxable income	Maximum rate threshold[a]	Standard tax-exempt threshold[1]	
Bulgaria	27.5	4	15	29	236	43	42
Croatia	41.1	4	15	45	438	...	37
Czech Republic	36.6	4	15	32	186	21	48
Hungary	37.7	3	20	40	94	7	46
Lithuania	27.6	1	33	33	..	26	34
Poland	31.4	3	19	40	374	14	45
EU15	40.5	..	..	46	..	..	..

Note: Data for Croatia apply to 2004. [1] % of average gross wage net of social security contributions calculated as (annual income to which the maximum rate or the exemption applies)/12*average gross monthly wage*(1-SSC paid by the employee expressed as % of taxable income) .. = not available. ... = not applicable.

Sources: UNECE (see UNECE, 2004, tables 5.2.1 and 5.2.3 for further details) for CEE countries, except Croatia; IMF & MoF for Croatia; Eurostat for EU15.

With the exception of Lithuania, which like other Baltic countries applies a flat-rate income tax, the tax system is progressive, with an increasing marginal tax rate. From this point of view Hungary is an outlier, with a maximum rate applied very early in the income scale, below the level of the average wage. The higher maximum marginal rate in Croatia applies instead only to incomes far above the average wage, thus making it irrelevant for the majority of households. Bulgaria presents both the lowest maximum rate and the highest standard tax-exempt income as a share of the average wage among the countries under consideration.

Table 8.8 presents the evolution of the tax wedge over time. The data for Bulgaria and Croatia are not fully comparable as they refer to workers earning the average wage for the general economy while the lower average wage for production workers in manufacturing is used for the other countries. This overestimates the relative tax burden of these two countries. To provide a term of comparison, the tax wedge in 2003 for a worker earning 167 per cent of the average wage for production workers in manufacturing was 46.2 per cent in the Czech Republic, 55.8 per cent in Hungary, and 43.9 per cent in Poland. The steep increase in Hungary is due to the characteristics of the personal income tax underlined above.

It is particularly interesting to look at the fiscal burden on low-wage earners, defined as people earning two-thirds of the average wage for a production worker in

Table 8.8   Tax wedge as a percentage of labour cost for single persons without children earning the average wage, selected CSEE countries, 1995–2003

	1995	1996	1997	1998	1999	2000	2001	2002	2003
Czech Republic	43.2	42.6	42.9	42.8	42.7	43.1	43.1	43.5	43.8
Hungary	51.4	52.0	52.0	51.6	50.7	49.6	49.0	49.0	45.7
Lithuania	..	..	..	..	..	48.0	..	..	46.0
Poland	44.7	44.7	43.9	43.2	43.0	43.0	42.7	42.8	42.9
EU15 (unweighted average)	43.3	43.4	43.5	43	42.7	42.4	41.4	40.6	..
OECD (unweighted average)	37.3	37.3	37.5	37.2	36.6	36.9	36.4	35.9	..
Bulgaria	39.1	44.1	41.8	42.7	42.9	43.6	41.4	40.7	40.3
Croatia	48.3	48.5	46.8	46.4	44.4	41.6	39.9	41.1	..

Notes: For Czech Republic, Hungary, Lithuania, Poland, EU15 and OECD: average wage of production worker in manufacturing sector. .. = not available.

Sources: OECD for Czech Republic, Hungary, Lithuania, Poland, EU15 and OECD; USAID for Bulgaria; World Bank for Croatia.

manufacturing. As can be seen in table 8.9, the countries under consideration impose a tax wedge of around 40 per cent on low wage earners, with the exception of Bulgaria (no data are available for Croatia), a level that is above the EU15 average in 2000–03. Hungary was characterized by the highest fiscal burden on low wage earners, but in 2003 a five percentage-point reduction took it to a level comparable with the other CEE countries. Bulgaria once again emerges as the country with the least burdensome fiscal regime.

Table 8.9   Tax wedge on low wage earners, selected CSEE countries and EU15, 1996–2003

	1996	1997	1998	1999	2000	2001	2002	2003
Bulgaria	40.3	37.8	39.1	37.1	39.4	36.5	35.2	35.2
Czech Republic	41.4	41.5	41.4	41.4	41.6	41.6	41.8	42.0
Hungary	46.8	47.8	47.4	48.2	46.2	45.8	46.0	41.0
Lithuania	37.6	39.3	39.5	39.7	42.0	42.2	41.3	39.5
Poland	43.6	42.9	42.1	41.9	41.9	41.4	41.6	41.6
EU15	39.7	40.0	39.3	38.5	37.9	37.0	36.9	37.2

Source: Eurostat.

A reduction of the tax burden on wage earners would be useful to encourage participation in formal employment and raise disposable income. This is made difficult, however, by the fiscal constraints that these countries face. Increasing the tax base by favouring the transformation of informal work into formal employment would be a satisfactory solution, but it is interesting to note that the country with the highest estimated informal economy, Bulgaria, has the lowest tax imposition on labour. This suggests that intervention in regulatory fields besides taxation may be crucial to achieving a reduction of the degree of informality characterizing the economy.

8.6   CONCLUSIONS

Two characteristics of the wage determination system in the countries under consideration have been conducive to high wage flexibility. First, collective bargaining is rather limited: for the majority of the workforce remuneration is determined on an individual basis and bargaining takes place mainly at a decentralized level. Croatia represents an exception in this regard. Second, informal arrangements are widespread. Payments above the officially declared level or below the contractually agreed level are in some countries common practice. Flexibility stemming from non-respect of regulations is of a perverse type and its reduction should be high on the agenda. High fiscal pressure on labour surely represents a strong incentive to evade regulation, but the Bulgarian case suggests that this is not the only aspect. A comprehensive approach to reform, involving several regulatory fields, should be applied. Greater involvement of social partners at the decentralized level could also contribute to increased compliance. A broadening of the fiscal base would allow a necessary reduction in the high tax burden on labour, particularly in Hungary.

Wages have displayed high downward flexibility during the transformational recession at the outset of transition and during macroeconomic crises thereafter. High inflation has been the mechanism used to reduce real wages and it remains an open issue whether earnings would display such a high level of flexibility in a low-inflation environment should circumstances require it. In such an eventuality, coordination mechanisms at national level could prove useful and should therefore be introduced beforehand or strengthened in the countries where they already exist.

A broad correspondence between the paths of real earnings and productivity emerges in the countries under consideration. In Bulgaria, however, the connection between wages and productivity is looser, with real earnings failing to follow productivity increases. Several other indicators also point to a 'weakness' of wages in Bulgaria.

Increasing the responsiveness of wages to local conditions could represent a further tool as part of a policy package aimed at reducing regional disparities. This is particularly true in countries such as Croatia and the Czech Republic. A contribution to this could be made by developing the regional dimension of social dialogue, which has already started in some countries. Introducing differentiated minimum wages along the regional dimension would also serve this purpose. More differentiation would make it possible to take into consideration differences in price levels, and thus in the purchasing power of wages, across regions. A tendency to introduce some form of differentiation in the minimum wage has been reported for some countries. Extending this to other dimensions would enhance the effectiveness of the minimum wage in a segmented labour market. A more differentiated minimum wage would also help to fight underreporting, as the Bulgarian experience with social security minima suggests, without introducing regressive elements in the social security system. Introducing a stronger relation between previous earnings and unemployment benefits would also represent an incentive to report wages.

Wage policy has a strong influence on the capacity of a society to provide the means to a decent standard of living and to handle change. The negotiation of a combination of flexibility and security applied effectively to the whole workforce is one of the most important tasks facing these economies.

POLICY CONCLUSIONS 9

Sandrine Cazes and Alena Nesporova

9.1   A SUMMARY OF FINDINGS

The comparative analysis of the national labour markets in Central and South-Eastern Europe as well as the five national studies have pointed to important changes both in labour market trends and in labour market institutions and policies since the end of the 1990s. Our findings could be summarized as follows:

1. Economic growth has accelerated in the region and coincides with declining unemployment. However, employment increased in only five of the Central and South-Eastern European (CSEE) countries and even there only modestly, so that one should still speak about *jobless growth* across the region. The fall in unemployment continued to feed inactivity more than employment: labour market participation has continued to decline in the majority of these countries, including two of the five countries with improving employment performance. Another channel of outflow from unemployment has been labour migration, accelerating after the enlargement of the European Union (EU) on 1 May 2004, in particular from countries struggling with high unemployment. The most worrying labour market situation is in Poland, with the highest unemployment rate and low and declining labour market participation and employment rates, despite good economic performance.

2. Persistent extensive inactivity among the working age population combined with very high long-term unemployment and an increasing ratio of youth to average unemployment rate indicate important barriers to labour market (re-)entry, especially for young persons, older workers, ethnic minorities, low-skilled workers, women returning from maternity leave and persons with health problems, many of whom are pushed to use the available social welfare schemes to actually withdraw from the labour market. Some of them are also involved in informal activity to make ends meet.

235

3. The share of temporary employment has accelerated. However, in contrast to the 1990s, it has taken the form of fixed-term and short-term contracts rather than civil contracts, which were reduced as a result of a stricter stance taken by the labour market and financial institutions in many countries. In addition, the Hungarian and Croatian chapters point to much higher incidence of time-limited contracts among newly concluded contracts compared with their much lower and only slowly increasing share in all contracts. This indicates important labour market segmentation between workers of usually prime age and with higher skills enjoying full-time contracts without limit of time and young or older workers, typically less skilled, who are trapped in temporary jobs. In contrast, part-time employment remained limited in most countries except among young and old workers, at least some of whom may actually prefer to combine part-time employment with study or leisure time (youth) and old-age or disability pension (the elderly), as evidenced in the Hungarian chapter. Apart from declining subsistence farming in Poland, there has been no clear trend in self-employment development across the region. Contrary to the 1990s, multiple-job holding has declined in the majority of these countries. Although data on informal employment are scarce, they also indicate a certain contraction in informal employment.

4. The gender difference in labour market participation and employment rates persists across the region. However, there has been a slight tendency towards this gap closing in the case of labour market participation, while the opposite has been true for employment since 2000. The unemployment situation has also improved more for men than for women. In terms of employment, men have thus benefited slightly more than women from economic growth.

5. Labour turnover has declined since 2000 in all the countries for which we have data, indicating a certain stabilization of their labour markets. Both accession and separation rates have fallen, which suggests that enterprises are no longer resorting to mass redundancies (or forced 'voluntary quits') but are still unable to create many new positions, and employment performance remains poor. This explains the continuing perception of high employment and job insecurity, as indicated by the continuing tendency towards a countercyclical development of labour turnover that we have found. During economic upswings workers are less ready to quit their jobs voluntarily for newly created ones since the job creation capacity of the economy is low and people do not trust the stability and quality of new jobs. In turn, during economic recessions enterprises struggle to survive, strengthening their competitiveness by increasing labour productivity and cutting labour costs, including downsizing the workforce. The link between economic and employment growth has remained weak in the 2000s. Economic recovery has brought only a significant decrease of flows from employment into unemployment, while we have not found any significant correlation between economic growth and outflows from employment to inactivity or flows from one employment to another.

6. Stabilization of the labour market has also been confirmed by a slight lengthening of average job tenures. An analysis of the employment distribution by duration of job tenure revealed that between 1999 and 2003 this distribution polarized towards a higher share of short-term (below one year) and long-term (above ten years) job tenures, which is further evidence of the tendency towards labour market segmentation cited in point 3 above.

7. The trend towards liberalization of employment protection legislation (EPL) which started in the 1990s has further continued. In 2003 EPL in the countries of Central and South-Eastern Europe was on average more liberal than that of the countries of the European Union, although still less so than the average among the countries of the Organisation for Economic Co-operation and Development (OECD). Nevertheless the differences are minimal. The CSEE region now has a fairly liberal regulation of temporary contracts compared with both the EU and the OECD, while its regulation of permanent contracts is slightly more restrictive. The major deregulation in the CSEE countries concerned collective dismissals, which moved slightly below the EU but still remained well above the OECD average. Our analysis has shown that strictness of employment protection legislation has no statistically significant impact on important labour market indicators such as labour market participation, employment (including the incidence of flexible forms of employment), unemployment, labour turnover or job tenure. Moreover, as the Hungarian study shows, actual employment protection through legislation is even lower. This is due less to non-compliance than to non-eligibility, as those workers made redundant from exempt enterprises or sectors, or whose lay-offs are classified as temporary, are not covered by EPL. Calls for further labour market deregulation through the liberalization of EPL in the hope of increasing employment and reducing unemployment would thus appear not to be substantiated. With regard to increasing labour productivity and reducing production and labour costs – considered a priority by employers – deregulation itself does not lead towards higher recruitments, nor does it improve the labour market situation.

8. There have been important developments in other labour market institutions and policies. Protection at the workplace has decreased, not only as a result of more liberal regulation of employment termination but also because levels of unionization and coverage of workers by collective agreements have declined in the region: the Hungarian study presented evidence that in companies with strong trade union organizations and collective agreements, labour turnover significantly decreased. In Croatia, social security coverage has been extended to fixed-term and part-time employment, to reduce the gap in coverage between these and permanent contracts and thus increase their attractiveness for workers. Employment security outside the workplace has been strengthened in the majority of the CSEE countries by improving passive and active labour market policies. Passive policies have focused on increasing the level of unemployment benefits (as, for example, in Croatia and Lithuania) and the length of their payment, in

237

particular for persons of pre-retirement age (for example in Croatia, Lithuania or Poland) or parents at home with children (in Hungary). Many of these measures serve to reduce the labour supply, particularly of those individuals with problems re-entering the labour market. Other countries, such as Bulgaria, have given priority to activation strategies and ensured higher access of jobseekers to active policies, improving their employability, strengthening their link to the labour market and providing them with subsidized employment. Difficulty remains in facilitating the transition from subsidized employment to regular jobs and in ensuring sustainability of employment of vulnerable groups of workers, since many of these repeatedly re-register after relatively short spells of employment. Public employment services have improved their capacity to provide job placement services and vocational guidance to jobseekers and to collaborate with enterprises, although much more can still be done. All five of the country studies document an overall tendency away from protection at the workplace towards broader security in employability and assistance in redeployment, including to subsidized jobs and self-employment. Nevertheless, the proportion of expenditure on passive and active labour market policies to GDP remains low, particularly given the high levels of unemployment. Informal employment remains high, despite recent reductions, and requires more determined policies to gradually formalize informal jobs and improve the protection of informal workers against all kinds of labour-related and social risks. Another challenge is the low degree of coordination within the workers' and employers' movements and their insufficient capacity to deal with labour market issues, which significantly limits the role of the social partners in formulating and implementing effective labour market policies, despite formal mechanisms in place for their involvement. Finally, labour taxation has been reduced in the subregion but still remains well above the average of the EU and OECD.

9. The multivariate analysis of the effects of labour market institutions on the main labour market indicators displayed partially different results from those for the 1990s. First of all, no difference was found between the CSEE and the OECD countries for the factors explaining all five labour market indicators. This would indicate a generally convergent development, certainly strengthened by the EU accession process. The results confirmed the outcome of the bivariate analysis, i.e. that EPL had no statistically significant impact on economic activity, employment and unemployment trends. The correlation found in the 1990s between EPL on the one hand and employment and labour market participation on the other has become statistically insignificant. The significant impact of collective bargaining on the level of labour market participation, employment and unemployment identified in the 1990s has now disappeared. However, for youth unemployment and long-term unemployment our results show a negative effect of trade union density. This suggests that strong protection of core workers by trade unions seems to work against recruitment or may lead towards more lay-offs among less competitive workers and thus contribute to higher youth and long-term unemployment.

10. Active labour market policies have further strengthened their positive effect on promoting economic activity and employment and reducing overall, youth and long-term unemployment in comparison with the end of the 1990s. In contrast, we have found that high payroll taxes seem to contribute not only to higher unemployment but newly also to lower labour market participation and employment. The analysis also indicates that longer duration of payment of unemployment benefits has a negative impact on reducing economic activity and employment and on increasing youth and long-term unemployment. This result may be largely driven by the OECD countries where unemployment benefits are paid on average for much longer periods. Nevertheless, in our view this also reflects the considerable difficulties experienced by young people, low-skilled, older workers and others in finding employment in a situation of persistent low demand for labour. These individuals are then forced to stay on unemployment benefits as long as possible while in fact many of them are passive jobseekers and thus inactive.

11. Higher levels of unionization and coverage by collective agreements (as well as sectoral-level bargaining in Croatia) are pushing wages upwards. Many countries have also tried to increase the attractiveness of work over social welfare by increasing the minimum wage, which has thus become a binding wage floor. Income protection against risks of enterprise insolvency and bankruptcy has been ensured by establishing wage guarantee funds in an increasing number of CSEE countries. With regard to wage flexibility vis-à-vis fluctuations in GDP, wages have generally contracted in the period of transition crisis but economic recovery has seen diverse wage development across the subregion. However, in the period 1997–2003 real wages moved in line with GDP per capita trends. Countries also differ in the extent of territorial, sectoral and occupational variation of wages as well as in the wage premium on education.

9.2 POLICY IMPLICATIONS

The most important objective of employment policy in the subregion is to address the challenge of jobless growth. It must endeavour to translate economic growth into positive and sufficiently high net job creation, such that it results in higher, good-quality employment. This calls for a sound, balanced macroeconomic policy which would stimulate sustainable economic development through interventions on the supply and demand sides of the economy. Since this is not the topic of this book, we provide only a very general outline of such a policy.

On the supply side, macroeconomic policy should concentrate on creating an environment conducive to private business development. This implies legislation promoting fair competition and protecting property rights; a transparent tax system that does not overburden enterprises but generates sufficient revenues for important public activities, such as promotion of research and development, education, development of infrastructure and social policy; and well-functioning, relatively stable and clear administrative and financial systems for enterprises. A well-developed technical infrastructure that encourages competitiveness among domestic enterprises and attracts foreign investors needs investment. The State should stimulate such funding by allocating public resources or providing concessions to private investors, while in the latter case regulating the risk of monopolies. A number of CSEE countries have recently offered special conditions and subsidies for foreign direct investment (FDI), which has contributed towards their increased inflows and helped create new jobs. Such policies can bring lasting effects when they support production links between foreign and local investors, rather than discriminating against domestic producers. To the extent possible, they should also stimulate investment flows to technologically more advanced production. This will utilize and further upgrade human capital and increase the competitiveness of the enterprise sector.

Since all the CSEE countries have open economies largely dependent on external trade, they also need trade policies conducive to growth and employment. EU accession has had a positive impact on their merchandise trade, reducing deficits or even changing them into surpluses, as a result of removing remaining trade barriers within the EU and accelerating FDI. To make these improvements sustainable, there is a need to provide support to exporters to reach and maintain new markets. The countries should establish and/or further develop specialized institutions offering services to exporters, such as export credits and credit guarantees; information and counselling on markets, prices and trade connections; business and trade missions and international fairs; and trade departments at foreign embassies.

Finally, small enterprises need promoting in order to survive and expand. Promotional measures include lower taxation, simplified accounting and other administrative rules, better access to finance and the provision of small business support services.

On the demand side, high economic growth and the abolition of overly restrictive financial policies has contributed to fast recovery of wages and incomes and helped boost demand for consumer goods and services. Wages and labour productivity have so far moved in parallel and there is in general no inflationary pressure or imminent threat to competitiveness in the CSEE economies. Financial institutions have further stimulated consumer demand by offering extensive consumer credit schemes. Massive provision of relatively cheap credits and mortgages for housing, coupled with government-subsidized saving and/or credit schemes for house buying or renovations, has contributed to the revitalization of the construction industry and housing market in a number of the CSEE countries. Public investment in infrastructure and increasing greenfield investment by foreign and domestic investors have also stimulated demand for building materials and construction works and to some extent also the demand for investment goods of domestic origin. All this has had a positive effect on economic growth and should continue. However, there is a danger that the increasing indebtedness of households may threaten future demand and economic stability. Governments should therefore be vigilant and intervene in this issue if necessary. In the catching-up process, governments should also consider strengthening their commitment to upgrading the technical infrastructure and combine their public resources and bank credits with resources from the EU. This would further stimulate demand for construction, to the benefit of the whole economy.

Sound macroeconomic policy undoubtedly contributes towards stimulating economic growth and business development. However, for it to create more and better employment opportunities for the population and for all social groups to have equal employment opportunities, macroeconomic policy has to be combined with effective employment and labour market policies. In this respect the national studies (Chapters 3 to 7) have pointed to important skill mismatches, which are pushing low-skilled individuals, individuals with skills no longer in demand, and young people without work experience into unemployment or out of the labour market. The progressive ageing of the population in the subregion will sharpen skill mismatches in the absence of further reforms of the national education systems. The reforms should focus on increasing the educational and skills level of the population but they should also create conditions for the continuous adjustment of skills, on the principle of lifelong learning through universal, high-quality general education and equity in access to higher education. Vocational education and training (VET) needs to be made more responsive to changing demands for skills both in terms of form and content, through more broadly based, modular schooling, including interdisciplinary studies. The same applies to adult training of workers with low or obsolete skills to help them retain their jobs, redeploy within an enterprise or move into completely new jobs, while properly reflecting the special needs of adult trainees.

Reforms of VET require, inter alia, education and training facilities to work in close partnership with enterprises to define and adapt their curricula and teaching/ training methods. More generally, their labour market success is conditioned by the involvement of the social partners on the one hand and public employment services on the other in shaping and implementing VET policy. The feasibility of such reforms is often questioned from the point of view of the very restricted public funds available. Solutions should be sought in changing priorities to support new economic and employment strategies, better linking resource allocation to education outcomes (saving resources currently spent on the immediate retraining of school leavers or trainees unable to find a job after completing education or training), but also in combining public and private resources.

As argued in the introductory chapter, balancing flexibility and security has both an economic and a social rationale. Our comparative analysis, supported by the national and wage studies, has shown that the balance between flexibility and security has indeed improved in the CSEE countries since 1999, but is still far from sufficient. Even though national employment protection legislation may already seem quite liberal, the situation is not uniform in all the CSEE countries and for all provisions. Some rules may be too restrictive while others may provide only low protection or discriminate against some groups of workers and contribute towards labour market segmentation. Since both the social partners and the State are asserting often diverging interests on behalf of their constituents, the review of labour legislation and the subsequent legislative changes should be agreed in tripartite social dialogue that also involves representatives of less competitive groups of workers and jobseekers.

Weak enforcement of labour legislation remains an important challenge, despite the considerable improvements in recent years evidenced by the country studies. The length of time taken to resolve industrial disputes in the already overburdened civil courts is a persistent problem. Even if the court finds in favour of the workers and awards financial compensation, they win a Pyrrhic victory, since often the process itself has already damaged their careers. This discourages other workers from raising complaints and allows employers to continue in bad practices. Countries should therefore consider establishing specialized labour courts.

A number of employment protection and promotion issues which go beyond the basics provided by legislation could be effectively tackled by collective bargaining. While in most countries legislation promoting collective bargaining as well as mechanisms for bipartite and tripartite dialogue are in place, their existence is often only formal. The authors of the national studies rightly point to the lack of sectoral dialogue, which should complement enterprise-level bargaining and provide protection to non-unionized workers, particularly those in smaller enterprises. Also regional tripartite structures play no role in local and regional economic and employment development. Social dialogue should thus be further developed, especially at the sectoral and regional levels. In particular, the social partners should strengthen their capacity in the field of employment policy with effective support from the State as well as international employers' and workers' organizations and the ILO, and should actively engage in dialogue on flexibility and workers' protection instead of insisting stubbornly on their positions – in the case of employers on complete deregulation and in the case of trade unions on preservation of existing jobs and protection of core workers at the cost of youth and other vulnerable groups.

High payroll taxes, despite their recent slight reduction in many countries of the subregion, have been identified as one important factor of unfavourable labour market performance and as contributing to higher informality of employment. Governments should therefore consider their further reduction while shifting some social expenditure to general taxation and improving tax collection.

Apart from tax cuts, governments should also strengthen labour inspectorates and financial offices to combat informal labour. However, a determined policy towards gradual formalization of informal employment should comprise improvement of legislation and its enforcement, tax reforms and better monitoring and sanctions, alongside positive motivation for employers and workers to engage in formal employment relationships with wages and taxes paid in full.

Another factor negatively affecting labour market performance is the duration of payment of unemployment benefits. This might appear to invite a stricter stance on unemployment insurance schemes, in particular for vulnerable groups. However, since the main problem lies not in the generosity of unemployment benefits in the subregion, which is low compared with the EU15 average, but rather in the lack of employment opportunities for less competitive workers in a context of persistent depressed labour demand, the solution should be sought in an activation strategy. Public employment services should pay much more attention to harder-to-place persons, to understand their specific obstacles to employment and address them through individual employment plans. Such plans would include intensive job placement assistance and/or training, placement in temporary subsidized jobs, vocational rehabilitation or other assistance according to their needs. Measures could also include incentives for workers, such as early job take-up premiums, and for employers, in the form of wage subsidies, grants or tax deductions. Regional differentiation of the minimum wage corresponding to differences in living costs could stimulate recruitment of harder-to-place persons, as could negative income taxation of low wages. By contrast, the refusal to accept a suitable job or to participate in an active labour market programme without any serious reason should lead to the suspension of unemployment benefits and/or social assistance. However, activation polices should be combined with a decent level of income support during the period of active job search, training or rehabilitation, to motivate individuals and prevent their falling into poverty or turning to informal activity. Those persons (of working age) who cannot work for health reasons or opt for inactivity to take better care of their small children or elderly family members should keep their access to appropriate social welfare schemes.

The impact of active labour market policies (ALMPs) on increasing economic activity and employment and reducing aggregate, youth and long-term unemployment has further strengthened since the 1990s. Although ALMPs alone have only a limited capacity to create new employment, their main contribution is in expanding the labour supply and improving its quality, facilitating labour market transitions, reducing labour market imbalances and cutting frictional and structural unemployment, and addressing equity problems as described above. This reinforces the importance of active intervention in the labour market required by the European Employment Strategy. The extent of ALMP should be broadened to reach all jobseekers in need of assistance and their application fine-tuned to provide appropriate but also cost-effective assistance for successful re-employment.

The main providers of ALMP, public employment services, should improve the extent and quality of the services they provide to their clients – jobseekers and enterprises – to gain their trust and expand their influence on the labour market at all levels. This requires further capacity building of public employment services in terms of their staff numbers and skills, equipment, computerization of their operations, creation of nationwide databases of jobseekers and vacancies, optimal decentralization of decision-making, ensuring smooth horizontal and vertical collaboration and effective work organization. Close public–private partnerships with governments at their respective levels, and with the social partners, enterprises, private employment agencies, education and training providers and non-governmental organizations, can further strengthen the overall impact of active policies, as illustrated by the Croatian study, for example.

The human development and employment activation strategy, in combination with decent income support for those actively searching for jobs or unable to work, is of course not cheap. Even if the limited available funds were to be used in the most effective way, they would need to be increased, in particular in those countries with a high level of unemployment. In the face of the current pressure to reduce public budgets and maintain the balance of public finances within the Maastricht criteria, such a recommendation may look unfeasible. However, this issue is not one that should be left to politicians to decide alone; it should become the subject of social dialogue. It is up to the government together with the social partners and representatives of vulnerable social groups and jobless persons to determine their country's employment and social development. Through dialogue, they must decide whether the country will accelerate its development in line with the EU Lisbon Strategy and the ILO Decent Work Agenda towards a triple objective of full and decent employment, high labour productivity, and social coherence and inclusion, or whether it will remain driven by predominantly economic goals.

BIBLIOGRAPHY

Arro, R.; Eamets, R.; Järve, J.; Kallaste, E.; Philips, K. 2001. *Labour market flexibility and employment security: Estonia*, Employment Paper Series No. 2001/25 (Geneva, ILO).

Auer, P.; Berg, J.; Coulibaly, I. 2005. "Is a stable workforce good for productivity?", in *International Labour Review*, Vol. 144, No. 3, pp.

—.; Cazes, S.; Spiezia, V. 2001. *Stable or unstable jobs: Interpreting the evidence in industrialized countries*, Employment Paper Series No. 2001/26 (Geneva, ILO).

—.; —. (eds.). 2003. *Employment stability in an age of flexibility: Evidence from industrialized countries* (Geneva, ILO).

Babrauskiene, T. 2003. "Lithuania", in ETUI – European Trade Union Institute: *Collective bargaining in Europe 2002* (Brussels, ETUI).

Bandelj, N. 2003. *Varieties of capitalism in Central and Eastern Europe*, paper presented at the Society for Comparative Research Graduate Student Retreat, Princeton University, NJ, available online: http://www.princeton.edu/~scr/papers03/ [June 2006].

Bardasi, E.; Lasaosa, A.; Micklewright, J.; Nagy, G. 2001. "Measuring the generosity of unemployment benefit systems: Evidence from Hungary and elsewhere in Central Europe", in *Acta Oeconomica*, Vol. 51, No. 1, pp. 17–42.

Becker, G. 1964. Human capital: *A theoretical and empirical analysis, with special reference to education* (New York, Columbia University Press).

Bednarski, M. 2000. "Social agreements accompanying privatization as a part of changes in ownership structure of the Polish economy" (in Polish), in *Polityka Spoleczna*, No. 4, pp. 14–17.

Beleva, I.; Tzanov, V.; Tisheva, G. 2005. *Flexibility and security in the labour market. Bulgaria's experience*, Flexicurity Paper 2004/3 (Budapest, Subregional Office for Central and Eastern Europe, ILO).

Bertola, G.; Boeri, T.; Cazes, S. 2000. "Employment protection in industrialized countries: The case for new indicators", in *International Labour Review*, Vol. 139, No. 1, pp. 57–72.

Blanchflower, D.; Oswald, A. 1994. *The wage curve* (Cambridge, MA, MIT Press).

Boeri, T. 1995. *Is job turnover countercyclical?* EUI Working Papers in Economics Series No. 12 (Florence, European University Institute).

—. 2000. *Structural change, welfare systems, and labour reallocation: Lessons from the transition of formerly planned economies* (Oxford, Oxford University Press).

—.; Terrell, K. 2002. "Institutional determinants of labor reallocation in transition", in *Journal of Economic Perspectives*, Vol. 16, No.1, pp. 51–76.

Botrić, V.; Rašić, I.; Šišinaćki, J. 2004. *Comparative analysis of regional unemployment and regional GDP in Croatia and selected transition countries*, Paper prepared for the 44th Congress of the European Regional Science Association, available online: http://www.ersa.org/ersaconfs/ersa04/ [June 2006].

Burda, M. 1993. "Labour markets in Eastern Europe", in *Economic Policy*, No. 16, Apr., pp. 101–37.

Calmfors, L.; Driffill, J. 1988. "Bargaining structure, corporatism and macroeconomic performance", in *Economic Policy*, No. 6, pp. 13–61.

Card, D.; Krueger, A. 1995. *Myth and measurement: The new economics of the minimum wage* (Princeton, NJ, Princeton University Press).

Carley, M. 2002. *Industrial relations in the EU Member States and candidate countries* (EIRO: European Industrial Relations Observatory), available online: http://www.eiro. eurofound.ie/ [June 2006].

Cazes, S.; Nesporova, A. 2003. *Labour markets in transition: Balancing flexibility and security in Central and Eastern Europe* (Geneva, ILO).

Commander, S.; Faggio, G. 2003. *Labour market reallocation in Central Europe, Russia and Ukraine during the 1990s: A review of the evidence*, mimeo (London, London Business School).

Djuric, D. 2003. *Social dialogue in Southeast European countries*, final research paper at Open Society Institute, Center for Policy Studies, available online: http://www.policy. hu/djuric/ [June 2006].

Dolado, J.; Kramarz, F.; Machin, S.; Manning, A.; Margolis, D.; Teulings, C. 1996. "The economic impact of minimum wages in Europe", in *Economic Policy*, No. 23, Oct., pp. 319–72.

Ederveen, S.; Thissen, L. 2004. *Can labour market institutions explain unemployment rates in new EU Member States?*, paper presented at the conference of the Accesslab European 5th Framework Program, 30 June (Vienna, WIFO).

European Bank for Reconstruction and Development (EBRD). 2003. *Transition Report 2003: Integration and regional cooperation* (London).

Fazekas, K. 2001. "Local government practices of providing income support and public works for the working age unemployed", in K. Fazekas and J. Koltay (eds.): *The Hungarian Labour Market – Review and analysis* (Budapest, Institute of Economics, Hungarian Employment Foundation), pp. 254–63.

—. (ed.). 2002. *Munkaerőpiaci Tükör 2002* (Budapest, Hungarian Academy of Sciences).

Feldstein, M. 1976. "Temporary lay-offs in the theory of unemployment", in *Journal of Political Economy*, Vol. 84, No. 3, pp. 937–57.

Frey, M. 2001. "The financing of unemployment assistance" (in Hungarian), in K. Fazekas (ed.): *Munkaerőpiaci Tükör 2001* (Budapest, Hungarian Academy of Sciences), pp. 75–81.

Gábos, A.; Szívós, P. 2001. "The share of unemployment benefits within household incomes", in K. Fazekas and J. Koltay (eds.): *The Hungarian labour market – review and analysis* (Budapest, Institute of Economics, Hungarian Employment Foundation), pp. 206–13.

Galasi, P. 1996. "The job search behaviour of the unemployed" (in Hungarian), in *Közgazdasági Szemle*, Vol. 43, No. 9, pp. 805–15.

—.; Nagy, G. 2001a. "Criteria for benefit entitlement and chances of re-employment", in K. Fazekas and J. Koltay (eds.): *The Hungarian labour market – review and analysis* (Budapest, Institute of Economics, Hungarian Employment Foundation), pp. 221–28.

—.; —. 2001b. "Assistance recipients and re-employment following the exhaustion of insurance benefit", in K. Fazekas and J. Koltay (eds.): *The Hungarian labour market – review and analysis* (Budapest, Institute of Economics, Hungarian Employment Foundation), pp. 242–53.

Gardawski, J. 2003. *Trade unions: numbers, composition and opinions. Results of the survey* (in Polish) (Warsaw, CBOS), available online: http://www.cbos.pl [June 2006].

Ghellab, Y.; Vaughan-Whitehead, D. (eds.). 2003. *Sectoral social dialogue in future EU Member States: The weakest link* (Budapest, Subregional Office for Central and Eastern Europe, ILO).

Grgurev, I. 2002. "Collective agreements in Croatia", in *Bulletin of Comparative Labour Relations*, No. 48, pp. 273–92.

Grotkowska, G.; Socha M. W.; Sztanderska U. 2003. *Social dialogue on the formulation, implementation and monitoring of employment policies in Poland*, paper prepared for the research project Social Dialogue on the Formulation, Implementation and Monitoring of Employment Policies, conducted by the Research Institute for Labour and Social Affairs (RILSA), Czech Republic, and the ILO (Warsaw).

—.; —.; —. 2005. *Flexibility and security in the labour market. Poland's experience*, Flexicurity Paper 2004/4 (Budapest, Subregional Office for Central and Eastern Europe, ILO).

GUS. 1998. *Undeclared work in Poland* (in Polish) (Warsaw, Central Statistical Office).

—. 2004. *Information on the Social and Economic Situation of the Country: 2003* (in Polish) (Warsaw, Central Statistical Office).

—. 2005a. *Information on the Social and Economic Situation of the Country: 2004* (in Polish) (Warsaw, Central Statistical Office).

—. 2005b. *Statistical Yearbook of the Republic of Poland* (Warsaw, Central Statistical Office).

Halpern, L.; Koren, M.; Kőrösi, G.; Vincze, J. 2004. "The budgetary effects of the minimum wage" (in Hungarian), in *Közgazdasági Szemle*, Vol. 51, No. 4, pp. 325–45.

Haltiwanger, J.; Vodopivec, M. 1998. *Gross worker and job flow in a transition economy: An analysis of Estonia*, mimeo (University of Maryland, MD)

Hamermesh, D. 1996. *Labor demand* (Princeton, NJ, Princeton University Press).

Havas, G.; Kemény, I.; Liskó, I. 2002. *Roma children in primary school* (in Hungarian) (Budapest, Oktatáskutató Intézet, Új Mandátum).

Hristoskov, Y.; Shopov, G.; Beleva I. 1997. *Non-institutionalized employment and self-employment in Bulgaria* (in Bulgarian), mimeo.

Huber, P.; Brücker, P.; Köllő, J.; Traistaru, I.; Mickiewicz, T. 2002. *Regional and labour market development in candidate countries: A literature survey* (Vienna, WIFO), available online: http://accesslab.wifo.ac.at/ [June 2006].

International Labour Organization (ILO). 1996. *World employment 1996/97: National policies in a global context* (Geneva).

International Monetary Fund (IMF). 2003. "Unemployment and labor market institutions: Why reforms pay off", in *World Economic Outlook 2003* (Washington, DC), pp. 129–50.

Jenkins, S.P. 1995. "Easy estimation methods for discrete-time duration data", in *Oxford Bulletin of Economics and Statistics*, Vol. 57, No. 1, pp. 129–38.

Katz, L.F.; Loveman, G.W.; Blanchflower, D. 1995. "A comparison of changes in the structure of wages in four OECD countries", in R.B. Freeman and L.F. Katz (eds.): *Differences and changes in wage structure* (Chicago, University of Chicago Press).

—.; Meyer, B.D. 1990. "Unemployment insurance, recall expectations and unemployment outcomes", in *The Quarterly Journal of Economics*, Vol. 105, No. 4, pp. 973–1002.

Kertesi, G.; Köllő, J. 2003a. "Industrial wage differentials in Hungary, Parts 1 and 2" (in Hungarian), in *Közgazdasági Szemle*, Vol. 50, No. 11, pp. 923–38 and No. 12, pp. 1049–79.

—.; —. 2003b. *Fighting low equilibria by doubling the minimum wage – Hungary's experiment*, IZA Discussion Paper No. 970 (Bonn, IZA).

—.; —. 2003c. *The employment effects of nearly doubling the minimum wage: The case of Hungary*, Budapest Working Papers on the Labour Market 2003/6 (Budapest, Institute of Economics, Hungarian Academy of Sciences).

Kézdi, G. 2002. "Business sector and budgetary institutions", in K. Fazekas and J. Koltay (eds.): *The Hungarian labour market – review and analysis* (Budapest, Institute of Economics, Hungarian Employment Foundation), pp. 92–101.

Köllő, J. 2001. *The patterns of non-employment in Hungary's least developed regions*, Budapest Working Papers on the Labour Market 2001/1 (Budapest, Institute of Economics, Hungarian Academy of Sciences).

—.; Mickiewicz, T. 2005. "Wage bargaining, privatisation, ability to pay and outside options. Evidence from Hungary", in *Post-Communist Economies*, Vol. 17, No. 4, pp. 465–83.

—.; Nacsa, B. 2005. *Flexibility and security in the labour market – Hungary's experience*, Flexicurity Paper 2004/2 (Budapest, Subregional Office for Central and Eastern Europe, ILO).

Kornai, J. 1992. *The socialist system: The political economy of communism* (Oxford, Clarendon Press).

Kőrösi, G. 2000. *Corporate labour demand* (in Hungarian), Budapest Working Papers on the Labour Market 2000/3 (Budapest, Institute of Economics, Hungarian Academy of Sciences).

—. 2002. *Labour adjustment and efficiency in Hungary*, Budapest Working Papers on the Labour Market 2002/4 (Budapest, Institute of Economics, Hungarian Academy of Sciences).

—.; Surányi, S. 2002. "Dynamic adjustment" (in Hungarian), in K. Fazekas (ed.): *Munkaerőpiaci Tükör 2002* (Budapest, Hungarian Academy of Sciences), pp. 157–60.

Kozek, W.; Kulpińska, J. (eds.). 1998. *Collective industrial relations in Poland: View of changes* (in Polish) (Warsaw, Scholar).

Kwiatowski, E.; Socha, M.; Sztanderska, U. 2001. *Labour market flexibility, employment and social security: Poland*, Employment Paper Series No. 2001/28 (Geneva, ILO).

Kyle, S.; Warner, A.; Dimitrov, L.; Krustev, R.; Alexandrova, S.; Stanchev, K. 2001. *The shadow economy in Bulgaria* (Sofia, Agency for Economic Analysis and Forecasting/Institute for Market Economics/Harvard University).

Lado, M. 2002. *Industrial relations in the candidate countries* (EIRO: European Industrial Relations Observatory), available online: http://www.eiro.eurofound.ie/ [June 2006].

Layard, R.; Nickel, D.; Jackman, R. 1991. *Unemployment: Macroeconomic performance and the labour market* (Oxford, Oxford University Press).

Liwiński, J.; Sztanderska, U. 2003. *Determinants of lifelong learning in Poland* (in Polish), part of the Research Project on Educational Preferences of Polish Households, mimeo.

Markova, E. 2003. *Sectoral collective bargaining develops* (EIRO: European Industrial Relations Observatory), available online: http://www.eiro.eurofound.ie/ [June 2006].

Micklewright, J.; Nagy, G. 1994. *Flows to and from insured unemployment in Hungary*, EUI Working Papers in Economics No. 41 (Florence, European University Institute).

—.; —. 1999. *The informational value of job search data and the dynamics of search behaviour – Evidence from Hungary*, Budapest Working Papers on the Labour Market 1999/14 (Budapest, Institute of Economics, Hungarian Academy of Sciences).

Ministry of Labour and Social Affairs (MgiPS), Poland. 2003. *Making social expenditures rational. Green book* (in Polish) (Warsaw).

Ministry of Labour and Social Policy, Bulgaria. 2003. *New social policy strategy*, Ministerial Strategy Paper (Sofia), available online: http://www.mlsp.government.bg/ [May 2006].

—. 2004. *National Action Plan for Employment* (Sofia).

—. 2005. *Second Report on the Progress made by the Republic of Bulgaria on the Joint Assessment of Employment Priorities* (Sofia), available online: http://www.mlsp. government.bg/ [May 2006].

—. 2006. *National Action Plan for Employment* (Sofia).

—.; European Commission. 2002. *Joint Assessment of Employment Priorities in Bulgaria* (Sofia/Brussels), available online: http://www.mlsp.government.bg/ [May 2006].

Ministry of Social Security and Labour, Lithuania. 2004. *National Action Plan for Employment* (Vilnius).

Nagy, G. 2001a. "The generosity and targeting of unemployment benefits", in K. Fazekas and J. Koltay (eds.): *The Hungarian Labour Market – Review and analysis*, Institute of Economics (Budapest, Hungarian Employment Foundation), pp. 174–80.

—. 2001b. "Unemployment compensation: Types, measures and eligibility criteria", in K. Fazekas (ed.): *Munkaerőpiaci Tükör 2001* (Budapest, Hungarian Academy of Sciences), pp. 70–4.

—. 2003. "Regional differences in employment probabilities" (in Hungarian), in K. Fazekas (ed.): *Munkaerőpiaci Tükör 2003* (Budapest, Hungarian Academy of Sciences), pp. 57–64.

National Labour Inspectorate. 2003. *The Report of the Chief Labour Inspector on the Activity of the National Labour Inspection in 2002* (in Polish).

Neumann, L. 2002. "Does decentralised collective bargaining have any effect on the labour market?", in *European Journal of Industrial Relations*, Vol. 8, No. 1, pp. 11–31.

—. 2005. "Collective agreements" (in Hungarian), in K. Fazekas and L. Neumann (eds.): *Munkaerőpiaci Tükör 2005* (Budapest, Hungarian Academy of Sciences), pp. 131–38.

Nickell, S. 1987. "Why is wage inflation so high?", in *Oxford Bulletin of Economics and Statistics*, Vol. 49, No. 1, pp. 103–28.

—. 1997. "Unemployment and labour market rigidities: Europe versus North America", in *Journal of Economic Perspectives*, Vol. 11, No.3, pp. 55–74.

—.; Layard, R. 1999. "Labour market institutions and economic performance", in O. Ashenfelter and D. Card (eds.): *Handbook of labour economics*, Vol. 3 (North-Holland, Elsevier), pp. 3029–84.

Organisation for Economic Co-operation and Development (OECD). 1994. OECD J*obs Study, Part II: The adjustment potential of the labour market* (Paris).

—. 1995. *The regional dimension of unemployment in transition countries* (Paris).

—. 1999. *Employment Outlook 1999* (Paris).

—. 2003. *Employment Outlook 2003* (Paris).

—. 2005. *Education at a Glance 2005* (Paris).

ONYF (Országos Nyugdíjbiztosítási Főigazgatóság, Central Administration of National Pension Insurance of Hungary). 2001. *Yearbook of the Chief Directorate of Pensions* (in Hungarian) (Budapest).

Pissarides, C.A. 2001. "Employment protection", in *Labour Economics*, Vol. 8, No. 2, pp. 131–159.

Renooy, P.; Ivarsson, S.; van der Wusten-Gritsai, O.; Meijer, R. 2004. *Undeclared work in an enlarged Union.* Report presented to the European Commission, available online: http://ec.europa.eu/employment_social/ [June 2006].

Riboud, M.; Silva-Jauregui, C.; Sanchez-Paramo, C. 2002. "Does eurosclerosis matter? Institutional reform and labor market performance in Central and Eastern European countries", in B. Funck and L. Pizzati (eds.): *Labour, employment, and social policies in the EU enlargement process* (Washington, DC, World Bank).

Rutkowski, J. 1996a. *Changes in the wage structure during economic transition in Central and Eastern Europe*, World Bank Technical Paper No. 340 (Washington, DC, World Bank).

—. 1996b. "High skills pay off: The changing wage structure during economic transition in Poland", in *Economics of Transition*, Vol. 4, No. 1, pp. 89–112.

—. 2003. *Does strict employment protection discourage job creation? Evidence from Croatia*, World Bank Policy Research Working Paper No. 3104 (Washington, DC, World Bank).

—.; Scarpetta, S.; Banerji, A.; O'Keefe, P.; Pierre, G.; Vodopivec, M. 2005. *Enhancing job opportunities – Eastern Europe and the former Soviet Union* (Washington, DC, World Bank).

Schneider, F.; Enste, D. 2000."Shadow economies: Size, causes, and consequences", in *Journal of Economic Literature*, Vol. 38, pp. 77–114.

Socha, J. 2005. "Labour demand in manufacturing: Panel data analysis", in W. Wojciechowski and Z. Zolkiewski (eds.): *Determinants of employment of labour resources in Poland* (in Polish) (Warsaw, National Bank of Poland).

Socha, M.W.; Sztanderska, U. 2003. *Equilibrium unemployment rates for the Polish economy* (in Polish), mimeo (Warsaw, Warsaw University, Department of Economics).

Stata. 2005. *Stata Release 9*, Reference R-Z, pp. 266–69 (College Station, TX, Stata Press).

Svejnar, J. 2002. *Labor market flexibility in Central and East Europe*, William Davidson Working Paper No. 496 (Michigan, MI, William Davidson Institute).

Tonin, M. 2006. *Flexibility and security in the labour market. The wage dimension*, Flexicurity Paper 2004/6 (Budapest, Subregional Office for Central and Eastern Europe, ILO).

Tzanov, V.; Lukanova, P. 2000. *Unemployment in Bulgaria: Macroeconomic relationships and possibility for reduction* (Sofia, Kolbis).

UNECE. 2004. *Economic Survey of Europe No. 1* (Geneva, UNECE).

USAID. 2004. *Labor market in Bulgaria 2003* (Sofia), available online: http://www.pension. bg/index_E.html [June 2006].

US Department of State. 2003. *Country Reports on Human Rights Practices*, available online: http://www.state.gov/g/drl/rls/hrrpt/ [June 2006].

Vaughan-Whitehead, D. (ed.). 1995. *Reforming wage policy in Central and Eastern Europe*, International Symposium on Wages, Efficiency and Social Cohesion: Towards a Negotiated Wage Policy in Central and Eastern Europe, Budapest, Hungary (Budapest, Commission of the European Communities/ILO).

Večerník, J. 2001. *Labour market flexibility and employment security: Czech Republic*, Employment Papers Series No. 2001/27 (Geneva, ILO).

Williamson, O.E. 1985. *The economic institutions of capitalism: Firms, markets, relational contracting* (New York, Free Press).

INDEX

Note: Bold page numbers refer to tables and figures; footnotes are shown as subscript numbers.